10 THINGS EMPLOYERS WANT YOU TO LEARN IN COLLEGE

REVISED

10 THINGS EMPLOYERS WANT YOU TO LEARN IN COLLEGE

REVISED

THE **SKILLS** YOU NEED TO SUCCEED

BILL COPLIN

TEN SPEED PRESS
Berkeley

A previous edition was published in the United States by Ten Speed Press,
Berkeley, in 2003.

Library of Congress Cataloging-in-Publication Data
Coplin, William D.
  10 things employers want you to learn in college, revised : the skills you
need to succeed / Bill Coplin.
      p. cm.
  Summary: "A straightforward guide that teaches students how to acquire
marketable job skills and real-world know-how before they graduate"
—Provided by publisher.
1. Career education—United States. 2. College student orientation—United States.
3. Career development—United States. I. Title. II. Title: Ten things employers
want you to learn in college.
  LC1037.5.C68 2012
  370.113—dc23
                                        2012004869

ISBN 978-1-60774-145-9
eISBN 978-0-307-76849-0

Printed in the United States of America

Design by Chloe Rawlins, based on the previous edition's design by
Ed Anderson, SKOUT

10 9 8 7 6

First Revised Edition

To the memory of

MICHAEL K. O'LEARY

for his support as a friend
and colleague

CONTENTS

ACKNOWLEDGMENTS

This book benefited from the help of many students, alumni, and staff of Syracuse University and colleagues around the country who responded to the first edition. Hundreds of students have used the book and provided me with useful feedback for this new edition.

I would like to single out a few students who went beyond the expected. For the first edition, Gina De Rosa worked almost full time on it during the summer of 2002 and, despite her heavy schedule, contributed many hours during the fall semester as my primary research assistant on the book. For this revised edition, Lauren Ottaviano conducted research, solicited reviews, enlisted help from other students, and provided writing and editorial assistance. She played a major role in bringing the perspective of a current undergraduate and in keeping the whole process organized. Others who helped with this edition are Mary Beth Anagnost, Kelly Baug, Sean Heron, Zach Lax, Jeffrey Van Liew, and Elizabeth Zarecki.

Several alumni helped out their old professor by providing reactions and, in several cases, text that I quoted. They include Gwyneth Blevins, Sharon Ehm, Rebecca Holmes, Sarah Korf, Matt Marsh, John Mandyck, Lisa Mueller, and Gary Puddles.

Special thanks to Mike Pasqualoni, who supported me in training my students to use the library and its electronic services and who gave me excellent advice for chapter 7. Sue Shane of the Division of International Programs provided information and advice on overseas programs. Helen Murray, who headed the internship program, provided suggestions on the chapter on internships. Michael Cahill, Karen McGee, Ann Phelps, and Norma Shannon, who provide career counseling services on campus, introduced me to the latest developments in that field. Over the years, Michelle Walker, Angela Ward, and Carol Dwyer of my program staff have provided insight into job readiness. Blaine Delancey, the former recorder for the College of Arts and Sciences, prepared some written material for chapter 9 and provided perspective on the history of liberal arts. David Smith, former dean of admissions and vice president for enrollment management, provided detailed suggestions for the discussion of college selection in chapter 12. Chris Walsh, dean of financial aid, provided information on student debt. Special thanks to Tim Conway, a career and college coach as well as a college instructor, who has been a constant source of information and encouragement over the past few years and provided reactions and information used in this book.

I want to thank Grace Freedson, my agent, who hooked me up with Ten Speed, the best possible publisher; Brie Mazurek (first edition) and Emily Timberlake (revised edition), my editors at Ten Speed, who worked with me on the development of the final manuscript and came up with many bright ideas; and Jean Blomquist, who did a wonderful job copyediting.

Finally, thanks to my wife, Vicki, who shares with me the value of education for a purpose. She provided inspiration for this book, kept me on task for details, and encouraged me to complete the manuscript.

All of these people were helpful, but I take full responsibility for what you are about to read.

—Bill Coplin

"A COLLEGE DEGREE AND A DOLLAR WILL GET YOU FOUR QUARTERS."

—ANONYMOUS

If you are in college or intend to go to college, the single most irritating question that your family and others may ask you is this: "What are you going to do with your college degree?" This book will provide the answer: "I'm not just getting a degree. I'm developing the skills to succeed in whatever career I pursue, and when I finish my degree, I'll be able to prove that to my future employer—and you, too!" If you master the skills presented in this book, you can make this statement confidently because you know you will accomplish much more in college than simply completing courses and getting a degree.

Both good news and bad news face all college students, which is why this annoying question is asked so often. In the face of unlimited opportunity (the good news) and a high degree of risk (the bad news), everyone gets anxious. Here's a quick overview of the good and the bad news.

THE GOOD NEWS

- Over their work life, college graduates earn an average of $2.1 million dollars compared with $1.2 million dollars for high school graduates.

- Someone with a professional degree (MD, JD, or MBA, for example) will earn $4.4 million.[1]

- College graduates live longer, seem to be happier, vote more often, and are less likely to be unemployed or on welfare than nongraduates.[2]

- You and your parents and family will be proud.

- College tuition is likely to continue to increase at both private and public schools.

- Sixty-three percent of students who begin a four-year college do not finish in four years, and 42 percent do not finish in six years.[3]

- Two-thirds of college seniors who graduated in 2010 had student loan debt, with an average of $25,250.[4]

- In 2010, 85 percent of college seniors planned to move back home according to *Time* magazine.[5]

- The number of jobs not requiring a bachelor of arts will increase.[6]

- Research shows that the majority of college graduates do not improve key skills while in college.[7]

The bad news has gotten much worse since I wrote the first edition of this book in 2002. Costs have increased by 42 percent.[8] With the increase in college costs, the average amount of debt for those students leaving college with debt has increased by 17 percent in eight years.[9] The demand for students with college degrees in the humanities and social sciences has gone down.

College may be a day on the beach for some who live in the now, but it does not automatically lead to a beautiful life. Going to college is a risky business and getting more risky by the day. Like any investment requiring a lot of up-front money, four years of college can have a very big downside. Even if you get a good job, you may have huge debts to pay off. Paying off those debts may take a long time. If that doesn't scare you, think about this possibility: you drop out after two years and are saddled with $25,000 in debt. That's definitely bad news.

This book gives you the tools to avoid becoming one of those "bad news" statistics. It will help you avoid those risks and disappointments and take advantage of the big payoffs that a college education can provide. Aside from luck and other uncontrollable factors—such as the state of the economy at the time you graduate or some kind of family crisis—the key to a successful career is what you can *do*. This book will describe the skills you need to acquire in order to convince a job recruiter to hire you, as well as the tools you need to master so employers will find you—and your work—invaluable. Knowing how to

do what needs to be done is the key to success in your job and life—
and that's what this book is all about.

SEE COLLEGE AS A HUGE INVESTMENT IN TIME AND MONEY

Perhaps the most important aspects of making your college education
work for you are time and money. A college education is a massive
investment that is intended to shape your future, not just careerwise
but in every aspect of your life. Failure to recognize that it is an
investment and to use that investment wisely will create challenges in
your life that could have been avoided. Using the investment wisely
will, conversely, open up opportunities that you never thought possible.

Students who are aware of college costs and understand that
college is an investment will leave college with a clear career path and
a job. Those students who see college as four years of "camp" regardless of who is paying usually are faced with a more difficult path after
college. All too frequently they go to graduate school with no career
goal in mind or return home, where they take jobs just to get some
spending money.

Serious consideration of the financial ramifications of college for
you and attention to how college will help you develop your skills and
explore careers can be basic training in many of the skills that will
lead to a successful career.

The biggest risk you face with respect to money is the amount of
debt you accumulate by the time you leave college. As noted earlier,
67 percent of college students have debt averaging more than $25,000.
To retire that debt, you will pay approximately $250 a month for ten
years (depending on the type of loan and other factors). If you buy a
car, you will pay about the same amount for a car payment. Facing a
huge debt may also limit your career opportunities because you might
feel the need to take a higher paying job doing something you don't
like to do or are not good at.

A crucial step in the right direction on treating your time and
money commitment to college is to be aware of the costs of your college
education. Even if your parents are paying the full freight, you should
know how much they are paying. Parents sometimes make a mistake
in shielding students from the cost; don't let yours do it. If you are
going to graduate college with debt, always know the amount of the

debt. When I talk to students and ask them whether they are going to leave college with debt, they frequently cannot even give me a ballpark estimate. They don't know whether it is $5,000 or $50,000. These students make decisions about taking extra courses in the summer or going on some type of special summer program overseas without ever considering the financial implications. Too often you flip through the pages of a newspaper or turn on a national news channel to read or hear a story about a college graduate who graduated from a top university with $100,000 in debt and no job. You do not want to be like these people. These students will frequently blame the college for letting them take on so much debt when they would never complain about a car dealership talking them into a more expensive car and a higher loan.

MAKE THE BEST OF YOUR INVESTMENT IN COLLEGE

Your college years can be some of the best years of your life. College is a place and time to make your family proud, party, get a credential, find a significant other, or grow up so people will take you seriously. College helps you discover yourself, learn your likes and dislikes, develop your mind and your love of learning, and build an undergraduate record so you can get into a professional school, if that's what you want to do.

But college should also prepare you for finding a good job and a rewarding career. Your college years can be a training period in which you develop your general skills in order both to get a great job right out of college or graduate school *and* to succeed in the workplace. By taking advantage of the opportunities that college offers, you can build the base of skills you need not only to land your first job but also to excel at it. Once that happens, you will be on your way to a lifetime of rewarding work.

College can be a truly significant time in your life. That's why it's important to use this time well, including preparing yourself for a good job after you finish. Use your college years to gain and polish the skills necessary for a successful career. You'll be glad you did—and your employer will be, too.

You may be thinking, "Well, skills may be nice, but won't prospective employers be looking at my GPA?" Prospective employers look at your grade point average (GPA) as a measure of your persistence and your basic intelligence. However, the list below, which was published by the National Association of Colleges and Employers (NACE) in 2010, indicates that employers are really looking for skills. At the top of the list are communication skills, strong work ethic, initiative, interpersonal skills, and problem-solving skills.[10]

EMPLOYERS RATE THE IMPORTANCE OF CANDIDATE QUALITIES/SKILLS

Communication skills

Strong work ethic

Initiative

Interpersonal skills (relates well to others)

Problem-solving skills

Teamwork skills (works well with others)

Analytical skills

Flexibility/adaptability

Computer skills

Detail-oriented

Leadership skills

Technical skills

Organizational skills

Self-confidence

Tactfulness

Friendly/outgoing personality

Creativity

Strategic planning skills

Entrepreneurial skills/risk taker

Sense of humor

What's not on this list? A high GPA. In a previous NACE survey, it was listed as 17 out of 20. I bring this up because some students think a high GPA is the most important achievement they can have in college. It may be important for graduate schools and some employers, but it is not as important as being able to demonstrate that you have the skills employers want.

A respectable GPA reflects some of the skills discussed in this book. It also measures how well you play the system by figuring out what your professors want and then delivering the goods. In some ways, meeting the standards of professors is similar to pleasing your boss. Your boss is not likely to ask you to fill up a blue book or take a multiple-choice test, but she or he will expect you to follow directions. For these reasons, you want to have a respectable GPA. A 3.0 is respectable in architecture, the physical sciences, and engineering, but a 3.2 is the bottom line in the social sciences, humanities, and some professional schools. However, while the GPA provides some information to employers, it is not nearly enough for them to make a judgment about your job potential. This was true before the days of grade inflation; it is doubly true today.

Your GPA alone is not a reliable indicator of your potential as an employee because your course grades do not reflect the range of skills that today's employers need. A very strong recommendation from your internship supervisor at a respected corporation about your people and problem-solving skills is much more important than a high GPA. But a high GPA may get you the interview.

Demonstration of good word-processing and spreadsheet skills will get you your first job faster than a GPA of 3.6 and even a master's degree. Just as college admissions officers look beyond SAT scores when they make their admissions decisions, employers look for qualities beyond your GPA to make hiring decisions. One of my students was hired over several students who had master's degrees in the department of education from a northeastern state. Why? She knew how to use spreadsheets. The interviewer, who was looking for the spreadsheet skills, asked about pivot tables. The other applicants had no clue what those were, even though they listed Microsoft Excel on their resumes. They may have taken an introductory course, but they clearly did not have extensive experience using Excel. (Taking a course is like being told where the swimming pool is. It does not mean you know how to swim.) The spreadsheet maven was hired; she worked her way up the ladder and eventually did policy work for the organization (and directed others to do the spreadsheet work for her). She is now a senior manager in a charter school.

The emphasis on skills may seem like common sense to you, but when you get to college you will find that courses rarely focus primarily on skill development. In fact, employers have long complained about the poor preparation of most college students. According to a *New York Times* article, a "1999 report by the Business–Higher Education Forum condemned graduates for lack of skills in problem solving, time management, analytical thinking, and basic writing and speaking."[11]

It is not that colleges don't provide opportunities for students to develop problem-solving, time-management, analytical thinking, and basic written and verbal communication skills. Rather, most college students do not know how to take advantage of those opportunities. This book will show you how to use your courses to build your skills in what I refer to as the ten "Skill Sets." Let's take a brief look at those ten sets now. (Each of the next ten chapters will focus on one Skill Set.)

MASTER THE SKILLS THAT MATTER

On the basis of forty-five years of advising experience as well as extensive discussions and interviews with recruiters, successful alumni, and a variety of employers and human resources specialists, I developed ten basic categories of skills. The ten basic Skill Sets are like the five food groups. Just as you need to eat enough from each of the food groups to be healthy, you also need to develop enough of the skills within the ten Skill Sets by the time you graduate to be successful.

THE TEN SKILL SETS

1. Taking Responsibility
2. Developing Physical Skills
3. Communicating Verbally
4. Communicating in Writing
5. Working Directly with People
6. Influencing People
7. Gathering Information
8. Using Quantitative Tools
9. Asking and Answering the Right Questions
10. Solving Problems

Although lists provided by experts and employers may use different terms and groupings, the ten Skill Sets reflect a broad consensus concerning the skills necessary to succeed in today's workplace.

WHAT'S YOUR SKILLS SCORE?

Employers from every sector—big, medium, and small—would love to have a number that tells them how well you perform the skills that make up the ten Skill Sets. Because colleges do not provide this kind of assessment, employers use their interview processes, including written tests, to come up with their own estimate of a similar list of skills. They do not call it "skills for success," but that's really what they are measuring. Although employers may use different terms, they do know which skills they want their employees to have. Show them that you have those skills, and you're on your way to a great future!

This book is also useful regardless of the field you want to pursue. Some reviewers of the first edition said that the book only applies to people wanting to go into business. Nothing could be further from the truth. The ten Skills Sets are necessary for success whether you are working for a nonprofit or government agency or large corporation. Teachers, social workers, government officials, and more can all benefit from having a high Skills Score—just as much as salespeople, business managers, and finance specialists. Even artists, writers, and other types of creative people will need the ten Skills Sets if they want to succeed professionally. They all have to provide value to someone who will pay their freight. For that reason, the success of both the professional surfer in California and the Wall Street banker depends on all of the ten Skills Sets.

WHAT YOU'LL LEARN IN THIS BOOK

This book will help you identify and develop the skills necessary for a successful career. Part one identifies the skills, and part two tells you how to develop those skills. Part three provides tools that will enable you to plan and schedule your time to make the most of your college experience. It will help you position yourself for your first job, which in turn will provide the foundation for a viable career path. Used well, these tools will confirm—to yourself, your parents, potential employers, and others—that your college education was a good investment.

Although this book is most useful to those just entering college, it can also be helpful to high school students and students further along in their college careers. Even if you are a college junior or senior, it is never too late to start improving the skills presented in this book. Those in part-time learning programs, which extend over a long period of time, can benefit by embracing the philosophy and suggestions provided here.

A high Skills Score will not only help you achieve a high GPA and get you hired when you graduate college, but it will also give you the basic tools necessary to continue learning new skills in order to reach the top of your field. In college, you lay the fundamental groundwork that provides you with unlimited job options. If you follow the advice in this book, you will earn a high Skills Score that will wow your job interviewers and put you ahead of the class when you start work.

USEFUL RESOURCES

A short list of useful resources at the end of each chapter can help you develop the ten Skill Sets and ultimately a successful career. I've selected the books and websites that I feel will be most helpful to you. The three websites listed below can be used for many, if not all, of the chapters. I encourage you to request email alerts from these sites so you can see what's new. Just one alert could make a big difference in your success.

ONE CAUTION: Don't spend so much time online that you don't develop your skills. You learn skills by practicing them, not just reading about them.

WEBSITES

www.billcoplin.org My site provides web links and videos on all thirty-eight skills in the ten Skill Sets. It also has an online version of the worksheets that appear in the appendix on page 265.

www.howcast.com Howcast offers free videos via YouTube on every conceivable topic, some of which are also available on billcoplin.org. Use the drop-down menu to quickly find a specific skill or task (like resume writing) about which you want to learn more. Try the categories "Careers and Education" or "Business and Finance."

www.mindtools.com Mind Tools provides a broad range of materials that will help you develop many of the skills covered in this book, especially those in chapters 8 and 9.

PART ONE

EXPLORING THE TEN SKILL SETS (AND BEYOND)

"WE ARE WHAT WE REPEATEDLY DO. EXCELLENCE, THEN, IS NOT AN ACT, BUT A HABIT."

—ARISTOTLE

CHAPTER 1

TAKING RESPONSIBILITY

MOTIVATE YOURSELF · BE ETHICAL ·
MANAGE YOUR TIME · MANAGE YOUR MONEY

Why do some people work hard and others just can't seem to get started? You could blame it on genes, family, poor academic preparation, or bad luck, but blaming won't do us much good here. Instead, let's just call it a "skills deficiency." We'll look at how you can remedy that weakness by using your college experience in a way that will have employers drooling. Taking responsibility is by far the most essential of the ten basic Skill Sets. Accepting that you are responsible for your success, character, time, and money will help you concentrate on developing all the other skills employers want.

To develop the skills you need to succeed in college, and being ready for a career requires hard work and a commitment to your future. On many occasions, you will need to defer gratification. The best way to think about this is to ask yourself where you would place yourself between two opposites. Are you Bart Simpson, who never thinks about the future? Or are you like Bill Gates, who left college to start Microsoft and is one of the richest men in the world? Bill Gates has always thought about the future, first for himself and his company and now for improving conditions throughout the world.

You may not have to be Bill Gates to develop the skills for success, but you can't be Bart Simpson. A fruitful balance between the two would be more than enough. Live in the present some of the time but also invest in yourself a lot of the time.

Unfortunately, too many students do not take responsibility for their futures. They fail to do the difficult work in college that will prepare them for the work world. They don't understand that they need to take action now, not in April of their senior year. A long-term commitment to planning and follow-through has to become a habit.

Because you are reading this, you already are taking responsibility—a very good sign.

Whenever I advise students, I ask myself where are they on the "Simpson-Gates" scale or, as I say to myself, the loser-to-winner scale. If students are not ready to take responsibility for their actions, I am not interested in investing time to help them. They need to grow up, and that is not my job. People in authority, whether your teacher, adviser, or boss, don't have much patience for irresponsible people asking for their help.

The four skills in this chapter are about taking responsibility. The first two deal with character, and the last two require precise focus and self-control. All four are usually related to maturity, age, and experience. Your college years will give you ample opportunity to practice these skills. Let's see how.

MOTIVATE YOURSELF

"We cannot ensure success, but we can deserve it."

—John Adams

Motivating yourself is a matter of choosing targets of ambition wisely and then going after them with all you have. This means you set priorities and keep a commitment to be the best you can be. Self-motivation keeps you going long after the fear of sanctions by your boss or the sweet-talking by your coworker wears off. Just look around at your schoolmates. The truly successful ones are driven by some internal mechanism that won't let up.

A senior vice president at one of the leading financial corporations in the world had this to say about self-motivation: "If I had to police everyone in order to get the job done, it'd be faster for me to do it myself. I want someone who will get the job done and get it done right.

An employee needs to be a self-starter and self-driven. If I have to tell them what to do, they haven't done it."

Unfortunately for employers but fortunately for you, people with a strong will to do what it takes to achieve are in short supply. If you can provide evidence on your resume and in your interview that you are one of the few committed to working hard regardless of rewards and punishments, you will clinch the job. If you deliver on the job, you will be on your way to unimagined success.

A corporate executive with one of the world's largest multinational corporations has another way of saying motivate yourself. He calls it "energy/passion/self-confidence." He writes, "In the first few minutes of an interview, I can tell whether a candidate is ready to play in our company's ballpark. You can have all the skills in the world, but if you aren't excited enough about what you're doing, you should reevaluate the job."

This on-the-move executive emphasizes self-confidence and says that it is "the only way to make it through a stretch role or some of the tough days." He writes, "There will be a period of time—not necessarily short, either—where the job is tough. Self-confidence keeps you on your path, focused on a goal, and able to keep everything in perspective."

Whether you call it enthusiasm, energy, passion or self-confidence, the bottom line is that to succeed you have to get off your butt and do something positive. That is your responsibility and no one else's.

COURSES: There are no courses in sociology or anywhere else on how to motivate yourself, but every course you take tests your motivation. This may mean you decide to get an A in every course, but not necessarily. A high GPA indicates that you are focused and motivated enough to work hard, but you may have to choose your grade battles. On some occasions, you may consciously decide to sacrifice the A because you want to devote your time and energy to studying related material that will not be on the test or you have to do triage between two or three courses. However, if you rationalize that you don't need to proofread your semester-long paper, for example, because you really want to party, then you are falling short on the skill of self-motivation.

Plan carefully so that you will earn at least a C in every course, realizing that you may have to make a tradeoff between higher grades and non-course activities. Set targets ahead of time, knowing how to do the work to get the grade you want. If you do this throughout your courses, you will establish the good work ethic you want to take to your first job.

NON-COURSE ACTIVITY: Practicing self-motivation in whatever internship, part-time, summer, or student activity you undertake is as essential as practicing self-motivation during your course work. However, it can be harder to stay self-motivated outside of the classroom, where guidelines are not as clear. In your courses, you know what you need to do (assuming the professor's standards are clear), but in an internship or a job what constitutes "high motivation" is not so clear. Staying after your assigned hours may indicate high motivation—but only if you work hard during the hours you are assigned. Being proactive in solving problems also takes extra motivation—but be careful not to solve the "wrong" problem. Once you have gained the confidence of your supervisor, start doing more than is required. But wait to impress your supervisor by going above and beyond until you have clearly demonstrated you can do what is asked of you.

BE ETHICAL

"Honesty is the best policy."

—Miguel de Cervantes, author of *Don Quixote*

The term *ethical* is used to mean both being honest and doing the right thing. People do not always agree on what the standards are for these two. The reason that most people lie is that they think it will save time and maximize interests. Some people are pathological liars, which too often leads to self-destruction. If you are one of them, get help. For the rest of you, the key to being ethical is knowing how to cope with the pressure to cut corners to the point that it violates the trust others have in you and you have in yourself. The direct way to possess that key is to recognize that dishonesty and unethical behavior can sooner or later lead to career failure.

Honesty is more than telling the truth to others. It is also a matter of telling the truth to yourself. In the world of action, this usually means being dependable and taking responsibility for the promises you make. Promising to do a job either within or outside your normal duties and then not delivering is a form of deception that has no place in the behavior of a person destined for success.

Employers want to trust their employees to do what is right, not just in calculating their travel expenditures but also in their dealings with clients and coworkers. They need to be able to trust their employees to fulfill the commitments they make. Given the business scandals at the beginning of the twenty-first century, companies now demand that students in graduate business programs receive instruction on integrity or ethics. Once you have done something to raise concern about your trustfulness, you will face a very hard time gaining back trust. Dishonesty and irresponsibility are the most powerful and quickest ways to lose another's trust in you.

A lobbyist and senior vice president of government affairs/trust services for a university says this about honesty: "As a lobbyist, you are essentially trying to convince the legislature to support things that they're not necessarily inclined to do, and for me to be successful, I have to be honest and truthful even if it may not benefit my client at that time. If you lose your credibility . . . you can never get it back." This may sound strange given all the bad publicity about lobbyists, but to influence politicians, they have to trust you. This is true for all careers.

COURSES: To explore concepts of right and wrong, you may want to take courses in philosophy and religion in which rational and metaphysical writing about right and wrong and other moral and ethical questions are explored. Courses based on studies where questions of ethics come up can be found in professional schools like management and might be more useful than philosophical debates over the meaning of right and wrong. More helpful would be your commitment here and now not to cheat either on tests or through plagiarizing papers. This recommendation is made for two very important reasons. First, if you can avoid the temptation of cheating in college, you are likely to avoid it in your work life. Cheaters, like alcoholics, usually tell themselves "this is my last cheat." If you cannot resist the pressure of dishonoring yourself in order to move from a B to an A, how can you avoid shredding documents in order to preserve your job or get a raise when you have a family to help support?

Second, if you get caught cheating in college, there are dire consequences for your job search, including losing a possible job reference from a professor or having an F on your transcript. University of Virginia is known for its integrity policies and has gone as far as revoking diplomas from students. Liars and cheaters in the workplace usually get fired or worse. Some have trouble finding another job, and others actually go to jail.

NON-COURSE ACTIVITIES: Honesty in your jobs, internships, and student activities should be a high priority. There will be plenty of opportunities to fudge your timesheet or text during work hours or lie to your supervisors and colleagues. Don't be like one of my alums who had a very good job at a very large corporation but lied on a travel expense form and was fired. If your supervisor at an internship or a job catches you in a lie, you will have lost an opportunity for a strong recommendation when going after your first full-time job.

*"Let all your things have their places.
Let each part of your business
have its time."*

—Benjamin Franklin

In most cases, managing your time well is a result of planning and setting priorities. Handing in papers three days late, forgetting assignments, and stressing out over how much you have to do are all symptoms of poor time management. This occasionally happens to the best manager of time, but if it is persistent, you need to do something *now*.

Procrastination for most people is a form of poor time management. Those who say "I'm a procrastinator!" are not taking responsibility for poor time management. There is no procrastinator gene as far as I know. "Procrastinators have higher rates of smoking, drinking, postponing seeing a doctor, digestive ailments, insomnia, and cold and flu symptoms than the student population at large" according to a study by psychologists at Carleton University.[1] For those who can't seem to give up procrastinating, factors other than poor time management may be involved. If you can't break the habit and you really try, make an appointment with your counseling office for assistance.

Time management is really pretty simple. You have X number of tasks that must be done at different times and that take different amounts of time to complete. To complicate it a little bit, some tasks have to be done before others. Knowing how to manage your time properly, therefore, simply means listing what has to be done, estimating the time it will take, and noting in what sequence you will do it. If you can do that, then you can figure out when you should not take on more tasks for a while, and you'll have sufficient time to do the tasks you have to do. What it comes down to is learning to plan and follow a schedule that will allow you to complete your tasks with minimum stress and maximum quality. The ability to handle multiple assignments over a two- or three-week period, as well as to not miss highly routine activities, such as submitting weekly reports, is key to every professional job.

You will frequently hear the term "multitasker" to describe a person who juggles several balls in the air and never drops one. With the speed of decision making made possible by computers and the increasing ability of people to deal with a variety of responsibilities, the ability to excel at multiple projects at once can be critical to your success. However, as with everything, you need to find your balance: I find that many students who pride themselves on "multitasking" only *think* they've finish a task completely, when in fact they've cut too many corners.

Employers are not impressed with workers who stay late to finish tasks that should have been completed during regular work hours. Missing more than two important deadlines is usually grounds for immediate dismissal.

COURSES: Some colleges have a study skills course that may help you with time management, but, before you take it, see whether it provides other skills you need. A whole course in time management is not worth the time. I sometimes see time management courses as a way to avoid dealing with poor time-management because it adds another set of tasks when the student already has too many to do. Take at least one course each semester in your junior and senior years that requires a major project that must be completed over at least a four-week period. You should be able to do this in most majors, but if not, take a course outside your major that requires a long-term project. Long-term projects require careful planning, attention to detail, and the ability to set and meet your own deadlines. By completing a long-term project, you will practice the same skills that enable you to successfully manage a weeks- or months-long project in your first job.

NON-COURSE ACTIVITIES: Treat college as a 9-to-5 job. That will leave you about thirty hours to do homework, which should be more than enough. Use early evening to play and then be in bed no later than 1 a.m. Do not be afraid to have 8:30 a.m. classes in your schedule! Not only will you avoid pulling all-nighters, but you will also be in a class where your regular attendance contrasts sharply with the majority of the class members. That will impress the professor and maybe even lead to a higher grade than you would otherwise get.

A senior who has accomplished a great deal in his college career has this to say:

"Time management is one of those things that can make or break a student. I laugh when I see a student who is habitually late ask a professor why he got a C on a paper or ask a question that the professor answered five minutes before the student walked in. In college classes, showing up is half the battle. If you're sitting there, you'll get something out of the course even if you don't pay full attention. As for 8:30 a.m. classes, you'll want to get away from them as soon as possible, but don't. The real world starts at 9 a.m., not 2 p.m. when you wake up. My best recommendation for time management is to get a planner, because keeping a schedule will greatly improve your time-management skills."

MANAGE YOUR MONEY

"Money makes the world go 'round."

—John Kander and Fred Ebb, songwriters and lyricists for the musical *Cabaret*

If you are careful about your own cash flow, you will be generous to your future. If you are in constant debt, working extra so you don't fall behind, you will have a very unpleasant future.

Managing money to reach your goals requires careful attention to detail, not only in reading the fine print on a credit card application but also in balancing your checkbook and paying your taxes. Managing money is not just a matter of keeping your expenses in line with your income but also deciding how you will invest your money in the future. Every time you buy something for immediate gratification, you reduce your income to be invested in the future. Money management means thinking through the trade-off and then having the discipline to implement the necessary decisions. Such a trade-off might mean resisting the urge to cash in by selling a textbook for a course you just completed, knowing that you might need it a year later for another course in your major.

Knowing how to manage money well is key to getting and keeping good jobs. First, money problems while in college can hurt both your GPA and your Skills Score. Taking that extra part-time job or worrying about bills reduces the time you have for studying and maintaining your health. It could mean giving up a great nonpaying internship experience. Although many students say they have to work more than twenty hours a week to make ends meet, my experience suggests that at least half of them are working for "wants" and not "needs." I find it very strange when students tell me they don't have enough money to buy books in January, and then in April, they tell me about the great time they had in the Bahamas over the spring break.

More and more students need extra money to pay for tuition, living expenses, and books—not just to have fun. If that's you, careful spending and time-management skills are crucial. For example, you may be able to avoid book expenses by taking the time to go to the library to use books on course reserve, or to order them used. You may need to avoid costly activities that serve as entertainment, and you may need to take on more debt than you would like. However, careful money management while you are in college can lead to huge payoffs years down the road.

Second, when you graduate, you may be forced to take jobs that you would not otherwise take because you have significant personal debts to pay off. You may be so consumed by the fear of not paying your bills that you take the first job that comes along. Roughly speaking, for every $10,000 you have in student debt, you will pay $100 a month for ten years. If the debt is $50,000, the payment will be $500 a month, which usually is a significant portion of your rent. You may even find yourself living with your parents because of this debt.

Finally, no matter what job you take as you move up the ladder, you will have increased responsibilities for expenditures in your department or division. You will face projected and actual budgets, and you will learn to make forecasts and monitor expenditures. If you learn good money-management techniques for yourself, you will be prepared for the budget exercises you will face on your road to being the CEO of IBM, the executive director of the Boys and Girls Clubs of America, or the secretary of education. You should also be aware that many employers do a credit check on their new hires, so your money-management skills are very important.

COURSES: Courses in management and consumer studies that introduce you to tax policy and personal financial management are available at most colleges and universities. They can be extremely helpful in preparing you for the work world. You should take at least one of these courses at the introductory level. A really useful course, if offered, is one that deals with starting a business or entrepreneurship. Even if you don't plan on having a business career, you can benefit from a course in which you come up with an idea and develop a plan to finance it and keep it going. Taking a personal finance course is also a very good idea.

NON-COURSE ACTIVITY: Develop a yearly budget of income and planned expenditures that you update regularly. There is a form in the appendix that will help you develop a semiannual budget. Completing this form will help you improve your money management skills. If you have an opportunity to become treasurer for a student organization, take it. Finding yourself in a position to tell your frat brothers not to buy another keg of beer because you will go into the red is a great learning experience.

Avoid running up debt on your credit cards. If you do have debt, figure out exactly how much interest you will be paying. If you are lucky enough to have parents who pay your credit card bills, your insurance bills, and everything else, ask them to work out a budget with you. Then, twice a year, have them deposit in your account the amount from which you will pay your bills. This is what the parents of one of my students did. The student writes:

> *"During my first two years, my parents paid all of my school bills, like tuition, housing, all the fees, etc. If I wanted any spending money though, it was up to me.*

It didn't take long for me to realize that I'd have to get a job on campus if I wanted any money to be left in my bank account by the time the semester ended.

"When I moved off campus junior year, our deal changed. They still paid my tuition, fees, and rent, but I had to pay for all of my own utilities. I also had to pay for my own phone, cable, Internet, and any other household needs. I wasn't given money on a regular basis either. At the beginning of the semester, my parents gave me a check that covered that semester's rent and the amount of money they would have spent on a meal plan. I was responsible for writing the checks every month. I was free to spend it however I want, but if I chose to spend my rent money on a stereo, I had to come up with the rent myself. In this way, they taught me to get used to making careful financial decisions, but still kept a safety net under me as I moved into the 'real world.'"

If you have someone bankrolling part or all of your college costs, ask for a deal like the one described above. It will be a great training device in money management. If you're paying your own way and keeping your debt as low as possible, then you're already getting that training. It may not seem like it now, but one day you will count it as one of the most beneficial experiences of your college career. The payoff will begin with a resume that says, "Financed 100 percent of my college education," and it will carry through to everything you do.

USEFUL RESOURCES

BOOKS

Been There, Should've Done That: 995 Tips for Making the Most of College, 3rd edition, by Suzette Tyler (Front Porch Press, 2008). This book is useful for learning more about developing many of the skills discussed in chapters 1 through 10 as well as the actions suggested in the remaining chapters.

Brain Rules: 12 Principles for Surviving and Thriving at Work, Home, and School by John Medina (Peer Press, 2009). This clever book connects health, time management, and related topics to success.

The 80/20 Principle: The Secret to Achieving More with Less by Richard Koch (Nicholas Brealey Publishing, 2007). This book explains the theory and practice behind the belief that 80 percent of your work is completed in 20 percent of your time, whereas the remaining 80 percent of your time is spent trying to complete the last 20 percent of your work.

The Money Book for the Young, Fabulous & Broke by Suze Orman (Penguin Group, 2005). This book is easy to read and contains useful suggestions for minimizing debt and spending wisely.

QBQ! The Question behind the Question: Practicing Personal Accountability at Work and in Life by John G. Miller (Putnam Publishing Group, 2004). This short, clever, inspirational book is about taking responsibility in the business world. You can easily apply it to your college activities and, at the same time, use it to help you prepare for your career.

Rich Dad, Poor Dad by Robert T. Kiyosaki (Warner Books, 1998). The author details the ins and outs of financial management for beginners.

Secrets of College Success: Over 600 Tips and Tricks Revealed by Lynn F. Jacobs and Jeremy S. Hyman (Jossey-Bass, 2010). Written by two professors, the book provides a variety of suggestions for both the academic and the nonacademic components of a college education and emphasizes the importance of time management.

The 7 Habits of Highly Effective People by Stephen R. Covey (Free Press, 2004). This classic book, which has sold more than 15 million copies, will inspire you to take responsibility for your success in an ethical way.

WEBSITE

www.usnews.com/professorsguide Check out this site for the weekly education column by Lynn F. Jacobs and Jeremy S. Hyman, authors of *Secrets of College Success* (see above).

"A SOUND MIND IN A SOUND BODY IS A SHORT BUT FULL DESCRIPTION OF A HAPPY STATE IN THE WORLD."

—JOHN LOCKE, SEVENTEENTH-CENTURY ENGLISH PHILOSOPHER

CHAPTER 2

DEVELOPING PHYSICAL SKILLS

STAY WELL • LOOK GOOD • TYPE WELL • WRITE LEGIBLY

Most people don't think of physical skills when considering college unless they are jocks or sports nuts. However, physical skills are very important. First of all, many majors require specialized physical skills. Some are obvious, like the skills required for art and music careers, and some not so obvious, like chemistry, where spilling stuff is not really a good idea. There are too many programs and too many physical skills associated with them to provide a discussion of the specific skills for each. If you choose a field that requires physical skills, make sure you add them to your list. We will, however, discuss some general physical skills that are valuable in the world of work— and in college, too.

The first two skills—stay well and look good—are obvious, but they're still important to address. The last two—type well and write legibly—are just as important to you as the speed and accuracy with which bricklayers mix and apply mortar. Fast and accurate typing and legible writing will raise your chances of success in college and the work world more than you can imagine.

"Eat not to dulness [sic]. Drink not to elevation."

—Benjamin Franklin

Wait until you get mono, strep, and pneumonia all at the same time, only to have those followed by tonsillitis. Avoiding these and other diseases is not just a matter of genes, your general physical makeup, or luck. It also depends on your ability to eat a balanced diet, get enough rest and exercise, and avoid destructive behaviors.

Good health means you'll have the energy and alertness necessary to do a good job. Employers prefer workers who show up on time and are ready to work. "Alertness" is a word frequently used in interviews and published lists of characteristics of a good worker. Good health will also mean higher grades and the energy to undertake leadership activities (which employers appreciate) while you are at college.

An accounting professor I know tells his students that while socializing is part of the job interview, don't drink alcohol even if the interviewer does. He says you need your full faculties to answer the questions well. He has heard plenty of horror stories about reckless talk and behavior resulting from interviewees thinking they are at a keg party. On the other hand, a recent graduate with a great job maintains—on the grounds that it is important to be yourself—that one drink is okay with dinner, if you usually have one.

As far as drug use is concerned: what you may not realize is that *any* contact with the law on drug charges can harm your chances of getting government jobs. The question of whether or not you have been arrested almost always appears on job applications, especially those for the government, and you don't want to be in a position of lying or admitting to a drug or alcohol-related arrest.

COURSES: Courses in nutrition are available on many campuses and may even fulfill liberal arts or general studies core requirements. Courses on self-damaging behaviors such as drug and alcohol abuse may be found in psychology and sociology departments. There also may be exercise courses that allow you to work out for credit.

NON-COURSE ACTIVITIES: "Wellness floors," which encourage healthy lifestyles (including no drinking, smoking, and/or drugs), are available in dormitories on many campuses. If you are on a floor with no theme, get your friends to argue for quiet hours after 11 p.m. Make a proposal at the first floor meeting and see who objects. If everyone living near you says "no," try to move right then and there. Floor mates are dangerous enough to your health because of the germs they spread. The hours they keep and the pressure they put on you to participate in destructive behavior is an even more serious threat.

One of my students has the following advice:

> *"It's not so easy to eat right if you live in the dorms and are given the choice between greasy dining hall food and takeout. Most of the time, though, the fear of gaining that 'freshman 15' will keep you from eating too much junk food and will steer you to eating complete meals. The free gym on campus is too tempting to pass up, and you can even take exercise courses. There's nothing more efficient then getting an easy A for a class that helps you stay in shape."*

Participating in an intercollegiate or intramural sport or a regular exercise program is a great idea—however, eating well and exercising are not the keys to staying healthy in college. What's most important is getting enough sleep and avoiding "destructive behavior," such as binge drinking and pulling all-nighters. It's easy to stay up until 4 a.m. hanging out, but get eight hours of sleep as often as possible. If you need to get your stomach pumped because you drank too much, you're not going to get anything done for a while. Be responsible (to yourself and others) when it comes to partying at school.

Likewise, take good care of yourself when it comes to smoking. If you arrive at college as a nonsmoker, don't get addicted. If you are addicted, use your college years to break the habit. Most smokers aren't happy about their habit—I've never met one who was. Smokers get sick more often than nonsmokers, and, by way of secondhand smoke, they jeopardize the health of others. Besides, smoking costs you valuable time and money—time and money that you could be spending on more important things. And on the job front, it's important to know that employers prefer nonsmokers. As an alumnus who works for a big stock brokerage once said to me, "Smokers typically smoke right before attending a meeting, so they stink, and smokers take more breaks . . . so they are unattractive hires." Smoking may not prevent you from having a successful career; however, in most cases, it won't do you any good either.

LOOK GOOD

"Clothes make the man. Naked people have little or no influence in society."

—Mark Twain

On the topic of looking good, Ben Franklin once said, "Harvard students learn little more than how to carry themselves handsomely and enter a room genteelly (which might as well be acquired at dancing school) and from whence they return, after an abundance of trouble and charge, as great blockheads as ever, only more proud and self-conceited."[1]

Ben Franklin was not a big fan of the elitism of higher education. He thought too much of it was "ornamental," which we will discuss more in chapter 12. But he knew the importance of clothes. When he was the ambassador to France, he did not compete with the fancy clothing of the French but dressed simply to make a statement about the democratic spirit of the American Revolution. Appropriate dress depends on the setting. Franklin did well with eighteenth-century women, if the truth was told, but I don't think he would cut it today.

When you decide what to wear for a job interview or to work, just remember you are not a revolutionary.

Let's face it: in the work world, first impressions usually do count, unless you are a hypercompetitive brainiac like Bill Gates, for whom looking good is beside the point. People make decisions on physical appearance quickly.

"Looking good" means being well groomed. Not everyone is born looking like Brad Pitt or Angelina Jolie, but the effort that you put into making yourself presentable says a lot about your character. Your appearance communicates who you are, and you must decide what you want it to say about you. If you come to a job interview or to work with your hair a mess, smelling bad either from a lack of bathing or too much perfume or cologne, and wearing clothes you pull out of the laundry bag without ironing, you show a lack of respect for both yourself and those around you. The best advice is to avoid shorts, jeans, and T-shirts.

COURSES: Too bad Franklin's description of Harvard doesn't hold up today for Harvard or anywhere else. Some physical exercise courses might work at least for good posture, but don't count on it. Actually, MIT at one time had a program in how to dress and act like a normal person, but most schools don't.

NON-COURSE ACTIVITIES: Put yourself in situations in which you interact socially or professionally with the kind of people likely to be your future employers. See whether you can get yourself appointed to a committee that works with alumni or the board of trustees. Go to local chamber of commerce meetings that are open to the public or to school board and local government meetings. In other words, hang out with the rich and powerful. Watch the way they dress and the way they carry themselves.

*"Typing 35 words per minute error free
is a set-in-stone necessity—kind of like
being able to find the job interview.
If you can't even do this, don't bother."*

—A senior vice president for a major investment firm

Although you may be one of the majority people who are on the computer and other electronic devices all the time, you need to check yourself to see whether you can type at least 35 words a minute with no errors. I still see a lot of students hunting for keys and pecking at the keyboard—even those who can perform at high speeds on their smartphones.

One of the reasons that speedy and accurate typing is important is that in almost any job you will have to write up reports. Gone are the days of typewriters—and of secretaries and typing pools who will transcribe your reports for you. That means that highly paid professionals are doing their own typing. For example, consulting companies who pay some of their analysts $200,000 dollar a year *don't* give them secretaries to type their reports. The faster and more accurately you can type, the better.

You can easily check your speed with one of the major typing tests available online and listed at the end of this chapter. If you don't meet the minimum of 35 words per minute, practice an hour a day for three days in a row and you will be surprised how much faster and better you type. Learning to type well is one of the clearest and easiest skills to master. It just takes commitment—and not looking at your fingers!

Meeting this standard will save you a lot of time during your college career. It will also open many doors for initial jobs and advancement. Good word processors can be hired at between $10 and $20 an hour by "temp" firms, but the minimum level for these firms is 45 words per minute. The temp opportunity alone makes having the skill worthwhile for its higher pay. But there is more! Jobs in temp firms frequently lead to permanent jobs. I know several successful, highly paid people who started in a temp position in their company. Chapter 13 provides more information on how temp firms can be important to your skills education, and chapter 16 shows how a temp job can lead to a permanent career.

Good typing will also allow you to be a team leader without the embarrassment of having to ask for the job. After all, if you are the one at the computer, you are virtually in control of the team because you filter your teammates' ideas as you type.

Aside from the obvious payoffs, typing well makes a nice impression on employers and supervisors because it shows you have enough discipline to do what it takes to succeed. Many employers worry about the work ethic of their new hires, because so many twenty-year-olds with bad attitudes act as if they are above making copies and typing reports. But demonstrating your good typing skills also signifies other important skills such as self-motivation, attention to detail, and the ability to edit and proof.

Every time I mention the typing skill, people in the audience come up and say something similar to what a special education teacher once said to me, "I never took a typing class, and it takes me four hours to write a four- or five-page report." Don't let that happen to you.

COURSES: Take courses that require typed papers in your freshman year. The practice will help you improve your speed. If your speed doesn't improve, the many extra hours you spend typing these papers will probably provide sufficient incentive for you to take the remedial action suggested below. Type everything you hand in.

NON-COURSE ACTIVITIES: Speedy and accurate typing requires continuous practice, and speed only comes if you do not look at your fingers. If you cannot stop looking at the keys, try a computer-based typing training program like Mavis Beacon, or get an unused keyboard and paint over the keys to practice typing without looking at the letters and numbers. Also, practice your accuracy when doing instant messaging and sending email.

"You may not be able to read a doctor's handwriting and prescription, but you'll notice his bills are neatly typewritten."

—Earl Wilson, twentieth-century journalist, author, and gossip columnist

I had not planned to include handwriting as an important skill until I read the following comment from a senior vice president at a very large company:

"Writing clearly and quickly does not seem like it would be important at a first glance; however, in many cases, it makes and breaks success. In many meetings, it is not socially acceptable to be pounding away on your laptop— a simple pen and paper will do fine. Pen and paper allow you to draw diagrams, add side notes, and color-code. Writing clearly is a huge benefit because it allows your notes to be distributed to people who could not attend the meeting, as well as for your future knowledge."

I was opposed to neat handwriting as a skill because when I take notes, which is rarely, I can't read them ten minutes later. I didn't want to include it because I couldn't face reality: I will never, ever be able to adequately master all the Skill Sets in my own book!

Having good handwriting that enables you to take decipherable notes quickly is a valuable asset. Aside from having a good personal record of what happened at any meeting, taking good notes can be used to influence future meetings and events. You can present what you have recorded faithfully but still organize the information in a way that helps express your point of view.

There is one more big advantage to clear handwriting. It will enable you to write professional-looking thank-you notes every time you go on an interview or get help from a mentor or future employer.

An email or typed letter just won't do it. A readable note that looks as if it was written by an adult and not by a child or medical doctor works wonders. Employers and alums who serve as mentors tell me how much they appreciate it. Receiving a short note from students for whom I've written a letter of recommendation makes me want to write more letters for them in the future.

COURSES: If you use your laptop to take notes in class, choose one or two courses where the note taking is limited and use a pen and paper. If you don't use a laptop and take notes by hand, make sure you can read the notes. Type your handwritten notes the next day to see whether you can read them accurately. If you have essay examinations in class, evaluate the legibility of your writing when you get your exams back.

NON-COURSE ACTIVITIES: Volunteer to keep the minutes for a student group and see how well you can type them up for the next meeting. Make it a point to look at your handwritten notes when you write cards to your family and love ones to see whether they are legible.

USEFUL RESOURCES

BOOKS

The New Professional Image: Dress Your Best for Every Business Situation by Susan Bixler and Nancy Nix-Rice (Adams Media, 2005). Consult the latest edition for up-to-date professional dress etiquette.

WEBSITES

www.webmd.com Consult this website for information on how to stay healthy.

www.computerhope.com Check out this site for a variety of suggestions for improving typing.

www.mavisbeacon.com Mavis Beacon Teaches Typing is the most widely used typing tutoring software. It provides a way for the very poor typist to develop speed and accuracy.

www.typing-lessons.org Use the free exercises on this website to improve your typing speed.

"SPEAK NOT BUT WHAT MAY BENEFIT OTHERS OR YOURSELF."

—BENJAMIN FRANKLIN

CHAPTER 3

COMMUNICATING VERBALLY

**CONVERSE ONE-ON-ONE • PRESENT TO GROUPS •
USE VISUAL DISPLAYS**

Verbal communication is a formal term for talking and listening. Some people are good talkers, and some are good listeners, but you need to be good at both. Good verbal communication leads to mutual understanding. As you will see, talking in an informal conversation is very different from speaking to groups.

This Skill Set is closely related to working directly with people, the topic of chapter 5. If you are skilled at establishing trust and cooperating with others, you will have an easier time communicating verbally. The two Skill Sets can enhance each other, but they can also be developed independently.

"Bore, n. A person who talks when you wish him to listen."

—Ambrose Bierce, nineteenth-century writer

Having a conversation with someone, in a job setting or elsewhere, requires both talking and listening. Communication is a two-way street and can only be effective if your desire and skill at talking is equal to your ability to be a good listener. In fact, most experts say that listening is more important than talking in good communications, which is why you have probably heard the saying that "God gave you two ears and one mouth."

Your style of speaking and the clarity with which you speak are just as important as using correct grammar. Equally important is the way you organize your conversation. It's important to stick to the point and not wander all over the place. In short, you need to be strategic about what information you are trying to provide and what information you are trying to get.

Effective one-on-one conversations require a variety of good habits: asking questions to check for mutual understanding, never talking more than thirty seconds at one time, not interrupting the other person, and using terms that both parties understand. Like most skills, reading about how to speak effectively is less important than being reflective about your communication effectiveness in your conversations.

Mutual understanding through good verbal communication in the work world is vital. Misunderstandings can lead to disasters in dealing with customers and coworkers. If you cannot understand what your boss wants you to do, you have the choice of asking for clarification or doing the wrong thing. The former is better, but getting it the first time is the best. A senior human resources person writes, "I think conversing one-on-one is my main skill set. A new-hire must be able to carry a conversation—willing to learn. The training process that all our new-hires must complete can be very confusing, and we expect each new-hire to ask questions in order to grasp a full understanding. If someone cannot hold a decent conversation, I am hesitant to even place them in a lower-end job, even if they have the education and training."

Solid verbal communication skills are critical for being an effective employee. In the following story, a senior vice president for a firm illustrates the importance of listening carefully and thinking about what the other person is saying by his phrase "pushing back the conversation":

"An eighty-year-old lady walks into a hardware store and says to you, 'I need a ladder, to climb onto my roof.' You ask her why she needs to climb onto her roof. She says, 'To reach my tree.' You realize there might be more to this story, so you ask her why she wants to reach her tree. She replies, 'My cat is stuck up in my tree and is afraid of heights.' You offer her a can of tuna fish that will solve the problem of the cat in the tree more effectively and less riskily than the ladder. If you had not talked with her, she could have gotten hurt and/or never solved her problem. If you were to offer her the can of tuna fish at the start, she wouldn't have understood your reasoning. Pushing back the conversation allows for empathy and builds a trust relationship between you and the client—sometimes they don't always know what they need, but they realize that they want their problem solved."

This story illustrates a pattern found in all jobs. Carefully listening to and questioning clients or coworkers is critical in building good relationships. Your goal is to help others who in turn will help you do the best job you can.

COURSES: The key to developing good one-on-one communication skills is to constantly reflect on how well you communicate. Your course work will give you a great deal of practice as you communicate with your instructor and with your classmates. Beyond that, courses that contain the words *human relations* or *interpersonal communication*, whether offered in business, psychology, or speech communications, can be useful. Also, look for courses in mediation and conflict resolution, because they put a high premium on effective interpersonal communication. Courses that require fieldwork, direct observation, video playback of classroom presentations, and team activities are most useful. Seminar courses, usually taken in the junior and senior year and usually within your major, can be useful in practicing one-on-one communication skills as you make presentations and react to the presentations of others.

NON-COURSE ACTIVITIES: Use your experience in your dorm during your freshman year as a place to practice and reflect on your ability to talk and listen as a way of developing mutual understanding. When there is a misunderstanding, reflect on why you think it occurred and talk to the individual with whom you had the misunderstanding. Many universities have programs within residence halls to develop communication and leadership skills. Ask the residence-life staff at your college about these programs; they provide solid experience to develop your one-on-one communication skills. Finally, if you are ready to devote the time and energy, join a Toastmasters group, which establishes small groups through which you can practice speaking in a supportive environment (visit the organization's website at www.toastmasters.org). In Syracuse, there are more than fifteen different groups within ten miles and two right at the university, so there probably is a group near you.

PRESENT TO GROUPS

> *"An effective speaker knows that the success or failure of his talk is not for him to decide—it will be decided in the minds and hearts of his hearers."*
>
> —Dale Carnegie

Talking to groups means presenting and listening to any number of people, ranging from a few to thousands! The techniques that you use will vary depending on the size and the group setting, but they are essentially different from one-on-one conversations. You will not be able to maintain eye contact with everyone in the group or ask questions about mutual understanding when speaking to a group. Successful group presentations require careful organization and specific ways to find out whether you are getting your message across. Learn to ask yourself, "How will I know whether my talk to a group has been successful?" before you give the speech. After the speech, take some time to reflect and see whether you passed your own test. Did you stay on task and talk at a reasonable pace? Did you make eye contact with different people in the room? Did you receive good questions and give clear answers?

One of the most critical skills you need to develop in order to speak effectively to groups is to not be fearful of a crowd. Some people who do very heroic things get sweaty palms and become speechless when placed in front of a group. The size is not always the determining factor. Some people can handle a couple of hundred strangers well but get nervous in front of a group of ten coworkers.

You also must recognize the short attention span of people, especially in a group setting. Getting an audience's attention in fifteen seconds requires real talent, but if you can hook them in sixty—the "golden minute" at the beginning of a speech—you should be safe.

The president of a growing communications business points out a well-known rule about speaking to groups. He writes, "If you want to have people remember something, they must hear it three times: first at the beginning when you summarize your speech, once in the middle when you explain your thesis, and once at the end when you summarize your topic again. Also, the most effective speeches should only make three important points."

Here's how the Dale Carnegie Institute, one of the premier sales and leadership training companies, promoted one of its "high-impact presentation two-day seminars":

> *"The end result of giving a powerful presentation should be that your audience comes away with useful information. Here are some guidelines on communicating with greater impact.*
>
> * *Have energetic body language and an upbeat tone of voice.*
> * *Maintain eye contact with your audience.*

- *Avoid being tied to a script or lectern.*
- *Get your audience involved by using examples and holding a Q&A session."*

These may be well-known and obvious points about addressing groups of people, but like many other commonsensical ideas, they are hard to put into practice. Use your college experience to develop good public-speaking habits that you can use when you enter the work world.

You do not have to be an accomplished speaker; you only need to be able to clearly accomplish limited goals in speaking with a group of people. Decide whether the primary purpose of your speech is to build trust, convey specific information, or motivate future action. You don't have to be entertaining to achieve this purpose.

The ability to talk to groups of people is critical in many work-place situations. Initially you will probably not be placed in front of a group but will observe how your superiors handle such presentations. A businesswoman who was interviewed for this book said that she does not expect an entry-level person to make presentations to strangers, but by the second year, that person should be able to make presentations to groups of his or her peers. Over the long run, being able to make good group presentations will catch the eye of people within your organization as well as outside of it.

COURSES: Start by forcing yourself to raise your hand in class. Take at least one speech communications course that focuses on presenting to groups, and take several other courses in which such activities are a requirement. Some colleges have business-presentation courses that are also useful. The best kinds of courses are those in which you are videotaped and then critiqued by the instructor and your peers.

NON-COURSE ACTIVITIES: Participate in activities in which you are required to make formal and informal presentations to groups. Any organization that you join will have leadership positions that require such presentations. A good place to start in your freshman year is in the residence hall in floor meetings and on councils of which you can easily become a member.

"There are many true statements about complex topics that are too long to fit on a PowerPoint slide."

—Edward Tufte, American statistician

A visual display does not necessarily mean a fancy PowerPoint presentation. It can be a single sheet of paper handed out to the group that outlines the topics you plan to discuss. You do need, however, to become proficient in using PowerPoint as well as creating visual displays on handouts, overheads, or newsprint-like papers that you place on the wall. Just remember the quote above and don't try to dump everything you want to say in a PowerPoint or a handout.

Visual displays can be critical even when you are talking one-on-one, but they are always critical when you speak to a group. Visual displays, by definition, help you move from simply telling the audience to showing them. By asking them to react to a chart or a diagram, you involve the audience in the speech, which will naturally keep them more interested.

There are two related tasks that you must perform well in order to use visual displays effectively. First, you need to master and organize your content well enough to integrate a display into your actual talk. Second, you need to produce the display, which ranges from simple layouts on an $8\frac{1}{2}$ by 11-inch piece of paper to a PowerPoint presentation. The first task always precedes and defines the second.

As a project manager who is in charge of important clients for a major financial firm said, "I always ask people how they would set up a meeting and prepare a presentation. I remember one woman I interviewed told me she used PowerPoint and set up the meetings two hours apart. Well, that's great, but I wanted to hear that the first thing she would think of is knowing her topic and doing research. I don't want a presentation with no substance and a bunch of pretty flowers."

Although the project manager is correct in saying that substance must precede form, your ability to make pretty displays and use PowerPoint to help your boss (who presumably knows the substance) shine can get you a big fat raise. Of course, you will have to understand what your boss is talking about. Most of the people you will be working for will not have the skills—and even if they do, they will not have the time—to take care of displays. Your display skills will make you indispensable. Just be careful to avoid the tag of "a great display maker, but what else can he do?" The best way to avoid such a label is to make substantive suggestions about the content of presentations that will show your superiors you are ready for more responsibility.

If you are making a presentation using a set of PowerPoint slides, avoid the common mistake made by far too many speakers: they read what is on the slides to the audience. Assume the audience can read and elaborate on one or more of the points on the slide.

Don't ignore the importance of a handout. Sometimes you will not even need a PowerPoint if you have a good handout. You should provide your audience with a copy of your PowerPoint presentation in some paper form so they can take notes.

COURSES: Some specialized courses in information or educational technology may be available to introduce you to all the possible bells and whistles of display making, but the fancy stuff is not necessary. It makes more sense to select courses that require group presentations, including ones with PowerPoint. They can be found in almost every field.

NON-COURSE ACTIVITIES: In whatever activity you undertake that involves talking to a group, force yourself to use at least paper handouts. This will teach you to integrate your talks with visual displays. Volunteer to make flyers and even simple brochures for a student organization or an academic department.

USEFUL RESOURCES

BOOKS

Crucial Conversations: Tools for Talking When Stakes Are High
by Kerry Patterson, Joseph Grenny, Ron McMillan, and Al Switzler
(McGraw-Hill, 2002). The authors provide helpful advice using
examples from a variety of situations.

How to Win Friends and Influence People by Dale Carnegie (Pocket
Books, 1982). This classic book provides valuable examples and principles on how to talk to people. It is the best place to start improving
your oral communication skills.

***Power Points!: How to Design and Deliver Presentations That Sizzle
and Sell*** by Harry Mills (Amacom, 2007). This book (with DVD
included) provides useful advice on developing presentations as well
as how to use PowerPoint. It is oriented to sales and covers more than
most would use in a career.

WEBSITE

www.toastmasters.org Consult the Toastmasters website for tips and
advice on giving speeches. Think about joining a local chapter.

"WRITING,
WHEN PROPERLY MANAGED . . .
IS BUT A
DIFFERENT
NAME
FOR CONVERSATION."

—LAURENCE STERNE,
EIGHTEENTH-CENTURY AUTHOR

CHAPTER 4

COMMUNICATING IN WRITING

WRITE WELL • EDIT AND PROOF •
USE WORD-PROCESSING TOOLS •
MASTER ONLINE COMMUNICATIONS

The purpose of written communication is the same as that of oral communication: promoting mutual understanding between two or more people. No matter what your major, college provides an excellent opportunity to practice and develop your writing skills.

"Writing is easy. All you do is stare at a blank sheet of paper until drops of blood form on your forehead."

—Gene Fowler, twentieth-century writer

Writer's block is okay for starving poets and novelists; it's just part of the process. But for anyone working for a boss, writer's block is a quicker way to get fired than producing poor copy.

At the other end of the spectrum is "writer's diarrhea," where once you start you cannot stop. Clients and fellow workers do not have the time to wade through unnecessary verbiage and figure out what you are trying to say.

Aim to come out of college with the ability to write quickly, effortlessly, and succinctly. In short, learn to write easily and well. A great (and very short) guide to excellent writing is the classic *The Elements of Style* by William Strunk Jr. and E. B. White. Here's a little Strunk and White wisdom: "Vigorous writing is concise. A sentence should contain no unnecessary words, a paragraph no unnecessary sentences, for the same reason that a drawing should have no unnecessary lines and a machine no unnecessary parts. This requires not that the writer make all his sentences short, or that he avoids all detail and treats his subjects only in outline, but that every word tell."[1]

Writing in the work world usually comes in response to a request for information or a directive to inform others. It almost always takes the form of a memo ranging from a paragraph to no more than two pages, and frequently requires the use of numbered points. Writing for your job will not be like writing for courses, in which the assignment is designed to help you learn something. Instead, the purpose of work writing is generally to brief others about a problem or situation and to possibly propose solutions.

A senior human resources director at a major company says, "Being able to write clearly is a must at my company. We have a database that holds problems and potential solutions—inputted by every employee in our implementation field. Our production team uses this database to fix problems that the rest of the company encounters. If they can't comprehend what the employee is trying to say, they can't fix it. We also collect writing samples from our potential employees. We ask a number of questions and ask them to respond—quite simple, but we can tell who can write and who cannot."

As one moves up the ladder, writing becomes even more important. If you have an idea that you can only explain verbally, you are limited to influencing only those with whom you speak. However, a one-page memo, circulated throughout the organization, can become part of a process that leads to the improvement and implementation of your idea. Also, putting your idea on paper makes it much harder for others to steal it.

COURSES: Most colleges have writing courses, sometimes titled "technical writing," which attempt to help you write for audiences you are likely to encounter in the world of work. Required lower-level writing courses can be helpful in improving your mechanics and also understanding the importance of writing for an audience other than yourself. In addition, take as many courses as you can that require you to write logs, planning documents, and evaluation reports. These can be found in the social sciences and in many of the professional schools. Courses in which you write for clients and get feedback from them, or in simulated situations like a legislative hearing, are the most effective. If your school has a communications program, take public relations and news writing classes, because they will help you write more succinctly as well as improve your grammar and punctuation. If you can find a course in grant writing, which actually requires you to write grant proposals, take it.

NON-COURSE ACTIVITIES: Pursue internships, part-time and summer jobs, and student activities in which you will need to write brief reports or plans. Working for a legislator at the state or federal level usually requires you to draft letters responding to constituents. This is excellent training for writing in many job situations.

EDIT AND PROOF

"If I had more time, I would have written a shorter letter."

—T. S. Eliot, twentieth-century poet

Editing and proofing require patience and attention to detail, as well as an ability to understand what the writer is trying to communicate and how the reader will interpret it. *Editing* refers to revising your first draft—organizing content between and within paragraphs, choosing the right words, and making sure the text is understandable and interesting. *Proofreading* is the last stage of the revision process, checking for misspellings, omissions, and grammatical mistakes. You should proofread your final draft before you submit it to anyone. Some of the proofing process is simply mechanical and is greatly helped by Microsoft Word with its spell-check and grammar-checking features. The editing part, however, requires as much practice and skill as writing.

Most college students develop poor skills in editing and proofing because they write their papers at the last minute. They consider themselves lucky if they have time to run the spell-check before they grab their papers out of the printer so they can hand them in on time. If this sounds like you, the most critical step in learning to edit and proof is to reserve time to do just that. This means planning to finish what you consider to be a final draft of your paper well enough in advance of the deadline; print it out so you can carefully edit and proof it. Proofing and editing your written assignment on the screen is never a good idea.

It is also a good idea to learn some of the basic symbols of editing, which can be found in most good dictionaries under "proofreading" or "proofreaders' marks." Marks include symbols to delete, begin a paragraph, and spell out. Using these symbols will help you revise not only your own work but that of your employer's as well. When you get into a job in which your boss wants you to edit and proof something she wrote, you can look professional by using well-known proofreading symbols.

A misspelling, which would lose you a couple of points on your paper in a course, could spell doom in the workplace. As a senior executive says, "Who wants to buy our multimillion dollar product when we can't even spell it right? Attention to detail is key in the workforce—without it, don't bother." Sound harsh? That's only because your teachers and professors have misled you with only minor point deductions for misspellings. To put the importance of editing and proofing in proper perspective, leaving a "not" out of a business proposal is about the same as a surgeon taking out your left kidney when your right one is diseased.

On the upside, if your boss knows she can throw a rough draft at you and you can edit and proof it so it is more readable, you will save her time and anguish. As long as you also excel in other areas, superiors consider editing and proofing a direct path to higher-level positions.

One way *not* to learn to edit and proof is to get someone else to do it for you. Many have roommates and friends do it for them. Others use the writing centers that most colleges and universities maintain. Still others use their Mommies and Daddies and even grandmothers. All of these sources in moderation may be helpful initially, especially when you are a freshman. However, they can easily become a crutch and will prevent you from developing your own proofing and editing skills.

COURSES: Some basic writing courses will help you develop your writing and editing skills, but you can benefit by more intense course work, such as one that trains you to be a writing consultant and earn credit helping others with their writing. A powerful way to develop your editing and proofing skills is to take courses that generate written products for someone in the community. Your professor will not want to be embarrassed by typos and misspellings and will subject you to a constant review process.

NON-COURSE ACTIVITIES: Try to get a job editing and proofing written manuscripts produced by one of your professors, or seek a job in which you are on a team that produces a large report. Write or edit for a school publication, even if it is a newsletter with limited distribution. These experiences will help you improve your editing and proofing skills.

USE WORD-PROCESSING TOOLS

"The real problem is not whether machines think but whether men do."

—B. F. Skinner, twentieth-century psychologist

Bill Gates is the man behind Microsoft and whether we love or despise him, we all need to thank him for Microsoft Word, which is the only word-processing tool you need to master. Other word-processing programs, no matter how cheap or quaint, are useless in writing for work. Most of you already know that and have some experience using Word. The rest of you need to get on board.

Even if you use Word, you may not know all of its features, some of which can speed up and clarify the writing process as well as help edit and proof what you write. Check out the menus and toolbar options. How many have you used? It's not necessary for you to use all of them, but you should know how to print out readable and attractive copy, to move text around, to save text for future use, and to check for grammar and spelling errors.

My favorite tool, and one that you will find very useful in a job situation, is tracking. Let's say your boss has sent you a business proposal (as a Word document) to review and make necessary suggestions or changes. Open the document and click on the "Track Changes" icon or select it from a drop-down menu. Then when you make a change or correction on the document, Word makes the change in a different color. When you return the document to your boss, she can see both the original version of the proposal and your suggested changes. This speeds up the editing and proofing process immensely. I cite this as one example of the hidden treasures offered by Word. You might find others. Word has terrific timesaving shortcuts that you can easily pick up by watching others or consulting reference books on Word.

Your ability to use Microsoft Word effortlessly and effectively will impress your supervisors, especially those who may not have kept up with the latest innovations. Conversely, if you are not familiar with the time-saving and quality-increasing features of Word, you could be in deep trouble if your colleague, or—even worse—your boss, is watching over your shoulder as you try to figure out the Find and Replace function five minutes before a report is due.

Although word-processing skills don't seem like a big deal, they should not be taken for granted. One of my former students, who was now completing a master's degree at one of the top graduate schools in the world, wrote this to me: "I am shocked by how many people in my program don't know how to do a lot of stuff in Word (formatting, tracking, etc.)—things I'm sure I only know because of my undergraduate experience on various projects."

Hopefully you will master this skill set as soon as possible to avoid "shocking" your future boss or your colleagues in graduate school.

COURSES: No college that I know of gives a course in Microsoft Word. Even if they did, it would not have much impact unless you continue using the skills after the course. Like developing your writing skills, your best bet for learning word processing is to take courses that force you to write and learn the necessary word-processing skills as you write your paper. If you take a course in which you are on a team that produces a paper, watch the person doing the typing and ask questions about some of the procedures he or she performs.

NON-COURSE ACTIVITIES: Find a friend who really knows Word and have him or her coach you on features you don't know. This works particularly well while you are actually writing a paper. While working on his or her own project, your friend can be in the same room with you, available to answer your questions when they arise. Another possibility (best done when you don't have a deadline) is to take an hour or two to check out Word's toolbar options and consult Microsoft Help.

MASTER ONLINE COMMUNICATIONS

"I live in a town of 2,000 but I can choose from among 5,000 virtual assistants."

—Gayle Buske, small business expert

Electronic communications are now used to create virtual jobs and virtual meetings. Workers who travel or work from home take directions from bosses, exchange views with colleagues, and complete tasks over email. Programs like Google Docs are used to create an electronic, document-based forum for teamwork so that a virtual office of people anywhere in the world can exchange views. The use of chat services and webinars where a telephone conversation is facilitated by shared displays or documents is also increasing.

As a former student of mine now at a large corporation writes, "In many jobs today you might not work directly with anyone or nearly anyone. At some point, you'll be virtual, and learning how to be successful when working remotely is a different and important skill from day-to-day management interaction. Global is a reality of today's companies."

In most jobs, email communication to one individual or a group is the norm. College is a great place to practice the art of virtual interactions. Microsoft Outlook or Outlook Express is most commonly used in the workplace, so learn your way around those programs.

Send emails with files attached to them or tables in the body of the email. Make sure you are also familiar with the Calendar tool; most companies will rely on the Calendar to set up meetings. Using the tool on your own is also a great way to practice organization.

Learning how to write properly formatted and easy-to-read emails is also important. Be careful that you do not use AIM or cell phone text message abbreviations in your emails or your employer will say "C U L8R, U R DONE." Make your point quickly. If you have a lot to say, either make a list or attach a separate document file.

Make an email signature. Just as a signature validates a letter, your signature should validate your emails. Typically it will include your name, email, and contact numbers. Many students also include their majors and graduation year.

If your cell phone is compatible, try syncing it to your email. Many companies will expect you to be reachable beyond the office. If a meeting time changes, you'll need to know about it. If they want feedback quickly, you'll need to be able to make suggestions. Learning to use mobile email is just as important as sending emails from an actual computer.

Web design and the online presentation of information are growing components of many of today's jobs. Students who have at least some knowledge in these areas will have an advantage over other applicants. No matter what industry you are a part of, familiarity with website creation and management will make you a more valuable employee. Pay attention to how people use websites and how they read information online. Understanding the concept of user-friendliness will improve your design skills dramatically.

Social media tools such as Twitter and Facebook are prominent marketing tools. You may have used them on your own before, but remember companies are using them to communicate with a target consumer demographic, not their friends. Learning how to use those tools in that framework and create content that has value to a specific audience will distinguish you from applicants who are only familiar with these tools on a social basis. LinkedIn is a tool in career connections. It is discussed in chapter 20 as a key tool in career networking.

Occasionally you will have to send information to another party that is too large to send by email and too small to bother hosting on a website. Familiarize yourself with online data storage tools where you can quickly upload bigger chunks of information for third-party access.

Communicating electronically can have its downside also. The constant interruptions that email brings, whether you work at a desk or use a portable device, can be a major roadblock to your success. It creates distractions that can interrupt thoughts when you are trying to write something. If you have become addicted to checking for messages from email or Twitter, you might be caught at a meeting and chastised. Bosses don't like to see this addiction even if they are addicted themselves. Learn to break the habit by turning off your portable device and fixing your desktop to not alert you to incoming email messages.

COURSES: Take courses in web design that teach you content management systems (CMS) like Wordpress or Drupal as a tool to fulfill project objectives. Avoid classes in computer science; they are too technical unless you plan to go into that field. If your professors communicate by email and use web tools to host assignments and course information, get into the habit of using them as well. Courses that explore marketing in a social media context will also help you develop your skills. When working in teams for classes, use Google Docs and other forms of shared electronic communications.

NON-COURSE ACTIVITIES: Get an internship where you work or intern for a company that uses such tools. Be careful when looking for government or nonprofit organization positions; they are not always up-to-date on the various electronic tools out there. Also, don't be afraid to explore graphic and web design software on your own. Many programs—Photoshop, Wordpress, and the like—have free trials you can download from the Web. Getting comfortable with a variety of different tools will help you learn how to use them on the job faster. Remember that the Internet itself has a variety of forums and resources that provide guides and tips on how to use these programs as well. Use the electronic communication tools described in this chapter in your extracurricular activities.

USEFUL RESOURCES

BOOKS

The Elements of Style, 4th edition, by William Strunk Jr., E. B. White, and Roger Angell (Allyn & Bacon, 1999). This book is short and very inexpensive. The emphasis on few words is right on.

On Writing Well: The Classic Guide to Writing Nonfiction by William Zinsser (HarperCollins, 2006). Zinsser looks at various types of nonfiction writing.

WEBSITES

http://office.microsoft.com This site provides video and written tutorials on using all Microsoft products.

http://owl.english.purdue.edu The Online Writing Lab (OWL) at Purdue University is widely used to help students at Purdue University and elsewhere, and it's free.

"NOTHING WE DO, HOWEVER VIRTUOUS, CAN BE ACCOMPLISHED ALONE."

—REINHOLD NIEBUHR,
TWENTIETH-CENTURY THEOLOGIAN

CHAPTER 5

WORKING DIRECTLY WITH PEOPLE

BUILD GOOD RELATIONSHIPS • WORK IN TEAMS • TEACH OTHERS

People skills are not just advocated by theologians but also by business people. Dale Carnegie quotes John D. Rockefeller, one of the hardest headed and richest SOBs of the late nineteenth and early twentieth centuries, who said, "The ability to deal with people is as purchasable a commodity as sugar or coffee. And I will pay more for that ability than for any other under the sun."[1]

Knowing how to work with others is critical to your career success, and it also makes life a lot more pleasant. Many human resources directors, employers, and experts rate people skills as the most vital of the ten Skill Sets. Because people skills are so important, they constitute two different Skill Sets in this book—working directly with people, which is this chapter's topic, and influencing people, which we will look at in chapter 6. While there is a fine line between "working with" and "influencing," the skills are different enough to warrant separate chapters. By creating these two Skill Sets, we give double weight to people skills in the calculation of the Skills Score. This is justified by the heavy emphasis that all employers place on the ability of their employees to work well together and to influence others, both within and outside the organization.

"The deepest principle in human nature is the craving to be appreciated."

—William James

Building good relationships with others is no easy task because it takes time and requires mutual trust and respect. Take the time necessary to work closely with others. Doing this well requires attention to a broad array of factors, including different cultural, ethnic, social, and economic backgrounds. Sensitivity to and understanding of these factors can often prevent struggles over power and authority or conflicts over competing interests, which sometimes irreparably damage relationships. Given the large number of factors, it's important to practice establishing good working relationships while in college.

One of the first tests of your ability to build a good relationship comes when you are interviewed for a job. Very literally, establishing a good relationship with your interviewer will determine whether or not you get the job.

Once you get the job, your success will depend on developing good working relationships with people throughout the organization. Having a relationship built on trust and mutual respect requires communicating clearly and working to resolve conflict in a positive way. Conflict is part of any relationship, and the challenge is to learn how to work with it effectively. You will deal with customers who may not trust you or your company. Your coworkers, especially if you do your work well, may see you as a threat; perhaps you will see them as a threat as well. Even more prevalent is the tendency for workers in one department to view those in other departments as incompetent or irresponsible. The only way to move past these conflicts is to keep the lines of communication open and to establish good working relationships based on cooperation.

Good working relationships make it possible to work more efficiently and effectively, not to mention more pleasantly. People with whom you have good relationships can also help you learn about or even obtain jobs throughout your career—this is usually called *networking*. Whether or not you have people who are willing to help you is a direct result of your ability (or inability) to establish good relationships. If, for example, you've developed a good working relationship with your boss, this could open unexpected possibilities for your future. One of the surest paths to career advancement is when your boss, who thinks you have done a great job, moves to another company and hires you six months later.

COURSES: Some psychology and sociology courses may introduce you to interpersonal and group dynamics that shape relationships. The more these courses require fieldwork and role-playing, the more helpful they will be. Your college may have courses in mediation and/or conflict resolution, which will be based more on experience than traditional courses in the social sciences. Social work courses may also be helpful, but they may not be open to you unless you are registered in a social work program. Other professional schools or programs like nursing and human development have courses that will prepare you to deal with future clients in those fields.

NON-COURSE ACTIVITIES: Fortunately, you will find opportunities to develop trusting and respectful relationships with others every day. Working things out with your roommate is a good sign that you are building interpersonal skills. A particularly useful non-course activity is to join a group that provides services to others, like Habitat for Humanity or a service fraternity or sorority. The internal cooperation among members as they seek to serve the outside world is very similar to what you will face in a job situation. Use Dale Carnegie principles in all your interactions with people at all levels. See the Useful Resources section at the end of the chapter.

"Never score without acknowledging a teammate."

—John Wooden, legendary UCLA basketball coach

You probably got a taste of working in teams in high school classes and, if you are like the majority of students I've interviewed, you didn't like it. The dislike of working in teams is natural because we live in a society that praises individualism and competition. If you are very competitive and want high grades, you do not want to depend on others. You want the control. If you are relaxed, you do not want the hyper people on the team bugging you.

Teamwork in high school classes, however, is not the same as teamwork in the world of work. You will have stronger common interests with your fellow workers than with your classmates, and the measure of success is not just what grade your teacher or professor gives you. Several of the Skill Sets already discussed are critical to your ability to work well in a team. They include time management, honesty, good verbal communications, the ability to proof and edit, and the capacity to form good relationships. Email skills will be important because email facilitates communication prior to and following meetings. Many businesses set up virtual teams in which the team members rarely meet face to face, if at all. There are also specific skills for working in a team, including reaching agreements with others, understanding the importance of concurring on how decisions will be made, running productive meetings, and designating roles like recorder. Accepting responsibilities assigned to you by the team and helping others do the same is also critical.

Perhaps the most important skill set you need for teamwork is patience and tolerance for the process. Teams rarely perform as well as team members think they should perform. The work of teams can take more time than expected and produce compromises that frequently lead directly to failure. Learning to be tolerant and to carefully pick your battles is essential to being a good team member.

College is the place to practice balancing your individual pursuit of excellence with the need to have a common goal and set of strategies. Don't make the mistake that many students do of seeing teamwork as one gigantic pebble in their shoe. See it as a challenge that you need to meet and as a setting in which you can enjoy the success of the team by doing your very best.

Expressing dislike or even a little uneasiness about working in a team will result in a short and unproductive job interview. Once you are in a job, failure to work well in teams leads to poor job reviews. Conversely, working well in teams gains you positive points throughout the organization and may lead to promotions that you would not otherwise get. You can whine about your team to your significant other, but always be positive about it at work in word and in deed. It's frustrating, but good teamwork is the law of most high-functioning organizations.

COURSES: Teamwork experiences can be found in every college program, especially in upper-division undergraduate courses. Look for professors who create team projects, especially those evaluated by someone other than them. Courses that prepare you for team mock trial competitions, teach you to set up a public relations campaign for the local Boys and Girls Club, or instruct you how to create a business plan for a start-up company provide excellent opportunities to develop teamwork skills.

NON-COURSE ACTIVITIES: The most powerful experience outside the classroom is probably in a fraternity or sorority, or in another tight-knit student organization that has to meet a budget projection or put on an event. Learning teamwork occurs best when failure has serious consequences. You can also gain valuable experience working on a college committee. These committees might involve faculty members and may give awards for teaching or select a speaker for commencement. They might be advisory groups to important programs like peer advising or residence life.

"A teacher affects eternity."

—Henry Adams, nineteenth-century author

Henry Adams, like most of us, may have been thinking of teaching as a situation of academic tutoring or one that involves a person lecturing at the chalkboard in a classroom. However, teaching occurs all the time in informal settings. It is as important in the world of work as it is in your everyday life with family and friends.

Teaching is a process in which one person—the teacher—takes action to improve what another person—the learner—does. Knowing how to teach is essential in every aspect of your life, whether it be teaching your little brother how to get dates or your roommate to stop throwing trash on your side of the room. You may even find yourself in a more formal setting, such as teaching CPR or training residence advisers on how to deal with out-of-control students.

The skills of a good teacher grow out of many of the skills discussed in this book. Verbal communication is critical, but so is asking and answering the right questions (more on that in chapter 9). Beyond that, teaching requires a consciousness about where the learner is and the ability to implement strategies that get the learner to move to where he wants to be. The best approach, according to a president of a growing and successful company, is to promote learning by doing. He writes, "If you want to teach someone something, show him or her how to do it and then get out of their way. If they get it wrong, well, at least they tried. Using this method has also helped me delegate better because teaching by doing requires the teacher to remember that everyone will do things differently."

This quotation not only provides good advice on how you can be a better teacher but also illustrates that even the president of a company has to be a teacher on a regular basis. The best companies are committed to encouraging or even requiring senior staff to guide and educate junior staff. You will need to become a teacher within your organization soon after you arrive; your capacity to "train" others to do your job will also help you move into other positions.

COURSES: Courses to develop your informal teaching skills are not necessarily offered in education departments or programs. The best kinds of courses for your development as a teacher are those in which you practice teaching. It might be an adult literacy course in which part of the requirement is to tutor adults, or it might be a course in social work or psychology in which part of the credit is earned by tutoring at a community center. Jump at the chance to be an undergraduate teaching assistant, if given the opportunity.

NON-COURSE ACTIVITIES: In many community service activities, you can find opportunities for doing one-on-one tutoring. You can also find jobs in tutoring with organizations like Kaplan, which provides training in SAT, LSAT, and GRE tests, Sylvan Learning, and Kuman Math and Reading Centers—or start your own tutoring service. Just search in Google using the term "tutoring" and you will find job opportunities. In addition, your work in any student organization will eventually involve teaching new members about the organization or training your replacement to do your job if you are given a promotion. Part-time jobs in a fast-food restaurant or retail store will require you to train new employees, even if you remain in the job for a short period of time. This practice will improve your teaching skills. Peer advising for your college can also improve these skills.

USEFUL RESOURCES

BOOKS

Coaching and Mentoring for Dummies by Marty Brounstein (IDG Books, 2010). This book includes a useful section on "teaching" in a job situation.

How to Win Friends and Influence People by Dale Carnegie (Pocket Books, 1982). Already mentioned in chapter 3, this book is the best way to gain a perspective on how to build trust with other people.

The 17 Indisputable Laws of Teamwork: Embrace Them and Empower Your Team by John C. Maxwell (Thomas Nelson, 2001). This book is reader friendly and will help you see how important and effective good teamwork can be and what you can do about it.

"BEGIN WITH PRAISE AND HONEST APPRECIATION."

—DALE CARNEGIE

CHAPTER 6

INFLUENCING PEOPLE

MANAGE EFFECTIVELY • SELL SUCCESSFULLY •
POLITICK WISELY • LEAD EFFECTIVELY

Oftentimes working with your colleagues and others outside the organization requires you to treat them as objects of influence. This may sound a little harsh, but it is reality. This chapter will introduce you to four different and relatively distinct roles that you may play when you try to influence others in the world of work.

Keep in mind that there are many styles of managing, selling, politicking, and leading. You will need to develop the style that is both effective and comfortable for you. Practicing these skills during your college years is important, because it will give you the opportunity to find your style through a process of trial and error.

Another theme in this chapter is the role of honesty and character in the actions you take as a manager, salesperson, politician, and leader. All of these roles require you to convince others to do something that they would not otherwise do. Deceit and the arbitrary or unjust use of power are tempting, especially if you are faced with a roadblock. Learn how to control that temptation in college, because in the long run, such control will serve you well in your professional career.

"The best managers think of themselves as playing coaches."

—Robert Townsend, author of best-selling book *Up the Organization*

In chapter 1, we discussed managing your time and managing your money as a key to the work ethic Skill Set. To manage time and money, you make decisions about allocating your own resources. Managing people is a whole different thing. Your task is to convince people to do their assigned jobs competently. In other words, managing people is using the human resources assigned to you over which you have some influence but little control. For this reason, management is always stressful, and effective managers are in short supply.

Effective managers usually come up through the ranks. They have performed well in their entry-level jobs and convinced those who managed them that they would be able to manage their former peers. To get the most from their people, managers need to build on many of the skills already discussed, especially those described in the previous chapter. They must also know how to use the tools their organization gives them, including salaries, benefits, and training programs, to motivate those they manage.

Good managers have to maintain the respect of those they manage while still encouraging them and listening to their feedback. As noted at the outset of this chapter, you need to find a comfortable management style. Situations that allow you to practice these skills in college can help prepare you to manage in the work world.

Management potential is a key consideration, especially in higher paying entry-level jobs, and it may be part of the interviewer's agenda when meeting with you as a prospective employee. For organizations to grow, they need to recruit people who can eventually take over the jobs of the top leaders, thus allowing the top leaders to move on to new fields. These leaders want you to do your job in a way that makes their task as your manager less burdensome.

Moreover, advancement within the company will ultimately lead to a management position.

COURSES: Courses that introduce you to the art and science of management are usually found in schools of management and public administration. Although more likely to be found at the graduate level, some upper-division undergraduate courses may be offered. In any case, take those courses that include role-playing and simulation or, better yet, observation and participation in the real world. For example, serving as an intern or assistant to a mid-level manager in a business or nonprofit organization will give you an opportunity to see how the manager interacts with subordinates and superiors.

NON-COURSE ACTIVITIES: The single most powerful way to develop management skills and demonstrate them to potential employers is to work your way up in an organization from an entry-level to a management position. On-campus jobs, such as one in food service, can allow you to move from server to a manager of servers. Every student I have ever met who had a management job on campus, whether for food service or some other "mundane" operation, has had no trouble in getting a job. This is not just because it looked good on their resume but also because they had evidence of a highly valued skill no matter what the field. Off campus, working your way up in a fast-food restaurant to shift supervisor or assistant manager will impress any job interviewer. Another valuable management experience is to run a fund-raising event or start a program by recruiting college students to offer tutoring at a local Boys and Girls Club.

"The main problem in sales is to find the basic need, or the main point of interest, and then stick to it."

—Frank Bettger, author of *How I Raised Myself from Failure to Success in Selling*

You probably think selling is about selling jeans at the Gap or about cold-calling to peddle charities, politicians, or products and services from kitchen knives to insurance.

If you are literary at all, you may be familiar with the play *Death of a Salesman* and do not want to end up like the main character, Willie Loman, who is considered an out-of-date, terrible salesman. It is part of our culture to see sales as a difficult and dirty business.

The traits of a good salesperson are dependent on almost every single skill group mentioned in this book. You have to work hard, stay well, have excellent communication and people skills, and be good at problem solving as well as finding and analyzing information. Several characteristics critical to being an effective salesperson are being able to handle sustained and continuous rejection, keeping pressure on yourself to work hard, and having solid product knowledge.

Get rid of negative thoughts about sales before you enter the workforce because those who make it to the top of every field are always good at selling themselves, their products, and their ideas. Sales skills are important to your future for the following reasons:

- Sales positions are plentiful even in the worst economy and are monetarily rewarding because there is always a shortage of good salespeople. When it comes to pharmaceuticals or financial products, we are talking about six figures in less than five years.

- Successful salespeople have a fast track to the top of the company: sales representatives become sales managers, who become marketing managers, who become VPs for marketing, who become senior VPs, who become CEOs.

- Selling is a very good training ground for all other professions because it involves synthesizing information and persuading people.

- Regardless of which career you pursue, you will ultimately be a salesperson if you are successful. The most successful lawyers are those who bring in new clients. The most successful government workers are those who sell themselves and their departments to others. Even teaching incorporates a sales component; selling your students on the importance of a subject may be more critical than giving good lectures. The highest position in academia, chancellor of a university, entails fund-raising, the most difficult form of sales. And, if you want to make the world better, you will be selling "change" to others.

- If you are a successful salesperson, by the time you are forty you will have lots of free time and excellent contacts to be a mover and a shaker. One of my alums sells carpets and works from home in his shorts and T-shirt a third of the workweek, visits clients another third of the workweek, and plays golf the remaining third of the week.

I am not suggesting that you take a sales job, although for reasons stated previously, sales can be a very good career choice. Instead, I'm urging you to develop your sales tools in college because they will be handy during your job interviews and in every job you take.

COURSES: Management schools offer courses in marketing, of which direct selling is a component. A marketing course might be helpful in alerting you to the dynamics of selling. Speech communication courses that focus on methods of persuasion can also help. Courses in negotiation and mediation might also contribute to your ability to close the deal. Courses that have simulations or fieldwork integrated into the course should be selected over those that do not.

NON-COURSE ACTIVITIES: There are enormous opportunities to learn sales in both internship and job activities. You can receive great basic training in sales by working for a political candidate during a campaign or in door-to-door solicitation campaigns of Public Interest Research Groups (PIRGs), which can be found in many colleges. Telephone sales skills can be practiced through a job with the alumni fund at your college. Cold-calling alumni provides you with plenty of rejection, an experience that employers love to learn you can handle. Summer and part-time telephone sales jobs or assisting those making the calls and visits can be important experiences in learning how to persuade people and how to think on your feet.

POLITICK WISELY

"One of the penalties for refusing to participate in politics is that you end up being governed by your inferiors."

—Plato

Plato was his usual elitist self here, but there is much to be said for this quotation. Politics has a bad name, whether we are talking professional politicians or the political types in corporations and organizations. You will find that playing politics is the price of career success, especially as you move up the career ladder. It you don't want to be political, don't complain about those who are. You could face much worse than being ruled by inferiors, as Plato says; you could be fired.

The skills discussed in this section have very little to do with running for office. Instead, they require understanding the role of power, authority, and self-interest. In short, the reality is that people, not reason, control decisions, and politics is the art of getting people on your side. As a human resources director from a large corporation says, "Don't step on people's toes. Know when to speak up, but do it with respect; play nice with everyone, but disagree with people politely. If you know when to speak up, this can lead to not only a promotion for you but also success for the company."

Wherever you work, you will face a long history of relationships and power structures. The easiest and perhaps least risky path to follow is to do what you are told and refrain from calling for substantial change, especially the first day or even year. A student of mine who was interning started out by going to his supervisor the first day and suggesting additional projects he could do. Fortunately, the supervisor called me and said she was planning to fire him because he appeared not to be interested in what he was hired to do. I gave him a heads-up to keep his mouth shut and just do what he was asked. He stayed on and actually got most of the opportunities he was looking for without asking.

While this path makes sense for the first year of your tenure, be ready to offer suggestions about policies and procedures that would improve the company and your job performance after that period. As we will see in chapter 10, effective problem solving requires a good grasp of politics.

Playing politics well requires that you avoid whining and complaining in the workplace. If you need to vent, wait until you get off work. You may be driven crazy by the fact that your boss is too slow to respond to a changing business environment. Don't complain to your colleagues, and never go over the head of your immediate supervisor unless you are prepared for the worst. Instead, realize that the political forces within the organization are generally averse to change, and you must always be planning as though it were a political campaign. Good politicians in any organization build coalitions to support their ideas.

Moving up the organizational ladder requires that you develop the very difficult skill of balancing interests. One of the primary reasons that all politicians are viewed with suspicion is that their job is to balance different interests. Consequently, anything they do will result in many of their constituents being disappointed. The first thing you need to learn from this is that people in those kinds of positions deserve a break, and the second is to realize that you will be in that position sooner than you think.

From this discussion, it should be clear that developing strategies and techniques to convince your superiors to make the decisions you want—whether it's giving you a bigger salary or altering an existing policy—are skills necessary for your career. From the day you start work, you will see and hear things that will push you to react. Reacting out of emotion or even out of clear evidence should be avoided until you know the political forces that lie behind what you see or hear. If you don't, you may find yourself looking for another job very quickly or languishing in a dead-end position.

You are likely to see corruption at various levels in the workplace. Your first experience might be a coworker padding an expense account. Given the corporate fraud and corruption making the headlines in the United States for the past decade or so, you should be aware that various kinds of tax evasion, incorrect reporting, and downright stealing occur on occasion. It may not occur more than 5 percent of the time, but eventually you will be confronted by it. The question then becomes, "What are you going to do about it?" Your political knowledge and skill will help you develop a strategy, but ultimately it is your character that will be most important.

In your college years, you will be confronted with many forms of corruption—dorm residents breaking dorm rules, resident advisers looking the other way, student organizations' leaders acting immaturely, classmates cheating, and faculty acting irresponsibly. Learn how to recognize these forms of corruption, how to avoid being corrupted, and how to politick wisely to work for change.

COURSES: Political science courses would be an obvious choice for learning about the politics of the workplace. However, these courses usually deal with public affairs–type politics and frequently are very heavy on theory. Courses that use simulation exercises or fieldwork experiences could be instructive, because they will confront you with the reality of politics with a small "p." There may be courses in public administration and sociology available to undergraduates that deal with theories on how organizations behave. They will be most helpful if they include some hands-on experiences.

NON-COURSE ACTIVITIES: You can learn a great deal by getting involved in student or residence-life organizations. The dynamics of power and authority will be very instructive. Equally valuable will be your appointment to a decision-making committee of a department or the college. You can become a member of the college or university body that represents faculty and usually involves students and administrators. Try to get appointed as the student representative to the board of trustees for the college or to a tenure and promotion committee. This will give you a picture of how the day-to-day flow of events is shaped by the rules and structures of the institution. Finally, some job and internship experiences may give you a glimpse into the politics of that particular organization. You might even find yourself playing a direct role by being asked to do something you think is wrong or being treated unethically. If so, try to learn as much as you can from the experience. The best general advice is not to act quickly but to think about the consequences. Make sure you can't live with it and decide whether you are willing to lose your job or internship for your principles. A student of mine worked for a community organization that required him to lie in a door-to-door campaign to get signatures and even donations. He quit the job even though he shared the overall goals of the organization.

LEAD EFFECTIVELY

"A leader is like a shepherd. . . . He stays behind the flock, letting the most nimble go out ahead, whereupon the others follow, not realizing that all along they are being directed from behind."

—Nelson Mandela

Most students want to have leadership experiences, if only because they think it will look good on their resume or graduate school application. It has to do with the American emphasis on individualism on the one hand and the natural drive for money and power on the other. Ironically, effective leadership is about limiting individualism and avoiding a preoccupation with money and power.

Leaders, by definition, have followers. Leaders are able to take the initiative based on a vision of making things better and then motivate supporters to follow their vision. All this requires special talents in problem solving, which we will discuss in chapter 10, and in the people skills discussed in this and the previous chapter.

Like managing, selling, and politicking, leadership styles vary greatly, so your goal in college should be to explore the kind of leader you might like to be. Do you prefer the autocratic and heavy-handed approach of someone like legendary pro-football coach Vince Lombardi, who was so successful that he had the Super Bowl trophy named after him, or the "lead from behind as a shepherd" approach of Nelson Mandela? Style is important, but so is the situation. Government and nonprofit organizations usually require a leadership that seeks consensus, while business organizations have more room for autocratic leaders. Small and start-up organizations may require an authoritarian leader while large and well-established ones require more consensus building. One of the things you will need to learn is which style is most effective in a particular situation or work environment. You may have a comfortable leadership style, but if that does not work, then you may be required to adopt one you find less comfortable.

Employers frequently say they want to recruit potential leaders, just as they want potential managers. In both cases, the top leadership of an organization wants to expand and needs solid candidates to manage things and lead in new directions. Employers value leaders who are good at stimulating their colleagues to take reasonable initiatives. They appreciate a little movement outside of the box, but not too much. Leadership that is revolutionary is rarely encouraged.

COURSES: Many universities offer leadership courses for credit. Some courses may be offered in traditional departments like political science and sociology, but others may be offered in what they call interdisciplinary centers or programs. Courses in entrepreneurial skills, which are associated with leadership, are frequently offered in management programs and schools. As with many of the other skills we have discussed, courses that are project-based and involve experiences outside of the classroom, or at least simulations, are preferred.

NON-COURSE ACTIVITIES: Becoming a member of the executive board of an established group can provide great opportunities to feel comfortable in a leadership role and to develop leadership skills.

If the position is elected, it will mean that you gained the confidence of the members of the organization. Establishing a new organization can be a great leadership development experience, even if the organization fails. All these kinds of activities require you to exercise the skills of motivation and vision that will get people to take responsibility for the organization. Many colleges have non-credit leadership development programs run by student affairs or resident-life departments.

USEFUL RESOURCES

BOOKS

Common Sense Leadership: A Handbook for Success as a Leader by Roger Fulton (Ten Speed Press, 1995). This inexpensive book summarizes a lot of good ideas about leadership in one-page sections.

How I Raised Myself from Failure to Success in Selling by Frank Bettger (Simon & Schuster, 1977). Even if you are not going to be a salesperson by profession, this book will help you be the salesperson you will need to be to succeed in whatever you do.

How to Win Friends and Influence People by Dale Carnegie (Pocket Books, 1982). Why not use the bible of how to get people to do what you want? This book will help you manage, sell, politick, and lead effectively.

100+ Tactics for Office Politics by Casey Fitts Hawley (Barron's Educational Series, 2001). Although this book deals with the business world, it will help you understand the role of politics in any career. You will also find parallels with your on-campus experiences while in college.

The One Minute Manager by Kenneth H. Blanchard and Spencer Johnson (Berkley Books, 1982). This book made quite a stir when it came out three decades ago but is still on target today. It's short and inexpensive, and its to-the-point presentation will help you manage not only others in your job but also your roommates and your parents.

WEBSITE

www.toastmasters.org Consult the Toastmasters website and click on Leadership for tips and ways to develop this skill.

"SEEK
AND YOU SHALL
FIND."

—JESUS CHRIST

CHAPTER 7

GATHERING INFORMATION

SEARCH THE WEB • USE LIBRARY HOLDINGS •
USE COMMERCIAL DATABASES • CONDUCT INTERVIEWS •
USE SURVEYS • KEEP AND USE RECORDS

Knowing how to collect information is critical to any job. Without the necessary information, you cannot perform your job. As this up-and-coming corporate type suggests below, information is an important key to advancement. He writes, "Hunt or be hunted. The majority of my accomplishments have come as a result of having information that someone else needed. The first step is to know what someone needs and why. The second step is being resourceful enough to know where to get the data and how to get it quickly. I can't stress the quickness enough. Organizations need speed, and when you're gathering information you have to be organized."

Getting information is more than a high-speed scavenger hunt in which you are given a list of things to find. It requires focus in the face of chaos. Not being sure what you are looking for creates substantial difficulties. If you have ever written a long paper, you know that you start with basic information to understand the questions you want answered, and then you need to find more information to answer the questions, which leads to more questions and more information. As you analyze your information, you will need to ask better questions. To make the whole activity even more aggravating, as you start to write your paper, you realize that your information base is weak and that you need to search for more specific information. Moreover, even after you have written the first draft of the paper, reactions from others may require you to go back and do more research. Collecting information is an unlimited, open-ended process.

But we have to start somewhere. This chapter features six Skill Sets that will provide you with the know-how to collect different kinds of information essential to most jobs.

"There's no such thing as a free lunch."

—Attributed to Milton Friedman, a twentieth-century Nobel laureate
economist and defender of the free market

Finding information on the Internet may seem easy, but finding the information you need *and* can trust on the Internet is much harder. Internet research can be risky and lead to poor results unless you have a solid grasp of web research (as well as many of the ten Skill Sets, especially those presented in chapters 9 and 10). If you can get information to your boss quickly, you will become indispensable. However, if your speedy delivery gives the boss inaccurate data, you may become disposable. The key is to assess the authors and publication sources providing the information. Learn about the strengths and weaknesses of various search engines and how to use them so you can learn more about the organization or people who have published the information you found. Are they reliable? Would others in your profession consider this website a good source of relevant professional information? Use your web-search and critical thinking skills to avoid giving your boss information that is incomplete or incorrect.

Librarians and faculty may try to get you off of Google and Wikipedia in order to discuss the commercial databases like ProQuest and LexisNexis (which are discussed in the next section). However, both Google and Wikipedia are a great starting point. Just recognize that for some specialized information categories, Google and Wikipedia may not always take you to all the information you or your boss needs. You may also get a lot of misinformation that requires you to check the accuracy of your sources.

Wikipedia was heavily criticized in its early years because anyone can write something on it. However, Wikipedia's collaborative editing policies encourage ongoing improvement of its articles. Moreover, documentation that links information to other reliable published sources is found in articles it publishes. David Ferriero, the tenth archivist of the United States, said it is a good enough source for him.[1] Wikipedia is a great place to get an initial factual briefing.

You can also find sites on the Web that will do things for you. For example, some sites can correct your citations, depending on the preferred citation style. (Professors in different disciplines use different citation systems, MLA and APA being two examples.) There are also sites that allow you to tabulate survey results or translate reports written in other languages into English.

Not only will being an expert at searching the Web help your GPA and make you valuable at work, but it will also help you find employment. The Internet is an essential tool for exploring careers, finding out about companies, and, most important, getting jobs.

COURSES: Any course that requires research will improve how you search the Internet. Such courses are usually upper level in your major, no matter what the field. All subjects taught in college are related to scholarly fields that have specialized publications and related websites. Research seminars frequently require each student to have a topic and produce a paper presented to others. This experience, along with any type of thesis or capstone project, will significantly enhance your capacity to use the Web.

NON-COURSE ACTIVITY: Get experience through part-time employment, an internship, or a summer job doing research. Businesses are often hungry for assistance with web-related projects and rarely have staff that have the time to devote to these projects. On-campus research jobs may also give you some experience in searching the Internet for useful and reliable information. For Google, experience is the best teacher. Play around with different key words. Most people know how to do a basic Google search, but everyone can improve his or her searching ability through practice.

"Libraries are not made, they grow."

—Augustine Birrell, nineteenth-century writer

The library used to be a place where you simply found collections of printed information. Today a library is a more complex system that houses some of that information but also provides electronic access to an almost unlimited amount of publications and multimedia formats. You need to know how to locate information in a large library by using that library's website, online catalog, and hard copy and electronic publications.

Your job may not require going to a large library, but it will require you to search for information. In addition, you may find yourself required to use the holdings of a corporate or other private archive to locate information, or perhaps even consult a government library, including federal, state, and local records. Efficiently and effectively using library research tools and actual holdings will prepare you to use those and other tools to research relevant topics such as mailing lists, government programs, and the work of relevant professional associations for future employers.

COURSES: Lower-division courses in information studies software are available at many colleges and universities, big and small. These courses help you understand the available tools, but they may be too general to give you focused experience. Courses in the social sciences and humanities that emphasize research will give you some additional skills in using the library. In every field of study, journals, magazines, newsletters, and a growing number of electronic services are used in upper-level courses. Look for courses that require you to do research. Because whatever job you go into will have specialized information needs, the purpose of this activity is to become familiar with the library search tools and not the specific sources.

NON-COURSE ACTIVITIES: Spend some time in the library just learning what information sources are available. Some colleges offer library-research skill education through self-paced online tutorials, videos, taped walking tours, or briefings by librarians. Most college libraries also employ students. Working at the library is another excellent way to learn how they organize information. Librarians will be very glad to give you general and specific briefings, if you don't approach them at the last minute.

USE COMMERCIAL DATABASES

"There is no better ballast for keeping the mind steady on its keel, and saving it from all risks of crankiness than business."

—James Russell Lowell, nineteenth-century writer

The term *database* has two very different meanings. First, it can mean a piece of computer software where you or your employer records information, like Microsoft Access, which we will discuss in chapter 11. Second, database also means a large set of published information available electronically. In this section, we will talk about the second type of database—the growing number of specialized bodies of highly organized information available in libraries and for purchase.

Because of the explosion of information in print and on the Web, people or businesses that need to find relevant and accurate information quickly are willing to pay for it. As a result, databases charge subscription fees in exchange for continuous archiving, organization, and delivery of that information. Sources one finds in these paid databases are usually more focused and more reliable than random source information found on the Web. One of the largest journalistic and legal database sources is LexisNexis. ProQuest also offers many database products with financial, academic, historical, and statistical information. There are exceptions to this rule; the free government websites are usually as reliable and useful as commercial databases. In fact, many commercial databases import vast amounts of free government information. Additionally, high-quality publications in the sciences, health care, and medicine are increasingly offered free online, especially when the research behind those published works is funded by the U.S. government. You need to be aware of these databases, how to find appropriate ones, and how to search them using their sophisticated search engines.

Specialized databases exist on every conceivable topic. These databases can be accessed through the Web (for a fee). Businesses frequently pay for them. Your library will purchase and make many of them available to you as a student. Whatever job you enter, several databases are likely to be used by the organization that hires you, regardless of whether you are in marketing, research, or production. Having some experience in any one of these databases will give you a leg up on your competition.

COURSES: General commercial databases like LexisNexis are likely to be a valuable source of information for you in many of your courses. More specialized databases may be used in upper-division courses in the social sciences, management, and communications. Look for mention of these databases in course syllabi and on your college library's website.

NON-COURSE ACTIVITY: Research jobs at business or government organizations may require you to work with databases they purchase. This is not usually the case with small nonprofits, which rarely can afford such services. However, a nonprofit could have access to databases created by government agencies or larger and wealthier nonprofit organizations, or the complex search engines of research institutes. So spend some time as a research gofer for the research, marketing, or public relations department of a business.

"An expert is one who knows more and more about less and less."

—Nicholas Murray Butler, early twentieth-century president of Columbia University

Getting information is like being a detective, and the best initial source of information is people who work in or study the field. The skill to find the right people, establish a basis for their help, ask the right questions, and probe for accuracy is, therefore, essential.

You probably already know how to do this if you are like one of my former students, who writes:

> *"Granted, you can get scores of questions answered on the Internet, but you can get information you trust from actual people, and you can get it fast. For example, asking a neighbor or a friend's parents about the best place in town to buy a car is a lot easier and more dependable than searching through tons of automobile websites. To get the information you want, you need to figure out who are the best people to ask and what are the best questions to ask that will get you what you need. Start small, first asking your close contacts for information or for names of people who can better help you, and then you'll be able to work your way toward the experts."*

The single most important reason for conducting effective interviews is to save time. With little background, you can get more basic information and leads in less time than going to the library or searching databases and websites. Even if you only ask someone who knows something about the subject questions like what is the best book, article, website, or database, you will be way ahead of the game. If you are good at interviewing, you will be able to help your boss when he says, "Find out about X and brief me on it." This principle applies to any kind of information search. To illustrate, the most important part of a job search is getting information from career counselors, from future employers at job fairs, and in "informational" interview situations.

COURSES: Courses in sociology, psychology, political science, speech communications, journalism, and writing sometimes provide training in conducting good interviews. Any research course could provide you with opportunities to interview experts, as you educate yourself about your topic.

NON-COURSE ACTIVITY: You can obtain excellent experience in developing your interviewing skills merely by spending time figuring out which major fits you best or which courses are good to take. Figuring out the best person to ask and the questions that will provide you with the most useful information are critical to making good program and course choices. Moving from there, get yourself involved in a student group that tries to get something from the administration or from the student government. As both groups give you the runaround, you will develop your ability to find good information sources and ask the right questions.

USE SURVEYS

"If one or two people tell you that you're an ass, you can ignore them. But if three or four people tell you you're an ass, you might think about putting on a saddle."

—Yiddish saying

There are many different kinds of surveys, ranging from customer surveys and focus groups to market research and public opinion polls. Learn how to appreciate the limitations of all surveys and how to adjust for those limitations in using them. Everyone who graduates from college does not need to know how to conduct a survey, but everyone certainly needs to know how to interpret survey findings.

Any job you take will be in an organization that works with a large number of people, either within the organization or as customers or both. Having information about the characteristics and attitudes of these people will be crucial. Surveys are frequently used to acquire that information. In some cases, you may even participate in designing and implementing a survey. At a bare minimum, you need to be a skeptical consumer of the surveys that come your way by asking the right questions about the quality of the sample and the biases in the surveys.

You should also be familiar with a product called SurveyMonkey, which, according to their website, is used by 100 percent of the Fortune 500 companies. It is a web product that can be used free on a limited basis to conduct surveys over the Internet. The product collects the information and dumps it into an Excel spreadsheet so you don't even have to enter the data. One of my interns was at a company that was about to hire a consulting firm to do a survey when she told her supervisor about SurveyMonkey and saved them $20,000. You can imagine what her supervisor thought about this intern after that!

COURSES: Although you do not have to become a professional designer of surveys, the only way to develop the skills necessary to be a skeptical consumer is to participate in the design, implementation, and analysis of a survey through a course. Courses that require students to conduct their own survey can be offered anywhere in the social sciences and in professional schools. They are usually more work than other courses, but the benefits are enormous.

NON-COURSE ACTIVITY: Volunteer to help a student organization do a survey or sign up with a political campaign to help conduct surveys. Professors and think tanks around the university frequently hire students to do the mundane work of conducting a survey, which you should do at least once. Create a survey on SurveyMonkey asking your friends a couple of questions about anything (for example, movies, significant others, teachers) and analyze the results.

"Without records, we have no way of knowing what we are doing."

—Frank Bettger, author of *How I Raised Myself from Failure to Success in Selling*

Record keeping may sound like the ultimate mindless activity, but, unfortunately, it is a critical skill. Use college to learn how organizations keep records and how you can assess their accuracy. Develop habits of good record keeping for what you do yourself.

Frank Bettger found that keeping detailed records was a key to his success as a salesman. By keeping records, he saw that 70 percent of his sales were made on his first call, 23 percent on his second, and only 7 percent on his third call. His conclusion was that he should make more first-time calls and fewer third-time calls. This doubled the amount of money he made per call.[2]

Whether you have a job in business, government, or the nonprofit sector, records of expenses and services are critical. Lawyers charge clients by fifteen-minute intervals on phone calls, and even nonprofits must show their funders what they are doing with the money through meticulously kept records.

Develop a capacity to keep good records for what you do, but even more important, learn how to use and assess the quality of the records that are important for making decisions in your job. Just in case you are not convinced, think about how important it is for your grades that your professors accurately record your test and paper scores or how fraudulent accounting practices contributed to the financial crisis in 2008.

COURSES: Record keeping is at the heart of the physical sciences, so a lab course will help you develop your capacity to make detailed and legible records. Many management courses will introduce you to different methods of record keeping. In several social sciences, you may find a course that requires you to collect data using code sheets. The key is to find hands-on courses in which you collect and record data or use data recording by existing organizations. Courses in which a log is required for an internship or fieldwork will also help you develop this Skill Set.

NON-COURSE ACTIVITY: The most powerful way to develop this skill is to do a good job in managing your time, which requires careful and detailed planning. If you can record when and where you want to complete a task and then check off when you have done it, you will be on your way to becoming a good record keeper. Become the treasurer or secretary of a student organization that requires good record keeping. You will review the work of the predecessor and learn how to assess accuracy while you learn the principles of good record keeping yourself. A surefire way to develop the capacity to keep good records is to use computer-based tools such as Microsoft Money and Quicken or online resources such as Mint.com on your own finances.

USEFUL RESOURCES

BOOKS

The Craft of Interviewing by John Brady (Vintage Books, 1977). Written for journalists, this book will help you in any situation where you are trying to get information, ideas, or attitudes from others.

How to Conduct Surveys: A Step-by-Step Guide by Arlene Fink (Sage Publications, 2009). Fink provides a basic introduction to the design and implementation of surveys that has less technical language than most.

WEBSITES

www.lexisnexis.com Learn about the database products available. Practice on your college library database, which should have the LexisNexis service.

www.proquest.com Go online to learn about the database products available. Practice on your college library database, which should have the ProQuest service.

www.surveymonkey.com SurveyMonkey is the most popular site for conducting an electronic survey. It's free for up to one hundred respondents, so, if you have not used it before, practice using it by creating a survey of your friends on some topic.

"IF ALL YOU HAVE IS A HAMMER, EVERYTHING LOOKS LIKE A NAIL."

—ABRAHAM MASLOW,
TWENTIETH-CENTURY PSYCHOLOGIST

CHAPTER 8

USING QUANTITATIVE TOOLS

USE NUMBERS • USE GRAPHS AND TABLES • USE SPREADSHEET PROGRAMS

This chapter introduces you to the three most basic quantitative tools you need to develop while in college. These tools are necessary for any job that you will take. Usually, you will use them immediately.

If you are not a numbers person, take a deep breath and read this chapter. Hopefully, you'll see that anybody can achieve the levels called for.

If you're a numbers person, heed this word of warning: getting 800 on your quantitative SAT, being a whiz at calculus, and knowing how to calculate the most exotic statistics are not the same as using quantitative tools. You may consider the Skill Sets in this chapter trivial, but unless you've used numbers and spreadsheets to make or recommend decisions, you will need to practice these skills during your college years.

"That is the news from Lake Wobegon, where all the women are strong, all the men are good-looking, and all the children are above average."

—Garrison Keillor, radio personality

If you did not immediately figure out what is wrong with the above quotation, you have a lot of work to do in developing a minimum competence in the use of numbers. Don't leave college without having the ability to (1) calculate and interpret percentages, (2) use simple statistical terms like average, range, and correlation, (3) put together a budget, and above all, (4) have a healthy skepticism when numbers are thrown at you. If you are one of those number-phobic people, learn to love numbers as much as you want money. It never ceases to amaze me how number-phobic people can calculate, in a flash, the amount saved from a 40 percent sale.

No matter what your job is, you need to calculate in your head what it means when your boss tells you that you are getting a 5 percent raise next year. Your performance will be measured in numbers just as the performance of your company or agency is measured in the number of sales, the amount of income, or the number of people served. For most jobs, you don't have to be a mathematical whiz, but you do need to be able to add, subtract, multiply, divide, calculate percentages, solve simple equations, and interpret simple graphs. Most important, you should be able to use these calculations to help you make decisions.

COURSES: Some mathematics courses may help you develop the basic number-crunching skills that you will need on the job, but don't count on it. Mathematics courses taught in college are usually taught as a science or an art form in which you master mathematical reasoning. A better alternative is to take courses on how to use statistics in a specific field like management, political science, economics, or sociology. Even in these courses, the level presented is usually way beyond what will be used in most jobs. Engineering, some areas of business, and many research jobs require the use of higher forms of statistics and math. The rest only require the ability to use and understand percentages and add, subtract, divide, and multiply. Try to find a research course in which you conduct a study for a real-world client like a business or nonprofit agency. They will want the results to be in simple charts, just like most of your potential employers will. Any course requiring you to look at budgets—real or projected—would be the best way to develop your applied number-crunching skills.

NON-COURSE ACTIVITY: The best training here would be to become a comptroller or treasurer of an organization with a real budget. If you can get on the finance committee of your student government, you will get a lot of practice in calculating and interpreting numbers.

Many activities that you might enjoy would improve your number skills. Shopping is one, especially if you start figuring out how much your use of credit will cost you or if you are purchasing a car and need a loan. Sports statistics is an enjoyable way to gain practice with numbers for sports fanatics. Stock market or business simulation computer games can also make exercising math skills fun.

The most important way to use numbers in college is to calculate your costs and your income, which, in most cases, will also mean your debt. Don't leave these calculations to your parents.

"A picture is worth a thousand words."

—Anonymous

You probably already know how to use simple graphs like those with bars and pie charts, and simple tables that show how numbers are related to each other. I include it as a Skill Set because, while the mechanics are easy, many people are not used to thinking with or are not good at using graphs and charts to make a point about a problem or decision that they face.

Whatever job you take will require you to analyze numbers and present them. Graphs and tables are important because you cannot just read lists of numbers to people. After the third number you give them, they'll either be asleep or thinking of something else. They're busy and want to know the bottom line—now. A carefully constructed graph or table that clearly illustrates a problem facing the organization (or better yet, a possible solution) will gain you considerable credit as you move to the top.

COURSES: Math and statistics courses rarely get into making tables and graphs. Besides, you probably already have the mechanics. You need practice in creating graphs and tables that help you make a point. For that reason, your best bet are research courses in any social science or professional-school field in which you present quantitative information in the papers you write. You may have to make up your own graph and statistics based on data you collect, or you may have to quote a variety of authors who use graphs and charts themselves. Taking courses that require the use of graphs and charts can improve your use of them in your internships and careers.

NON-COURSE ACTIVITIES: Work in a part-time position, an internship, or in student organizations where you make charts and tables. Use such situations as a learning opportunity. If you want to gain some experience with graphs and charts outside of class, pay attention to them when you see newspaper articles, especially in *USA Today* and the *New York Times*.

"Order and simplification are the first steps toward the mastery of a subject."

—Thomas Mann, twentieth-century novelist

One of the best-kept secrets for those not in the workforce is the revolutionary impact of spreadsheets for both analysis and action in a professional job. Spreadsheets are as important to the analysis of information as a map is to getting to Grandma's house. Spreadsheets bring order and simplify huge amounts of complex information so that you can make decisions.

If you don't even know what spreadsheet programs are, don't worry because you can easily understand the basics. A *spreadsheet program* helps you order information into lists and charts and conduct statistical analyses and make graphs. It is only slightly more difficult to learn than Microsoft Word.

The only spreadsheet software you will need to know is Microsoft Excel, the spreadsheet of choice for most business, government, and nonprofit organizations. Once you have mastered that, you may want to learn a database like Microsoft Access. However, the minimum standard for any college graduate who wants any kind of real-world job is Excel. Spreadsheets can be used to organize numerous pieces of information, such as that contained in a mailing list. That information can then be grouped in new ways for practical purposes. In the case of the mailing list, after you've entered the information into the spreadsheet program, you could then print out different lists by zip code, gender, or alphabetical order. As mentioned above, spreadsheets can also be used to generate statistics, tables, and graphs.

Organizing information in lists and tables as well as compiling and presenting statistics is becoming an increasingly important part of any job, particularly at the entry level. Solid Excel skills will get you in the door and make your boss forever grateful. Because spreadsheet programs are so widely used, temp firms are constantly looking for individuals to enter data for their clients. This means you can get a higher paying part-time job from a temp firm—much more than you would get parking cars or serving punch for the faculty. If typing well can give you a chance for a temp job, which can easily lead to full-time employment, then that goes triple for Excel!

Although Excel is presented here as a type of software, it is much more than that. Thinking in terms of spreadsheets means you can organize information in a systematic way, which is a key to problem solving. If both you and your boss can think in spreadsheet terms, you will be speaking the same language. If the rest of the staff is spreadsheet-challenged, you will leave them in the dust as you move on to bigger and better things.

One of my recent graduates who works at a large corporation and who is about as far from a computer nerd as anyone can be, writes the following: "I will deny this if you repeat it, but I totally underestimated your emphasis on Excel. It is slowly becoming my best friend. Lately I've had dreams about how to improve my pivot tables and use V lookups." Spreadsheets are also used in the nonprofit and government world. Those who become part of Teach for America are schooled on how spreadsheets are used to measure student performance.

COURSES: College courses rarely provide spreadsheet training, except perhaps in the management and engineering fields. However, courses that require the collection and analysis of quantitative data are likely to give you an opportunity to exercise your Excel skills once you have learned them. Take statistics courses in the social sciences or the professional schools that require you to use spreadsheets as part of the course. Be aware that most quantitatively oriented college faculty may use some other statistical program like SPSS. It will not hurt you to use such statistical programs as long as you learn to use Excel somewhere else. A word of warning here on certificates such as Microsoft Office Specialist (MOS) certification on Microsoft Office programs: they are not a substitute for real-world practice, but they do get the attention of the employer.

NON-COURSE ACTIVITY: If you have the basic skills in using a spreadsheet program, you should be able to find part-time and summer jobs within and outside the university that will give you additional experience. These jobs may become mundane and routine after a while, but you will be getting higher pay than if you were putting mashed potatoes and gravy on the plates of your dorm mates—and practice does make perfect.

Some colleges have an on-site testing center, where you can complete a self-study course in a Microsoft application. Once you are confident in your abilities, you can take an exam and become a Microsoft Certified Professional (MCP). It never hurts to have on your resume that you are certified by Microsoft in Word, Excel, or Access. These certifications may not earn you college credit toward a degree, but it does not hurt to ask.

USEFUL RESOURCES

BOOKS

Excel 2010 for Dummies by Greg Harvey (John Wiley, 2010). Like all Dummies books published on using programs, this one is a solid introduction but may not cover the version of Excel that you have.

How to Lie with Statistics by Darrell Huff and Irving Geis (W. W. Norton, 1982). Unlike most statistics books, which include a lot of formulas and try to teach concepts too complicated for everyday use, this book provides a thorough grounding in sampling and the use of percentages—tools you'll need no matter what field you enter.

The Visual Display of Quantitative Information, 2nd edition, by Edward R. Tufte (Graphics Press, 2001). This is the best and most thorough discussion of how to display quantitative information but way beyond what most people need to know.

WEBSITE

http://office.microsoft.com This website provides video and written tutorials on using all Microsoft products, including Excel.

"EVERY MAN IS FULLY SATISFIED THAT THERE IS SUCH A THING AS TRUTH, OR HE WOULD NOT ASK ANY QUESTION."

—CHARLES SANDERS PEIRCE, NINETEENTH- AND TWENTIETH-CENTURY PHILOSOPHER, PHYSICIST, MATHEMATICIAN, AND LOGICIAN

CHAPTER 9

ASKING AND ANSWERING THE RIGHT QUESTIONS

DETECT NONSENSE • PAY ATTENTION TO DETAIL •
APPLY KNOWLEDGE • EVALUATE ACTIONS AND POLICIES

Let's take Mr. Peirce's quote at face value and assume that it makes sense to search for truthful information even if we can never be 100 percent certain that we've discovered it. What you really need to do is develop the skill to discover information that is as accurate and useful as possible, which means asking and answering the right questions. The four skills in this chapter are the components of asking and answering the right questions.

Employers say they want their employees to have these skills, and college faculty, particularly in the liberal arts, say critical thinking is the most important of all "skills." However, "critical thinking" is so general that it needs to be defined more specifically. People who throw around the phrase are not really thinking critically because it means very different things to different people. I prefer to use the more specific terms "asking and answering the right questions" combined with the topic of the next chapter, "problem solving," instead of the general term "critical-thinking."

> ## *"Two-thirds of the things that are taught in college, even when they are well taught, are not worth knowing. The main thing is to learn the differences between appearances and reality."*
>
> —H. L. Mencken, twentieth-century journalist and commentator

College is really a place to learn how to determine the accuracy of information, and how perceptions and values bias much of the information you receive. H. L. Mencken's quote is right on.

You need to understand something about H. L. Mencken to see how insidiously appearance eats away at reality, even for the "Baltimore Sage," as he was called. Mencken is considered one of the greatest journalists and intellectuals of the first half of the twentieth century. His anti-nonsense style combined with a great sense of humor made him a darling of the reading public.

Mencken specialized in debunking politicians for their hypocrisy. This brilliant and anti-nonsense writer, however, expressed anti-Semitic views. It took Mencken more than five years after Adolf Hitler came to power to see through him, and even then, he never gave Hitler the vicious treatment he gave the American president, Franklin Delano Roosevelt. Having a German heritage, Mencken could not believe that his homeland could follow such a monster.

If you learn nothing else in college, learn how to see through what people say by looking at why they say it. Is it self-delusional, as it was in Mencken's case, or is it aimed at making a sale or garnering support? Even more critical, compare what people say with what they do.

Nonsense detection is critical to your job success. Whatever job you take will require getting the correct information about the tasks you need to perform and the conditions affecting your performance. This information comes from written sources as well as from statements by your boss, coworkers, those you serve, and others. Unfortunately, information is always generated for a purpose, and that purpose often gets in the way of the truth. Consequently, you need to develop a very strong "nonsense detector."

Having a broad range of background knowledge can help you detect nonsense. Blaine DeLancey, a longtime college recorder/academic adviser at Syracuse University and a champion of liberal arts, writes:

> *"In my experience, individuals who utter nonsense on one topic tend to make a habit of doing the same on every topic. If I can recognize, due to independent knowledge, that my coworker is uninformed about one topic—baseball, Mozart, epistemology, fill in the blank—then I am forewarned that my coworker is also likely to provide gibberish on other topics about which I know nothing—even work topics. Conversely, if I know that a colleague tends to speak only on topics about which she is well informed, then I need be less suspicious of her potential to spew nonsense."*

DeLancey makes a lot of sense. I will discuss the value of knowledge further in chapter 11.

COURSES: Every course you take in college will provide an opportunity to improve your ability to distinguish appearance from reality. First, examine carefully what professors say and do. Ask yourself questions about how accurately the course is depicted in the syllabus and how professionally a professor responds to questions from students. Second, most courses present different interpretations of the same events and patterns. Listening to different opinions about the causes of the Civil War or the meaning of a piece of literature gives you the opportunity to make judgments about conflicting ideas yourself. The ability to weigh different viewpoints is critical to getting beyond appearances and getting a better glimpse of reality.

Specific courses that could perfect your nonsense detector are more likely to be found in the fields of psychology, which looks at the mechanisms of the mind that generate self-flattering (and sometimes delusional) statements, and history, which focuses on how to resolve conflicting interpretations of fact and explanation. Beyond these two fields, most courses in the humanities and the social sciences are meant to provide different perspectives that, taken together, will help you get beyond appearances to discover reality.

NON-COURSE ACTIVITY: Whether you are a part of the pep band, a member of a fraternity or sorority, or a representative in the student government, you can learn a lot by watching your peers spin their webs. If you want an unlimited opportunity to distinguish appearance from reality, rush a fraternity or sorority and compare what was said to you before and after you pledge, especially about fees. If you decided not to pledge, ask a friend who did. This is only one of many sales situations you will face in your life with hidden and unanticipated costs.

While you are at it, don't forget to turn the nonsense detector on yourself, especially when you excuse your poor grades by saying, "My grade sucked because the class was so boring. If I am interested in a course, I will learn a lot and do well." Better you should tell yourself that you were too immature to suck it up and pay your dues.

PAY ATTENTION TO DETAIL

"To generalize is to be an idiot. To particularize is the alone distinction of merit."

—William Blake, eighteenth- and nineteenth-century poet

Blake must have been irritated with the science of the day. His quotation is a little over the top because, as we see in the next section, applying general knowledge is a key Skill Set. Moreover, the quotation itself is a generalization.

However, paying attention to detail is more important than generalizing because the effective use of generalizations depends on mastery of detail. In whatever task you undertake, get as many details as possible. You need to be like a medical doctor and piece the sequence of events together and create a pattern in your mind that helps you determine the reasons for an event. Can you create a story that explains why a patient is ill, a client did not buy your services, a student failed a course, or a person you supervise did the wrong thing?

Paying attention to detail will help you answer critical questions that could catapult you to the top of your career. Ignoring the details could result in a pink slip. Why does the boss keep criticizing you? What accounts for the sale of one item instead of another? Why does an individual praise or attack your organization? The answer to all of these questions often demands a strong focus on details.

An alumnus who has a very successful career in the federal government sent this bit of advice to my students:

"You may think five points for turning in a paper late, or two points here and there for formatting, is silly or bothersome. Guess what? There's an entire section of the Federal Acquisition Regulation (FAR), which governs federal contracts, that specifically speaks to formatting, deadlines, and the consequences. Not following the rules can get a multimillion dollar proposal thrown out without the evaluator reading page one! Try explaining to your employer that you just lost revenue dollars and jobs because you didn't use the right-sized margins or font. Two points doesn't seem so frivolous now, does it?"

COURSES: All your course work can be viewed as training in paying attention to detail. You will discover that success comes in mastering the detail consistently and carefully. Whether you are doing a lab experiment in science, completing an accounting exercise, criticizing a piece of literature, or presenting an analysis of a historic event, paying attention to detail is the difference between passing and failing. (How many points have you lost in your academic career for an incorrect citation format, a decimal in the wrong place, or just misreading a multiple-choice question?) Courses that use a lot of case studies are best. They can be found in history most often, but also in anthropology, economics, geography, political science, and sociology. Case studies are frequently used in business and social work but also in undergraduate professional programs in subjects like management and communications. The humanities, especially literature courses, develop the capacity to think about the causes and implications of things that happen. Courses that require fieldwork or community service along with weekly logs are especially useful.

NON-COURSE ACTIVITY: Participate in student groups in which collective decisions have to be made in writing, and take responsibility for getting by-laws written or grant applications made. An enjoyable activity to develop your ability to look at detailed cases is to watch one of the many TV shows like *Law & Order: SVU* in which the details about both behavior and the law are required to follow the show. Reading fiction and nonfiction that analyze events and behaviors is also helpful.

APPLY KNOWLEDGE

"Knowledge is power."

—Francis Bacon, sixteenth- and seventeenth-century
scientist and philosopher

Bacon's quotation is not quite correct. Knowledge is a source of power, but knowledge is power only if it is used effectively. You must continually ask, "What does this mean for my job and my organization?" The ability to get key statistics, find people who have the knowledge you need, and be alert to current trends in your field can help you in whatever job you have. Outstanding employees always look for the "best practices" that they can apply to their problems. You also need to be aware of "bad" and "mediocre practices" so you can avoid the mistakes others have made. Look at what other organizations do so you can bring up new ideas to your colleagues.

Whatever job you have will require you to do what medical doctors do with respect to continuous learning of new knowledge. You'll need to keep up with publications in your field, go to professional meetings, and translate the general knowledge that is relevant to your specific job. If studies related to your job exist, you will need to apply the principles of the scientific method to make judgments about how much faith you can put in those studies. You will also need to learn how to decide which sources can be trusted. An eagerness to learn and a curiosity about all aspects of your job field is the holy grail of success.

Employers also want their employees to be clear-headed about the knowledge they find. They do not want them bringing in irrelevant knowledge or chasing fringe ideas that have little factual backup. If the studies related to your job exist, apply the principles of the scientific method to make judgments about how much faith you can put in them. You will also need to learn how to decide which sources can be trusted. Finally, you may have to design and conduct a research project yourself to answer a specific question. If so, understanding scientific methods will give you more accurate results, even if you cannot get the precise and representative information required by such methods.

COURSES: Applied research courses are difficult to find at the undergraduate level in most colleges and universities. They are usually reserved for graduate students. However, some professors, especially in the professional schools, incorporate applied research in their curricula. Try to get into a course that supports that research or take an independent study with professors on one of their client-based projects.

To develop skills in the scientific method, start by taking courses in the physical sciences. Those that have labs integrated into the course are better than those that have no lab or that fail to make a connection between the lab and the content of the lectures and class discussions.

Science courses are only a beginning. Almost every course you take in college can provide you with a way of searching for patterns that can allow for generalizations about causes and forecasts about the future. Courses in all of the social sciences and many professional schools can give you additional practice with the scientific methods as well as knowledge of the limitations of those methods. The best courses to take are those that require fieldwork and real-world application because they are more likely to help you see both the value and the limitations of the scientific method.

NON-COURSE ACTIVITY: Participation in student activities such as residence hall councils or student government will give you an opportunity to look at the big picture and develop tentative ideas about why things are the way they are. This experience will help you generate hypotheses and then look for evidence to support, reject, or revise the hypotheses. The most powerful learning experience in applying knowledge will come from applied research work in part-time jobs, summer jobs, and internships both inside and outside the university.

EVALUATE ACTIONS AND POLICIES

"If you don't measure results, you can't tell success from failure."

—David Osborne and Ted Gaebler, authors of a
best-selling book on improving government

You cannot avoid the challenge of evaluating your own performance and the performance of others. Unfortunately, the task of evaluation is anxiety producing. Most students do not like tests and get sweaty palms before receiving a paper grade. The anxiety comes from the combination of the excitement of winning and the fear of losing.

For that reason, the natural inclination is to avoid evaluation or to see it as a win-or-lose proposition. People develop many clever ways to avoid evaluation. They may blame others or take actions that are "safe." They may procrastinate. If they are confronted with a failure, they go into a depression and blame themselves, or, in the terms of our current jargon, "lose self-esteem." If they decide they have been suc-cessful, they may conclude that they can do no wrong. These behaviors need to be avoided so you can develop a capacity to evaluate your own actions and the actions of others.

Success belongs to those who take risks and have some way of recognizing success and failure. Three steps are required to evaluate your behavior or the behavior of others:

1. Identify goals. Sometimes goals are not clearly stated or even shared by everyone in your organization.

2. Measure goals. You have to have information organized in such a way that you know when you have (or your company has) reached goals.

3. Determine success and failure. You need to develop an idea of what success or failure is in order to decide whether or not you want to make a change.

This process is critical for the world of work. By continually asking yourself "How am I doing?" you improve your job performance. By asking how your unit is doing or the company as a whole is doing, you contribute to a team effort to do the best.

To drive the point home, realize that your employer will conduct performance reviews periodically, and those reviews will determine whether or not and how much of a raise you receive as well as whether or not you will advance in your career.

The way to have a successful performance review, which might occur a couple of months into your job and then at least annually, is to say, "My goals have been X, Y, and Z, and I have met X and Y and made progress on Z." You will be in a much better position for a good review. It will also help your boss fill out the required human resources form and work with you to advance your career.

Evaluation skills are essential for improving the performance of your organization. You will be a better employee if you can help your organization focus on clear goals, measure performance according to these goals, and draw conclusions that will lead to future improvement.

I may seem to be stating the obvious here, but, as already noted, words like "evaluation," "assessment," and "performance" are threatening to the majority of people in the world of work. More often than not, people play evaluation games that require your nonsense detector to be fully operational. The evaluation game can be played by setting goals that are too low, by using poor information, by selectively reporting information, and, in some cases, by not even reporting the information at all.

To be successful in the work world, you need to distinguish between two types of evaluation. The first is evaluation to improve performance, and the second is to punish or reward you or others. The former is the most important over the long run and is part of what businesses call "continuous improvement." The latter can cause a lot of trouble, but it is used in most organizations as a major tool of promoting excellence. An organization that uses evaluation only as a reward or punishment is not a good place to work.

COURSES: Courses that provide direct training in evaluation are usually offered at the graduate-school level, but you can probably find some upper-level courses in the social sciences, management, and other professional schools that introduce you to the skills of evaluation. You can practice evaluation on your own performance in every course that you take by setting goals for both learning and grades, and then making judgments as to whether you have achieved them or not. You can also learn a lot about evaluation if you study how your instructors evaluate their courses. Ask yourself whether instructors are using end-of-semester surveys because they are forced to and will be rewarded or punished on the basis of them, or do they seem to really be interested in the results so they can improve the course? As a student, you would prefer the latter use.

NON-COURSE ACTIVITY: You can practice evaluation every time you do something, especially, as suggested above, in every course you take. Get into the practice of making a list of goals for every major new activity you undertake in student activities or in jobs, and then reflect on whether or not you achieved your goals. Using the forms in the appendix, which require you to assess yourself on the ten Skill Sets every six months, will sharpen your evaluation skills immensely. Chapter 18 provides detailed information on how to perform your self-assessment.

USEFUL RESOURCES

I hesitate to recommend books and other activities for the Skill Sets described in this chapter because there are many ways to improve these skills. Whether examining the sciences, humanities, and social sciences or the various professions like management, public communications, or social work, you will improve your skill in all four areas if you apply some serious study. So will playing games, especially chess, bridge, and poker. Arguing with others about sports, movies, or just about anything will also help if you try to use evidence and logic rather than argue for the sake of arguing. How you choose to practice your evaluation skills depends on your interests, background, and the way your brain is wired. Just follow the guidelines presented in chapter 18 when you evaluate yourself or anything else. Despite my hesitance in recommending books for this chapter, take a look at the following.

BOOKS

Evaluation Methodology Basics: The Nuts and Bolts of Sound Evaluation by E. Jane Davidson (Sage Publications, 2004). This book is as basic as it gets for understanding the value and pitfalls of evaluating anything, which is not saying much. Much of it will be too academic, except for students well versed in the social sciences. However, the first few chapters will provide an introduction to all four of the Skill Sets covered in this chapter.

How Wikipedia Works, and How You Can Be a Part of It by Phoebe Ayers, Charles Matthews, and Ben Yates (No Starch Press, 2008). The authors provide in-depth instructions on how to use Wikipedia and present the best possible research.

The Literature Review: Six Steps to Success by Dr. Lawrence Anthony Machi and Brenda T. McEvoy (Crown Press, 2009). This book provides an overview on how academics use knowledge. The word *literature* means academic publications on any subject.

Policy and Evidence in a Partisan Age: The Great Disconnect by Paul Gary Wyckoff (Urban Institute Press, 2009). This book shows how to use statistics and facts to assess the assertions of politicians. It also provides practice in all four of the Skill Sets covered in this chapter.

WEBSITE

http://en.wikipedia.org/wiki/Wikipedia:Verifiability The methods used by Wikipedia in verifying factual statements can provide practice for the skills in this chapter.

"YOU SEE THINGS;
AND YOU SAY,
'WHY?'
BUT I DREAM
THINGS THAT NEVER WERE;
AND I SAY,
'WHY NOT?'"

—GEORGE BERNARD SHAW

CHAPTER 10

SOLVING PROBLEMS

**IDENTIFY PROBLEMS • DEVELOP SOLUTIONS •
LAUNCH SOLUTIONS**

Effective problem solving starts with an attitude that asks "why not?" Why can't we do a better job? Problem solvers are into continuous improvement. Problem solving is much more than just pushing around a lot of information. Like the skills in the previous chapter, it is also part of what people outside of academia, and some who do applied work in academia, call "critical thinking." It requires you to use information to form a plan of action and then to make decisions and take action, or talk to others who can help you implement the solution.

The problem-solving Skill Set builds on all nine Skill Sets previously discussed. It requires character, good communication skills, excellent people skills, and good research and analysis skills. The Skill Set in the previous chapter—detecting nonsense, paying attention to detail, applying knowledge, evaluating actions and policies—is essential for successful problem solving. In addition, a problem solver must be willing to take risks and to think about the big picture. The willingness to see problems and do something about them is critical to success in a career. A senior VP writes, "While anger and fear are typical responses to change, optimism is the more appropriate one. Ironically, when people are worried about keeping their jobs, they are most resistant to change. They adopt the exact opposite behavior of what companies are looking for in their employees."

Employers rarely explicitly list problem solving as a key skill, but they do frequently mention critical thinking, initiative, adaptability, and leadership. These terms are frequently associated with employees' willingness to improve themselves and their organization. Employers want workers who are optimistic about change. They want to hire employees who, in the words of one employer, "know how big the problem is, the frequency, and how long it will take to solve." Willingness to recognize and provide evidence of problems helps your boss quickly understand what needs to be addressed and makes him or her ready to listen to your suggestions. Your interviewer may not use the term "problem solving," but he will be looking for it throughout your interview.

IDENTIFY PROBLEMS

"People tend to process solutions rather than identify the problem."

—Senior VP for a large investment corporation

Each unit in an organization is responsible for a specific function that, taken together, hopefully accomplishes the goals of the organization. So you will need to know the mission or goals of your unit and see the degree to which those goals are being achieved. The first and most critical step in problem solving is to see where what is happening is not in line with the goals of an organization. If you are in marketing, the problem could be not enough salespeople in some geographic area, or that goods are not being shipped fast enough.

Identifying a problem is more than just saying one exists. It also requires evidence that demonstrates the problem is real. You may use statistical evidence showing the increase in time it takes between the ordering and the shipping of the goods in a chart. You may use a survey to show the frequency of customer complaints. You may simply decide to show that everyone in your unit agrees that there is a problem. The key is substantiating in concrete terms that a problem exists.

One of the keys to good problem identification is making sure you *have* a problem before you even start to discuss solutions. Let's say the executive committee of a senior citizens' center decides that more publicity is needed to attract more people to their facilities. The committee will get into arguments about how best to publicize their center. They will do this without first understanding the real problem, which in this case, is the lack of participation. If they look at lack of participation as the problem, maybe they would realize that the real cause may be the lack of attractive programs and not the lack of PR. People tend to come up with solutions without adequately defining and measuring the problem. A problem-solving orientation will help you avoid this trap.

This example suggests that many of the skills presented in this book are needed to solve problems effectively. To identify the problem in such a way that the definition of it is clear and some evidence is available that it actually exists requires skills in working with people, information gathering, verbal and written communication, and quantitative analysis. Above all, it requires asking and answering the right questions.

COURSES: Identifying problems can occur in any academic field. Helpful courses can range from mathematics and science classes in which the problem can only be answered through logic or research to social science and professional school courses in which the answers come from working closely with those who have a stake in the problem. Literature courses, in which novels and plays, more often than not, pose a set of problems for the main characters, can also be useful. Research of similar problems through interviews and reading case studies can also be helpful in social science and professional school courses. Identifying problems in a measurable way could be practiced in methods courses.

NON-COURSE ACTIVITIES: Whether working in a student group, a committee with faculty and administrators, or an internship or job setting, looking for and clearly measuring problems can be practiced. Force yourself to observe how problems are identified and measured by a group trying to make a decision. Ask frequently and with forcefulness, "Now what problem are we trying to solve?" Read biographies of successful people who have made positive change.

"For every complex problem, there is a simple solution that is elegant, easy to understand, and wrong."

—H. L. Mencken, twentieth-century journalist and commentator

Once you have identified a problem, the next step is to come up with possible solutions. If we acknowledge the quotation at the top of this section, "solutions" is too strong a word in many cases. Difficult and persistent problems, especially if they involve many people, are never solved. These kinds of problems are not physical ones like fixing a dripping faucet, which can be solved. Problem solving is frequently about reducing the negative effects and not necessarily eliminating the causes of the problem.

In medicine, you treat a cough of unknown origins with cough syrup to reduce its severity. In the business world, your competitors' products and advertising are frequently the primary underlying cause of your poor sales. You cannot eliminate the competitors, but you can improve your product or advertising to win back sales. A preferred solution would be to put your competitors out of business, but that rarely happens.

I have purposely used the verb "develop" because solutions may be found by looking at what others have done in similar situations as well as creating new solutions. When it comes to solving problems, research and creativity are both required. Research into what has been done means searching for effective practices as well as those that have failed. Applying those practices to your problem requires creating an action plan that adapts the idea to a new situation. If your research does not yield a relevant effective practice, you need to think up an idea on your own. When car sales were slumping for Chrysler under Lee Iacocca, he came up with the idea of the minivan, which helped revitalize a company that was on the ropes. This was a creative idea that worked much better than trying to build better cars and use better advertising gimmicks than the competitors.

Employers want you to always be thinking about ways of solving problems that you, your department, and your organization face. They recognize that problem solvers sometimes are at risk if their ideas clash with their immediate superiors, which is why many use the suggestion box to get ideas from their employees. Many bosses not only want you to bring problems to them, but when you do, they also want you to propose a solution. If you just bring the problem, you may be perceived as whining. If you bring a solution with clear evidence of the problem, it shows that you are into continuous improvement, which is every boss's dream.

COURSES: Policy courses in the social sciences and all of the professional schools provide examples of solutions to problems in the profession or society in general. They are usually offered in the junior and senior year. A particularly valuable experience, no matter what job you take, is a course, increasingly offered in management programs, in which you propose a new business and develop a business plan to make the business profitable. This kind of exercise requires you to come up with solutions to problems you would face when starting a new enterprise. Even if you are not a business major, a course or two in entrepreneurship is a good idea.

NON-COURSE ACTIVITIES: Student organizations, including fraternities and sororities, and committees working within the college frequently develop actions to deal with problems. Problems range from what kind of entertainment to bring to the university, to how to increase the size of the pledge class, to how to allocate funds among student groups, to how to build membership for existing organizations. The key to these activities is seriously considering multiple solutions and then implementing the best one. When you are in a situation in which there are consequences to your actions, you will learn much more about problem solving than in hypothetical or simulated learning experiences.

"There is nothing more difficult to carry out, nor more doubtful of success, nor more dangerous to handle, than to initiate a new order of things."

—Niccolò Machiavelli

As a human resources person for a large corporation states, "You need to be able to make a decision and not be afraid of making a mistake. . . . I'd be more worried if someone couldn't make a decision rather than if they made the wrong one." Solutions can be discussed for only so long. Some kind of test, even if it is a pilot program, needs to be attempted after the research and discussion have been completed.

Your chances of successfully launching a solution will be greatly enhanced if you solicit the opinions of others in creating solutions. Part of the creative process is soliciting others' reactions to your initial ideas and then adjusting those ideas in response to legitimate criticism. Creating a solution alone is never as effective as creating a solution through mutual exchange with those who have influence over the action. You may have thought of the idea, but you should be happy to give ownership to those around you.

After you have clearly identified the problem and settled on a solution you think will work (at least partially), you face the most difficult and frustrating part of problem solving: either implementing the solution yourself or getting your organization to do it. The solution may be a collective idea, but you need to develop skills in getting solutions accepted.

Solutions, by definition, create change in the way things are done. People resist change primarily because they fear the unknown and are afraid they will personally lose something (like their job or a promised raise). The first and most important skill in launching solutions is to be tolerant of the resistance to change.

For changes that you do not completely control yourself, you will need a second skill: getting the problem and the solution on the agenda of those who have the power. Those who have power are usually very busy, and although they say they want solutions, they usually want them at no cost to themselves or their organization. Moreover, to get your solution on the table, you need to convince those above you that there is a very serious problem. To do this, while not offending those who are responsible for the problem, is no easy task. As Eldridge Cleaver, a famous black radical in the 1960s, said, "You're either part of the solution or part of the problem." Nobody likes to be told they are a part of the problem.

Finally, you need to be able to build support so that your solution is seriously considered. Building support requires getting others to buy into the idea: the more powerful, the better. Your people, communication, and analysis skills will be critical. Identifying a problem and developing an idea on how to "solve" the problem within your job responsibilities is not as difficult as launching a solution that eventually will need backing from above. When you start out, be satisfied with problem solving in your own job. Solving your own job problems will give you legitimacy; it will lead to raises and promotions as your boss realizes that you are improving the performance of the department he or she manages. After a few years of successful problem solving within your job, you may be ready to venture outside of it.

As you gain more experience, coming up with solutions will increase your worth to the company and make you more appealing if you decide to look for another position. A typical interview question is "What decision or action are you most proud of?" If you can tell how you built support within the organization for a solution, you will impress the interviewer. One of my students landed a high-paying job when he told the interviewer how he decided that computers were needed for kids in a small community center located in a housing project and that he was able to obtain eight used computers for the center. He said that the story convinced the interviewer to hire him.

Many people in the highest management positions see themselves as problem solvers or as creators of teams of people who can solve tough problems faced by the organization. Even entry-level interviews may touch on your capacity to improve yourself and others.

Because launching solutions is such a difficult and complex task, practicing it in your college years will get you started on a road to fame and fortune.

COURSES: History courses that focus on specific decisions, such as the United States action during the Cuban missile crisis, are valuable in learning about the processes surrounding decisions that lead to solutions. Political science courses that help you look at specific cases of political decisions and policy-making processes may also help. Courses that use simulations and fieldwork are likely to be more powerful than those that rely only on lectures, discussions, and readings. Entrepreneurship courses that include creating a plan for a start-up business judged by outside businesspeople will help you develop your skills at problem solving.

NON-COURSE ACTIVITIES: The only way to really learn about launching a solution is to launch one yourself. Whether you act within a student organization or alone, try to get something changed for the better while in your college years. The best way to do this is to get a leadership position such as treasurer, vice president, or president. You will be faced with plenty of problems and have the opportunity to come up with and implement solutions. A student of mine organized through the Student Association a free bus service for students to and from the university on holidays. She helped solve a problem that many students faced. This is less likely to happen at an internship or a part-time job, but keep your eyes open for the opportunity. After you gain your supervisor's trust, you may be able to suggest solutions to problems you know your supervisor is concerned about. Look for small and specific problems that can be easily solved.

USEFUL RESOURCES

BOOKS

The Maxwell Manual for Good Citizenship: Public Policy Skills in Action by Bill Coplin (Rowman & Littlefield, 2011). In this book, I introduce a problem-solving approach that can be used to create government policies but also can be applied to any clearly defined personal or professional problem.

QBQ! The Question behind the Question: Practicing Personal Accountability at Work and in Life by John G. Miller (Putnam Publishing Group, 2004). This inspirational book mentioned in chapter 1 also shows the importance of asking the right questions.

WEBSITE

http://athealth.com/Consumer/disorders/problemsolving.html
This site provides a short introduction to the steps you need to take to solve any problem.

"LEARNING IS NOT ATTAINED BY CHANCE, IT MUST BE SOUGHT FOR WITH ARDOR, AND ATTENDED TO WITH DILIGENCE."

—ABIGAIL ADAMS, WIFE OF PRESIDENT JOHN ADAMS AND ALSO HIS PRINCIPAL ADVISER

CHAPTER 11

MOVING BEYOND THE TEN SKILL SETS

GAIN SOFTWARE EXPERTISE IN ADDITION TO MICROSOFT WORD AND EXCEL • MASTER IN-DEPTH KNOWLEDGE OF ANY FIELD • DEVELOP FOREIGN LANGUAGE SKILLS • EMPHASIZE ARTISTIC AND MUSIC KNOWLEDGE AND/OR SKILL • CAPITALIZE ON SPORTS SKILLS • PURSUE PLEASURE ACTIVITIES

The previous ten chapters introduced a list of skills that will be essential in getting a job and in having a successful work life. With the world of work becoming increasingly competitive and complicated, your ultimate success will be boosted by having more than the basic skills and, in many cases, specialized knowledge. The items identified in this chapter represent only a beginning list. You may think of others, but the ones described here are most likely to be helpful. I have included these additional suggestions because you could be introduced to them in college or develop them from the base you already have when you begin college.

The opportunities discussed in this chapter could make a difference in your career, but more than that, some may simply help you live a more enjoyable life because of their intrinsic worth. This leads me to a very important point about this chapter. First, do not go after these added experiences in place of the skills listed in the previous ten chapters. Some of the suggestions might be a lot of fun and a diversion from the hard work of improving your basic skills.

Second, work only on the skills that you enjoy and are good at. Do not make the mistake that many students, who are goal oriented, make when they just add skills so they have more skills. Beyond the basic ten Skill Sets, you want to seek mastery of a few new skills rather than dabble in as many as possible.

In chapter 4, I stressed the importance of knowing how to use Microsoft Word as one of the written communication Skill Sets. In chapter 8, I included the use of Microsoft Excel as one of the quantitative analysis Skill Sets. Being able to use these programs well is integrated in many jobs today.

However, if you have basic competence in the primary operations of several other software packages, you will enhance your chances of landing a good job and succeeding in your job. Some of the most important programs are listed below by function.

GOOD COMPUTER SOFTWARE TO KNOW

ADOBE PHOTOSHOP Graphic editing software used to edit, manipulate, and design photos and prints

CONTENT MANAGEMENT SYSTEMS (CMS) Web authoring and editing software useful for creating layouts for websites, wordpress or Drupal

MICROSOFT WORD Word-processing software useful for writing reports and memos, designing resumes and cover letters, and working on other materials

MICROSOFT EXCEL Spreadsheet software useful for creating charts, tables, and graphs

MICROSOFT EXPRESSIONS A suite of programs including web, blend, design, and encoding features for building applications

MICROSOFT POWERPOINT Presentation software useful for making informational slides

MICROSOFT ACCESS Software used to record information case by case and create spreadsheets in statistical analysis

Some of the items on the list do the same thing (such as Photoshop and Expressions). Of the software listed above, those most important for most careers (especially in early stages) are Microsoft Excel and Microsoft Access, according to my alumni. Access is a step up from Excel and many organizations use or could use Access for a variety of purposes. Web-design skills that start with Content Management Systems (CMS) are important, not so much so you can become your organization's webmaster, but so that you can use your skills to ensure that the webmaster does what makes sense for the organization.

Many of my most successful alums have been helped by having some basic skills in web design, graphic design, social media, and blogging. Many jobs in marketing and sales require these tools. If you've had some basic experiences with these tools in college, you can work with technical people or pick up more technical skills on the job.

MASTER IN-DEPTH KNOWLEDGE OF ANY FIELD

I maintain that real-world skills beat the knowledge you can gain in college every time. That is true, but because life is a crapshoot, knowledge can sometimes make a big difference.

If two job applicants have the same level of competence in the ten Skill Sets but one is a Civil War history buff just like the boss, who do you think will get the job? And who do you think will be paying visits to the boss's house to move around toy soldiers, not to mention cannons, on a detailed miniature replica of the battlefield at Gettysburg? Areas of in-depth knowledge are valuable because they may possibly connect you with your boss or colleagues. In-depth knowledge will help you have bond-building conversations with colleagues.

What knowledge area is most likely to help you in your work life is not relevant here. With so many specialized areas, it makes little sense to pick something because it has a higher probability of a successful "hit." Follow your interests, and it's likely that on many occasions you'll find it useful in conversations with others at work.

In-depth knowledge, like some of the other extra skill areas to be discussed, is particularly useful in careers populated by those who think they are, or want to be, in the elite of our society. Showing off in-depth knowledge is part of your membership card to join the cultured and well educated.

As you move up the career ladder, you will come in contact with people who are more highly educated and who have the cultural benefits roughly associated with wealth. Having the knowledge frequently associated with "high-class people" can't hurt you, and not having it can hurt you. Give it a shot and see whether you can lose yourself in scholarly study, but don't let it get in the way of improving your skills in the basic ten Skill Sets.

DEVELOP FOREIGN LANGUAGE SKILLS

In this increasingly global society, developing foreign language skills is a good idea, especially if you are gifted in learning foreign languages. The major foreign languages to learn are Arabic, Chinese, Japanese, Russian, French, German, and Spanish. Some languages less frequently learned—such as Swahili, the languages of northern and eastern Africa—would be useful. Mastering a second or third language could open up career fields for you, but it also can help you in another way. Employers, colleagues, and customers will view your mastery of one or more foreign languages as an extra piece of evidence that you are smart and adaptable. Speaking Spanish can almost be a required skill in areas with a large Spanish-speaking population.

Taking language courses in college alone is not good enough for you to count language as a skill to be used in a career. You must be fluent in speaking, reading, and writing the language. Many college foreign language departments provide a foundation. Traveling to the country where the language is spoken and working hard to engage in conversations with the locals makes good sense if you are serious about foreign language skills.

EMPHASIZE ARTISTIC AND MUSIC KNOWLEDGE AND/OR SKILL

Interests that you may have started in childhood and continue as part of your college education can help you in your career. Just as with in-depth knowledge and foreign language skills, it's possible that someone above you in your organization will either have similar skills and knowledge or be impressed by someone who does. It will help you bond and converse with those you work with.

What type of art and music can be used to help your career? The answer is any type that has not been in the current pop culture mainstream for less than ten years, unless the artist or musician is dead, in which case five years is enough. Being a fan of Lady Gaga might help with colleagues close to your age, but it will probably lose cache with older coworkers, who might think pop music is short-lived and best left to the younger generation. Fifteen years from now, your expertise and love for Lady Gaga may be quaint and interesting; until then, it is less impressive.

Tennis and golf are the two sports with the highest potential payoff because they are the sports of the successful, especially in the business world. They are also important in the government and nonprofit world because those worlds want and need business support. So take some tennis or golf classes if available and/or make it your business to develop a high skill level in at least one. A word of warning: do not tell your boss you can play tennis when you have a serve that goes in a high arc, and he or she has one that knocks your racket out of your hand.

Participating on an intercollegiate sports team for at least one year, no matter what sport, is one of the most important extra credit things you can do for your career. The experience will give you something in common with a few individuals you meet in the world of work. Even if you were third string, you can use the experience to bond and engage in conversation. Many employers who played on intercollegiate athletic teams see the discipline and teamwork they developed when they played to be a key to their success. Playing on an intercollegiate team while maintaining a respectable GPA (above 3.2) sends impressive signals about your time management, discipline, and teamwork.

Colleges offer experiences in various sports, sometimes for credit, but always as an extracurricular activity. Joining the ski club or intramural sports can have big payoffs.

We have not talked about knowledge of sports here. Being able to talk intelligently about college or professional football or basketball can help you with your peers and supervisors. However, this is so common that I don't see it as a major benefit to your career future. Watching ESPN ten hours a day is not likely to prepare you for sports bonding. Fantasy football or baseball might, however, if you happen by chance to have a boss who is also into it.

Certain pleasure activities are treated as skills for credit in college. The most widely offered are wine tasting and cooking. These can be important in social situations. Horseback riding is another pleasure that you might want to pursue. Gardening can also be useful as an area of common experience. There are so many areas that might be viewed as leisure activities; it is important that you choose at least one pursuit and have extensive knowledge and experience in that area if it is to help in a career.

The kinds of knowledge and skills discussed in this chapter obviously have benefits beyond your success in the world of work. This is usually phrased as "learning for the sake of learning." Some would argue that, as a whole, learning as much as you can so that you are "well rounded" is the real purpose of a college education. I think that talking about the "real purpose" of a college education, in the abstract, is a meaningless exercise. Your purpose is the real purpose, which is why it is up to you. This book assumes that a major purpose of your college education is to prepare for a rewarding career, but it doesn't have to be the only purpose.

From the perspective of general preparation for your life or work, these skill and knowledge areas are clearly secondary to the ten Skill Sets that every employer wants you to master. You may become a professional in one of these areas, and that should figure in your job-specific skills, which will be discussed in the next chapter. For example, if your interest in literature stimulates you to seek a career in the book industry, then skills related to writing and editing as well as your content knowledge of trends in publishing will be important.

To make one or more of these areas pay off once you get into the workforce or even in your interview, you need to recognize two very important principles:

- Pursue an area because you enjoy it and have some aptitude for it. The term "dilettante" is used to identify people who dabble in many areas but lack depth in any. You do not want to be labeled a "jack of all trades, a master of none."

- The likelihood that any one of these areas beyond the ten skill sets will definitely impact your career is low. If they do, it will be a matter of happenstance. Being prepared for luck, however, is a matter of genuine and serious hard work.

USEFUL RESOURCES

The range of resources available is so broad that suggesting books is not useful. You can easily find the resources that will be helpful once you decide where your interests lie.

PART TWO

BOOSTING YOUR SKILLS SCORE

"YOU PAYS YOUR **MONEY AND YOU TAKES** YOUR CHANCES."

—PUNCH

CHAPTER 12

MAKING SMART ACADEMIC CHOICES FOR SKILL DEVELOPMENT

FOLLOW THE 50-50 PRINCIPLE • MAXIMIZE PROGRAM CHOICES • SELECT COURSES FOR SKILLS • INVESTIGATE PROFESSORS

Think of how the terms "it's academic" or "ivory tower" are used as negatives in our everyday speech—even by faculty members outside of the earshot of the public and their students. When it comes to gaining skills, the academic course work you take in college can help you, but only if you choose carefully and use it to its highest potential.

One of the unrecognized benefits of a college education is that it forces you to make choices that impact you directly, sometimes in the short run and sometimes in the long run. You will make more choices during your first two weeks of college than you have made in the previous year. The ability to make good choices and adjust to their consequences requires mastery of almost all the ten Skill Sets that are critical to your career success.

To make good choices about programs, courses, and professors, you will need to first think hard about your goals and then gather information that will enable you to estimate the benefits and risks of your decisions.

What do you want to achieve through your choice of a course or program—a high grade with or without a lot of work, gaining knowledge that you think is valuable, or developing important skills? Usually you will have several different goals, and sometimes you may not be clear yourself on what your priorities are. You need to think about your goals and reach some conclusions before you can make effective choices about courses and programs.

For purposes of preparing yourself for a career, the most important set of goals has to do with the ten Skill Sets. Knowing which skills you need to develop will help you decide which courses to take. If you need to improve your writing, for example, a course that requires a lot of writing might be a good choice.

Think critically about the information you received from college offices about the benefits and risks of choosing a given program or course. Think of all of the information that different programs provide as sales pitches to convince you to join their programs. Like all sales pitches, they accent the positive and minimize the negative. You know the saying "buyer beware." That also applies to decisions about college programs and courses. Get information from other students, surveys like Rate My Professor, as well as graduation and job placement rates from the school itself to offset the beautiful pictures painted by the informational brochures. You will have to be as critical of those sources as you are of brochures. Don't be one of those students who spends more time deciding which movie to go to than choosing a course.

I can't provide specific advice on many of the choices you will make in college because they are different for every student. Instead, I will provide some general comments on three choices you will be making that will most shape your academic activities: programs, courses, and professors. I will suggest how to make choices that will allow you to improve many of the ten Skill Sets necessary for career success.

THE 50-50 PRINCIPLE

As I pointed out in the introduction to this book, the majority of students do not improve their ten Skill Sets in college. There are many reasons for this, including the unwillingness of many students to spend time on their futures. But the biggest reason is the gap between what professors teach and what you need to know.

I can speak from my own personal experience here. Upon graduating from Johns Hopkins with a degree in the social sciences, I passed the written examination for the Foreign Service and had my oral examination in front of three high-powered State Department officials. During the interview, one of the three said, "I see you've had a lot of political science courses, so could you tell me what the Pendleton Act was?" I had never heard of this act, even though it established the rules for the civil service in America. I countered with "ask me about Thomas Hobbes or John Locke," two well-known political philosophers. They responded that they weren't interested in political philosophy. They asked me whether I knew anything about the civil service. At the time, I had no idea what the civil service was. At that point, I realized that I had spent four years learning "stuff" that even professionals in the field I intended to pursue didn't care about.

As long as classes have to do with reading textbooks, listening to lectures, and taking highly structured tests, the courses will emphasize theory and deemphasize application. They will be about the professorial scholarship rather than the application of skills. You may want to take a course in psychology because you want to improve your interpersonal skills, and you think knowledge about psychology will help. You will soon discover that your introductory psych course is an introduction to the field of psychology as a scientific discipline. This means learning a lot of definitions (like the term "cognitive dissonance") and studying what different scholars have had to say about various concepts. This basic introduction to the discipline of psychology has about as much value to those seeking to improve social skills as a book on how to swim will help you be a better swimmer.

This gap between your desire for career preparation and the faculty's theoretical and abstract knowledge can be confusing at best and discouraging at worst. It is not that academic course work provides no value with respect to skills and career exploration. It does, but it needs to be supplemented by activities outside the course work and by the selection of skills-friendlier courses. As discussed below, you can help yourself by choosing courses that have hands-on experiences that allow you to link the theories you learn in class to laboratory and fieldwork activities.

Course work and degree requirements will provide less than 50 percent of the skills required to be successful in whatever career field you choose. You may initially find this idea shocking because your degree is based on academic course work, but you will discover that what you learn outside the classroom is at least equally important for your skill development. The next three chapters tell you how your nonacademic activities in college, such as your social, internship, student organization, and job experiences, will help you improve in all skill areas. This chapter will suggest how your choices about academic programs, courses, and professors can help you practice the skills required for success in all fields.

MAXIMIZE PROGRAM CHOICES

The *academic program* refers to two different things—the school or college you are in and the major or majors you take in the school or college. If you are at a university, the first program choice is the college or school in which you are registered. Second, within any college, there may be different majors. If you are at a college rather than a university, you will just have choices about majors and minors.

PROGRAM TRADE-OFFS

One significant choice you face is between liberal arts and professional schools or programs, like management or engineering or communications. Some colleges specialize in liberal arts, but they also offer some professional school–type programs within the liberal arts. In liberal arts or arts and sciences programs, you major in one of the traditional disciplines or in an interdisciplinary program. A typical list follows.

TYPICAL MAJORS IN LIBERAL ARTS

African-American Studies

Anthropology

Astronomy

Biology

Chemistry

Earth Sciences

Economics

English

Fine Arts

Foreign Languages

Geography

History

Humanities

International Relations

Literature

Mathematics

Natural Sciences

Philosophy

Physics

Political Science

Psychology

Public Policy

Religion

Social Sciences

Sociology

Women's Studies

All programs can be used to improve your Skills Score if you plan carefully. From a career perspective, the biggest problem that students have when majoring within a liberal arts program is they wrongly assume their major is a gateway to a specific career. A liberal arts education prepares you for all types of careers and not just those that require graduate education.

Undergraduate professional school programs are also a good choice for raising your Skills Score. The following list names the programs that are usually housed within a school or college at the university or that can be floating programs in smaller colleges. Students who go into professional school programs may not end up in their intended profession because professional school programs offer a great deal of general education and a relatively small amount of technical training. As in all the generalizations presented in this chapter, there are major exceptions to this rule. For example, a program in drama can be run as one long audition and require that most of the course work be directed at developing actors. Another example is accounting in business or management schools in which graduates may be ready to pass the CPA exam and work as accountants.

PROFESSIONAL PROGRAMS BY SCHOOL

ARCHITECTURE	Architecture
EDUCATION	Communication Sciences and Disorders
	Education by subject (Art, English, Mathematics, Music, Reading, Science, Social Studies)
	Elementary Education
	Higher/Postsecondary Education
	Inclusive Elementary and Special Education
	Physical Education
ENGINEERING AND COMPUTER SCIENCE	Computer Science
	Engineering (Aerospace, Bio-, Chemical, Civil, Computer, Electrical, Environmental, Mechanical)
	Systems and Information Science
HUMAN ECOLOGY	Child and Family Studies
	Dietetics
	Exercise Sciences
	Hospitality and Food Service Management
	Nursing
	Nutrition
	Social Work
	Sports Management
INFORMATION STUDIES	Information Management and Technology
MANAGEMENT	Accounting
	Business Administration
	Entrepreneurship and Emerging Enterprises
	Finance
	General Studies in Management
	Marketing Management
	Organization and Management
	Real Estate
	Retailing and Marketing

PROFESSIONAL PROGRAMS BY SCHOOL	
PUBLIC COMMUNICATIONS	Advertising
	Broadcast Journalism
	Graphic Arts
	Magazine and Newspaper Journalism
	Photojournalism
	Public Relations
	Television-Radio-Film
VISUAL AND PERFORMING ARTS	Art
	Design
	Drama
	Fashion
	Film
	Museum Studies
	Musical Performance and Industries
	Rhetorical Studies

Liberal arts programs are not as irrelevant to your Skills Score as some think, and professional school programs are not as on target to getting you a job in a specific industry as others believe. That is why your selection of programs must in part be guided by the question "What skills am I good at and like performing?" rather than "What job will this major get me?" Chapter 17 will help you explore these questions. If you learn nothing else from reading this book, remember that the general skills you develop in college are the foundation for your success in the workforce, regardless of the career field you pursue.

To support this view, you should know that spokespeople for almost all graduate professional degrees like the JD, MBA, MPA, and MSW say that the degree you took as an undergraduate is not critical for admittance to their program. In fact, they emphasize diversity in the backgrounds of their students. These professional school programs actually look for the same skills as employers, along with high scores on the standardized graduate school examinations like the GRE, GMAT, and LSAT. In most cases, your GPA is not as important as your skills, experiences, and test scores.

Based on my experience with students over the past thirty years, I advocate a program in which you have a professional school major or minor and a liberal arts major or minor. Unless you are one of those few students who has a complete commitment to either becoming a scholar in a liberal arts field or following a highly specialized professional field like chemical engineering, you should have at least a minor in a field outside of your primary school program. If possible, try to take two majors from different schools if you are at a university. These combinations are important for your Skills Score because different programs emphasize different skills, and the ability to navigate between two programs will develop the skills described in chapter 9 (asking and answering the right questions) and chapter 10 (solving problems).

CONSIDER ROTC PROGRAMS

Although the military is not for everyone, the benefits to your Skills Score make the Reserve Officer Training Corps (ROTC) program, offered by the Army, Air Force, and Navy (which includes the Marines) at more than one thousand colleges, something you should explore. The programs carry full or partial scholarships to your college for many of the recruits and summer pay in exchange for an obligation to serve four years once you graduate.

The choice of academic programs is open, but scholarship opportunities are usually limited by your choice of major. The nonacademic component of ROTC and the courses specifically taught by military personnel can build your Skills Score as well. This is particularly true with respect to work ethic, physical skills, and the full range of people, communications, and problem-solving skills.

After graduating from college, you will be commissioned as a second lieutenant (or ensign) as a junior military officer (JMO). You would enter your respective service and attend specialty training in whichever career field assigned (for example, pilot training, intelligence, maintenance, logistics, security forces, services, public affairs, or communications). You would then be assigned to a base, post, or ship.

Once the active-duty service commitment is met, many officers leave the military and transition to rewarding civilian careers in government and business. College graduates who have had some military experience are in high demand in the world of work, according to an article by Dave Moniz in the *Christian Science Monitor*.[1] The article points out that when a business manager from Merck, a major pharmaceutical manufacturer, "screens resumes submitted in response to a newspaper's advertisement no more than 1 in 10 candidates is hirable. When he works with military headhunters, the number of employable candidates rises to about 7 in 10." Those odds may make it worthwhile to you to consider schools with ROTC programs.

SELECT COURSES FOR SKILLS

The course recommendations for the ten Skill Sets in chapters 1 through 10 make it clear that you have to plan carefully to find course work that will enhance your Skills Score. Concerning these recommendations, there is both bad new and good news. Here's the bad news:

- The majority of courses you take will not have skills as a primary goal.

- Some courses will be focused primarily on skills like writing, statistics, and speech communications, but even these courses may not deliver what they promise. They tend to be heavy on theory and light on practice.

- Many college professors rely on lectures and recall tests, which are not skill friendly.

But there is good news. These roadblocks can be overcome with a clear commitment to improving the ten Skill Sets. You can practice and develop your basic skills through much of your college course work while also getting good grades and your degree. The remedies below will show you how to make course and instructor choices and follow a proactive learning approach that will help you enhance your basic skills. If you do this, college is probably the best place you can be to develop the basic skills you need for success in the world of work. You will be able to use much of your course work to raise your Skills Score if you follow the suggestions in this chapter and in the course sections of chapters 1 through 10.

You will take many courses that are not directly related to your Skills Score for graduation requirements of one kind or another. Even these requirements can give you an opportunity to develop many of the skills, if you use them for that purpose. Business students taking a chemistry course as a general education freshman requirement can develop skills like paying attention to detail, using numbers to reach conclusions, and learning to ask the right questions. If the course has a community-service requirement in which they tutor high school students in chemistry, then almost every one of the ten basic Skill Sets can be practiced. Most courses will provide you with an opportunity to develop some skills—but only if you take advantage of the opportunity to do so.

Even the most academic and theoretical courses provide an opportunity to improve your Skills Score. They will also provide you with an opportunity to develop listening and writing skills or, if they use numbers, quantitative skills. Being required to take too many of these courses is far from ideal, but you can turn a negative into a positive with the right approach.

Above all, don't get frustrated with your college's course requirements because, if nothing else, they provide an opportunity for you to improve your ability to self-motivate and to solve problems. That said, do not rely on mandatory introductory skill courses to develop your skills, because most do not go as in-depth as they should. Most colleges offer "skill" or "tool" courses in writing, speaking, foreign language, and a vast array of quantitative and computer skills. Taking them, particularly at the introductory level, may help you get started on developing a skill. However, that is far from guaranteed and cannot replace the real-world application you need.

Many professors who teach "tool" courses tend to provide too much theory and not enough practice. In statistics, they focus on theoretical proofs for the equations that generate the statistics rather than when to use what tool and for what purpose. The more direct practice and application in exercising the skills, the better it is for you.

Even if you take a course that requires you to apply skills, skills are not something you get from one course. They need to be practiced over a long period of time and applied in different situations. So practicing in every course you take will ensure that you can apply the skills when you start on your career.

The instructor is always more important than the course, so do some serious investigation of the courses you choose. Online opinion sites like Rate My Professor should be used carefully because they tend to only express extreme views. Talking to peers you respect is much better, and using multiple sources of information is the best. The official course catalogue doesn't provide much information. The write-ups are brief and frequently neither informative nor accurate. Moreover, different faculty will interpret the official course catalogue description differently.

Instead, obtain a copy of the course syllabus before you sign up for the course. The syllabus can be viewed as a contract between you and the instructor. This advice sounds obvious, but may not be so easy to follow. First, many instructors do not prepare the course syllabus early enough to allow you to get the information ahead of time. If that is the case for a course you are interested in, sign up for one or two backup courses, go to the class the first day and get the syllabus. If the instructor has taught the course before, get an old copy of the syllabus. Second, the instructor might not stick to the syllabus, or it might be so vague that it tells you very little. The remedy for this is to check with students to find the "real syllabus." Finally, email the instructor or make an appointment to conduct a brief interview.

Find answers to these questions when choosing courses and instructors that you hope will significantly enhance one or more of the ten basic Skill Sets:

1. What kinds of tests and assignments are required?

Avoid courses based on multiple-choice exams, which rarely, if ever, measure the application of skills. Take courses that have off-campus field experience. (The vital importance of courses and programs that have incorporated some type of fieldwork will also be explored in the next chapter.) Look for words in the syllabus like "logs," "labs," "field-work," and "community service."

2. How is my final grade determined?

An instructor who weighs class participation and projects is likely to be looking more at your skill levels than your content mastery. Instructors who only give a midterm and final are not going to be concerned with your skill development. Be wary of instructors who grade on a bell-shaped curve. This practice occurs primarily in the sciences and mathematics but can happen in any course. It usually signifies that the instructor is not clear about standards, and that competition for the sake of competition seems to be the primary educational strategy. Curves may also reflect the tendency of faculty to teach too much at too high a level for the class so that grades are determined by how far the best can go. This is not usually a good way to help students develop their skills because the standards are muddled to the professor, and they will be even more confusing to you.

3. How are courses conducted?

Avoid professors who think teaching is telling or reading and who give recall tests. They may help you with your attention to detail skills and your ability to figure out what is wanted, but so will any course. Professors who use methods to engage students in debate and use active learning techniques like classroom exercises are always preferred. I'm not suggesting that you avoid a class from a professor who is a great lecturer, but instead check to see whether the examinations ask for more than recall or simply figuring out what the professor wants. Conversely, some professors who allow open class discussions that are unstructured and team projects that are not tightly evaluated are not helping you develop your skills any more than a teacher reading from notes that are thirty years old. Discussion sections, in which big lectures are broken into small groups and are run by a graduate student, may not allow for hands-on learning. Also, the quality of the discussion section depends on the quality of the graduate student. So ask students who've had the class what they think.

4. Are instructors both student oriented and standards driven?

These are two very important questions. Professors must finely balance two loves—the love for their subject matter and the love for their students. The balance is important for your own Skills Score. If the teacher throws the subject to you and then says, "Show me that you are almost as knowledgeable and as smart as I am," the skills value will be diminished. There may be value in this approach, especially with respect to the skills of asking and answering the right questions and problem solving, but there will be little opportunity for anything else. If the teacher tries to entertain you, the value to your skill development is minimized. An email to the instructor before the class starts may help you here. The answers may help you figure out the kinds of standards set for the course. If you get no response, the instructor may not be student oriented, well organized, or interested in having students. Most good professors welcome a student who takes the time to ask a question about a course.

5. Is the instructor accepting of the notion of skills?

Even professors who have the right combination of support for students and standards may not do a lot for your Skills Score. They may see their mission as developing you to become a scholar just like them. They can work with you on a one-on-one basis so that you understand the major research and theoretical questions they grapple with, but not much more. Unless you think you might want to be a scholar like your professor, this type of professor may do little to help you improve your Skills Score. Many professors tend to be more academically oriented than skills oriented, so you should explore this question.

Search for professors who send you out to test your knowledge and ideas in community service or related fieldwork. For example, if you are learning to master survey research, take the class in which the professor makes you design, conduct, and analyze a survey for a real-world client rather than one who has you read several books on survey research design and gives you a multiple-choice test. Almost every field can supply real-world experiences as part of the course, even if it is presenting your knowledge to a local high school class. If that is not possible, professors can run labs, simulations, and exercises;

give real-world case studies; or bring in outside speakers who are active in the field to give you a sense of the real-world dynamics. These are the professors who will boost your Skills Score the most.

6. What do the titles of professors mean?

Professor titles are sometimes bewildering, so here's a quick introduction. The title doesn't mean much in preparing for a career. A full professor or a part-time lecturer can provide you what you need in career guidance and skill development. It's the luck of the draw. The titles are not especially good predictors of the quality or relevance of a course. Unless you are trying to become a professor yourself and get into a PhD program, the title is irrelevant on letters of reference.

Two practices affect the titles of professors. The first is tenure. *Tenure* means professors cannot be fired unless they do something illegal or immoral or fail to meet their basic contractual obligations. For professors at teaching-oriented colleges, this means there is a lot of pressure on them to teach well. At research-oriented colleges and universities, the overwhelming pressure is to do research, and teaching sometimes suffers. Once they get tenure, some professors turn more of their efforts to teaching but in general the pattern set early in their career continues.

You can't draw any conclusions about a professor based on his or her title—a higher ranking doesn't necessarily mean better teaching. You are better off asking the opinion of peers, advisers, and the professors you trust rather than to look at titles. Don't be afraid to drop a course if you run into a professor you have trouble understanding for whatever reason. Give the professor a fair chance, but take action if you see trouble ahead. One more piece of advice: a lot of professors like to act mean and tough the first few classes. Check with your peers before you panic.

USEFUL RESOURCES

BOOKS

Our Underachieving Colleges: A Candid Look at How Much Students Learn and Why They Should Be Learning More, new edition, by Derek Bok (Princeton University Press, 2007). Bok is a former president of Harvard who has plenty to say about why skills for careers and citizenship are not at the top of the list of most faculty members.

Secrets of College Success: Over 600 Tips and Tricks Revealed by Lynn F. Jacobs and Jeremy S. Hyman (Jossey-Bass, 2010). This book is mentioned in chapter 1, but it's also helpful in navigating the academic choices you will have to make. Check out the authors' website (see below).

The Thinking Student's Guide to College: 75 Tips for Getting a Better Education by Andrew Roberts (University of Chicago Press, 2010). This book gives a different perspective and advice on getting the most out of the academic side of college.

You Majored in What?: Mapping Your Path from Chaos to Career by Katharine Brooks (Viking Adult, 2009). Parts of this book will help you explore academic programs with your focus on career exploration.

WEBSITE

www.professorsguide.com This is the website of Lynn F. Jacobs and Jeremy S. Hyman, authors of *Secrets of College Success*, mentioned above. The site provides current information and suggestions on a wide variety of topics related to making choices and succeeding during the college years.

"FOR THINGS WE HAVE TO LEARN BEFORE WE CAN DO THEM, WE LEARN BY DOING THEM."

—ARISTOTLE

CHAPTER 13

CREATING YOUR OWN APPRENTICESHIPS

EXPLORE APPRENTICE-BASED EDUCATION • BUILD YOUR BASE • LAND GOOD SUMMER JOBS AND INTERNSHIPS • MAKE THE MOST OF YOUR EXPERIENCES

Aristotle presents an ironic challenge to new graduates looking for their first job after college. Most job descriptions call for experience, but you can't get the experience without the job and you can't get the job without the experience.

Before the early twentieth century, the apprentice system, in which a beginner worked with a professional in the field, was the way to get the experience and grow into the job. That is how Benjamin Franklin became a printer with virtually no formal education. *Being an apprentice* means having a teacher and mentor who will encourage, demonstrate, provide ample learning opportunities, and correct you as you learn. In many countries around the world, an apprentice system is in place for large number of students—unlike in the United States, where it exists in very limited form.

Apprentice education is the best form of education in every field, but in the modern world there are too many wannabe apprentices and not enough faculty to serve the wannabes. Consequently, colleges cannot provide an apprentice system for the majority of undergraduates. Given the underlying economics and the trend toward distance and web-based learning, there is little hope for improvement. Email can help close the gap between the professor and the student but, in most cases, not enough to develop the kinds of apprentice relationships you need.

Even if there were enough college faculty members to provide apprenticeship experiences to all college students, they could not provide good apprenticeship experiences in most cases. Most college faculty, especially in arts and sciences programs, have studied their subject but have not been a "player" themselves. They can analyze the modern American novel but have not written a novel. They have written books on political leaders but have not been a political leader. Consequently, they are not equipped to give you an apprentice experience themselves. These faculty members are important to your general education but may be limited in how much they can help your Skills Score.

There are two important exceptions to this rule, however. First, students who want to take up the academic trade of scholarship and teaching can benefit greatly if a faculty member treats them as a junior colleague. This happens in many situations. Frequently, college students become research assistants to the point of being coinvestigators and even coauthors with faculty. Second, faculty members who have extensive nonacademic experiences can create apprenticeship relationships through their contacts or in their own work outside academia.

Fortunately, you can have limited but still useful apprentice relationships during your college years with experienced mentors and teachers both on and off campus that do not require professors to become part of your professional network. The solution to Aristotle's ironic statement is a string of educational work experiences or mini-apprenticeships. The apprenticeships will not be as long and intense as those Benjamin Franklin received from his brother and others to become a master printer, but they can be powerful learning experiences. Having a set of work experiences under the guidance of a professional can provide the support you need for an outstanding Skills Score. Recognizing the need for such experiences, most colleges are doing a good job in helping you get them.

Apprenticeship-type experiences are essential to your preparation for a rewarding work life for several reasons. First, every one of the ten Skill Sets can be developed during these experiences, depending on what jobs you are assigned.

Second, practicing the skills in real-world situations is a powerful learning engine. It means that when you do well, you will be praised in a genuine way, and that when you mess up, you will suffer real consequences. Receiving praise from a professional in the field you aspire to can motivate you to high levels of performance, just as being chewed out by the same professional can move you even higher.

Third, these experiences will help you build your professional network by creating opportunities to work with people in positions you may want to pursue. Whether you work as an intern in a nonprofit like a Boys and Girls Club or in a corporate setting, your immediate supervisor can write letters for you and also help you connect to others in your field of choice. (Networking will be discussed in greater detail in chapter 20.)

Finally, these experiences are important for your future work life because they give you a chance to see what kinds of jobs exist and whether or not you like them. The enormous haystack of professional fields that you face can be explored by these real-world experiences. You may find your work inherently interesting and the skills you exercise fulfilling, or you may realize that what you thought you would like to do is not rewarding. These experiences are more powerful and educational than reading books about careers and searching online.

For these reasons, what you do between semesters is as important for developing your basic skills as what you do during semesters. The time during both winter and summer semester breaks should be used to develop skills and acquire new experiences. Your public service, part-time jobs, or internships (paid or unpaid) are more important for your Skills Score than your major and the classes you take.

I base this assertion on what I hear from alumni, who routinely tell me that their internship and job experiences were the most important part of their education and urge me to provide even more opportunities. Often the difference between college graduates who obtain satisfying careers and those who don't is related to their summer jobs or internships between their junior and senior years. According to the National Association of Colleges and Employers, students who have internships are likely to obtain a job offer, accept that offer, and have 31 percent higher median salaries than those who have not had an internship.[1]

Employers are also unanimous about the value of summer work experiences. As one human resources director said, "Sure, it's great to have a fun summer job, but I'd rather see something with a lot of responsibility that requires skill."

There are four opportunities for apprentice-type experiences:

- Public or community service: These are usually in the local community but sometimes away from campus. They may be available through groups such as Habitat for Humanity or alternative spring break programs, which give students the opportunity to visit a poor area and build a house or do other philanthropic work for a week or longer. Such work is not paid and may or may not earn credit, depending on your college and program.

- Internships for a business, nonprofit, or government agency: Internships can be credit bearing and paid or unpaid. They can be taken during the semester or in the summer, and can be on or off campus, but are usually the latter. Some organizations will call paid positions "internships" in order to make it clear that it is not a permanent job and also to reduce fringe benefit costs. Internships can earn any number of credits depending on school and program policies and the availability of faculty oversight. The standard is forty-five hours of work for each semester credit hour.

- Part-time jobs during the academic year: These jobs can be on or off campus and, by the use of the term "job," are always paid. They usually do not generate academic credit, but give it a try.

- Full-time jobs during any period you're not a full-time student, usually in the summer: These jobs are paid, but they can also earn internship credit if you can demonstrate relevant "learning" to a college faculty member. The key feature here is that you work thirty to forty (or more) hours a week, and you receive wages.

I have lumped these four types together because they all have the potential to provide apprenticeship opportunities. The best opportunities for developing your skills come when the organization provides you with a staff member or an experienced volunteer to train and mentor you.

In addition, the four types frequently overlap. For example, the difference between an internship and a job is one of convenience for some employers. The term "internship" usually implies that academic credit will be earned. Internships frequently, though not always, are unpaid. For obvious reasons, paid internships are better than unpaid ones, but in certain fields paid internships are impossible to obtain. So the line between internship and job is not clear. Moreover, sometimes you can get credit for a job and sometimes public service morphs into a paid position. This is no different from the real world, where companies often give what are in effect internships before permanent employment. Think of these as opportunities in which you can have short-term apprenticeships.

What are the trade-offs among the four types of educational work experiences? All four types of experience can be powerful in raising your Skills Score, just as all can be an enormous waste of time. Public and community service is the easiest of the four types to obtain. The downside to public or community service from a learning perspective is that some of the agencies are not well enough organized to use you effectively, and frequently they provide little training or mentoring by the staff or volunteers. Things are frequently chaotic, especially if the agency deals with youth. Chapter 15 describes the benefits of service activities during your college years.

Internships have the most educational potential because inherent in the idea of an internship is that learning will occur. First, the organization offering the internship is likely to take some responsibility for making sure that you learn something and not just do gofer work. Second, as we have noted throughout the book, courses that integrate field experience are better suited for skill development. If the internship experience is part of a class and there are structured assignments and time for reflection on skills, you can make giant strides in many of the ten Skill Sets. Third, you earn college credit, which means that you have more time and less traditional academic pressure to limit your investment in the internship. Some college programs have a co-op requirement. A *co-op* is usually a semester-long (or even longer) full-time internship that is a requirement of the program and carries credit with it. It usually occurs in the junior or senior year, and you are expected to act as an apprentice for a company or agency. Frequently, a salary is paid by the host organization.

However, this is an ideal view of internships—their quality depends on both the college and the placement site. The site and your college may not have adequate resources invested to make it the kind of learning experience it can be. Many times internships are open-ended, poorly defined activity. This can work if the placement site has it together. However, if the organization is out of control and support from your college is weak, you may be in for an unpleasant experience. This does not mean you will fail to learn from the experience and should avoid it. It does mean that you have to put in extra effort to make it a learning experience.

Jobs, whether part time or full time in the summer, can make a major contribution to both your skill development and your career exploration. This is true even though the primary purpose of a job is for you to do what the employer needs to have done rather than your learning particular skills or knowledge about a business or an organization, as in an internship. However, you need to select a job that promises some education and is not continuously repetitive. Waiting tables, being a lifeguard or camp counselor, or driving a forklift are okay for your first summer, but they are not likely to be a learning experience worthy of the summer between your junior and senior years.

Some students opt to go for a higher-paying job even though it will provide poor career and skill development. They will choose the job that pays $12 an hour that they did last summer over one that pays $8 an hour but is directly related to a career goal. When you are paying $25,000 to $60,000 a year for your college education, going for a job that pays $4 an hour more, or $1,280 over an eight-week period, does not make a lot of sense. A summer job that gives you access to a full-time job when you graduate or, alternatively, helps you come to the conclusion that the field you have chosen is not so hot after all is worth much more than $1,280.

There are no clear-cut rules about paying versus nonpaying jobs. Even a job as a camp counselor, which some might view as just a summer of fun, can contribute greatly to your Skills Score. And a summer job scooping ice cream—if it also includes hiring, training, and firing workers—can mean more to a future employer than your having taken a management course or volunteered in a senator's office. Determine what skills you will be gaining from your experiences. Good choices about work and internship experiences are essential to a high Skills Score and, therefore, a top-of-the-line career.

Would you like to land a summer internship between your junior and senior year at a major corporation where you receive $30 an hour? How about adding to that salary a subsidized apartment, plane tickets home for a weekend, a broad and nurturing educational experience, and the promise of a job, if you perform well in your internship? If you think this is too good to be true, think again. Every year hundreds of students end up in this summer job heaven. Thousands find summer jobs that are not quite so profitable in the short run but just as valuable in the long run.

Most large corporations offer summer internship programs. However, only some of them are what you might label "dream internships." The table below lists internships considered the best by publications like *Business Week*, *Forbes*, and *Vault*.[2] The internships listed were mentioned in at least two of the three lists. These internships pay well—$15 to $35 per hour, depending on the gig. Most also have a high postinternship employment rate and offer benefits that range from housing stipends to health care plans.

DREAM INTERNSHIPS

DELOITTE & TOUCHE Opportunities are available in a range of financial services, including auditing, tax consultation, and business technology, among others.

ERNST & YOUNG Internships are available in one of their core practice areas: assurance, advisory, tax, and transaction advisory services.

GARMIN INTERNATIONAL Interns work in various engineering departments such as software engineering, design, electrical engineering, mechanical engineering, aviation systems, and engineering processes and components.

GENERAL ELECTRIC Program internships are offered in experienced commercial leadership, human resources leadership, financial leadership, and information management leadership.

GOLDMAN SACHS All disciplines are encouraged to apply; a financial background is not necessary.

GOOGLE, INC. Internships are available in departments such as sales, marketing, advertising, product management, finance, and business operations. Interns will learn the workings of the world's largest search engine firsthand.

JP MORGAN Interns work in asset management, finance, IB risk, investment banking, operations and business services, sales, trading and research, and technology.

KPMG The Build Your Own Internship Program allows students to combine audit, tax, or advisory disciplines to tailor their experience more personally. Successful interns are offered full-time employment.

NICKELODEON ANIMATION STUDIOS Interns will get experience in numerous departments, such as TV production, postproduction, casting, animation and live action development, computer graphics, special events, writing, college relations and recruitment, and business and legal affairs. Many interns are offered full-time positions after completion of the internship.

NORTHWESTERN MUTUAL FINANCIAL NETWORK Prime responsibilities for interns include identifying target markets, pursuing and obtaining clients, and maintaining client relationships. Students are able to contact clients directly, which is unique to the Northwestern program. All interns are responsible for passing the state licensing exam, either before or during the internship.

SMITHSONIAN INSTITUTE Various programs are offered that highlight the intern's personal, academic, and professional goals. Some of the programs may include work in the curatorial, archival, science research, and culture departments.

The following lists government and nonprofit summer internships that offer good pay.

CAPITAL FELLOWS PROGRAM Fellows work as full-time members of a legislative, executive, or judicial branch office of California. They are directly involved in policy making and help draft and analyze legislation, write speeches, and conduct policy briefings. Other benefits include readjustment assistance, health care coverage, and a high probability of postinternship employment.

CENTRAL INTELLIGENCE AGENCY Interns work with various experts in the field of foreign policy. Students in the following majors are encouraged to apply: accounting, area studies, business administration, computer science, economics, engineering, finance, foreign languages, geography, graphic design, human resources, international relations, logistics, mathematics, military and foreign affairs, national security studies, physical sciences, and political science.

DRUG ENFORCEMENT AGENCY Interns train with experts who work to combat drug smuggling in the United States and abroad in the following areas: accounting, acquisition, business management, forensic chemistry, human resources, information technology, intelligence, investigations, and telecommunications.

FEDERAL BUREAU OF INVESTIGATION Interns work closely with special agents and professional staff on important cases and management issues.

TEACH FOR AMERICA Interns help TFA staff run the training conferences for new TFA teachers in various cities throughout the United States.

These lists of internships are not at all comprehensive. There are many more internships, but they are highly competitive and frequently require a scientific or computer background. They can also disappear if the company hits hard times. While not all corporations offer internships like these, most do offer some kind of internship or co-op program for college students. All it takes to find them is persistence and research.

How do you get one of the dream internships or a great summer job? You follow a master plan that guides your activity from the first day you arrive on campus. That plan enables you to get such a summer internship between your junior and senior year. I am a firm believer in hitting the ground running. Students who begin their college career by building a base of experiences outside the classroom are almost always more successful than those who do not. If you are already beyond the freshman year, all is not lost. Get started now.

During the first semester of your freshman year, visit some faculty members or graduate students with whom you think you can connect because you are interested in their research or ideas, and offer to do some extra research. Take positions, either volunteer or elected, in your residence hall or with student groups. Do some off-campus public service. Do these things both to help you develop your skills and to make connections for bigger and better things. I am not a big fan of student government at the college level because it can become time-consuming and the drama can be distracting. However, try your hand at it if it interests you personally, especially the areas that deal with allocating money.

During the second semester of your freshman year, get involved in one serious commitment on campus and one off campus. I say "one," because you do not want to spread yourself too thin. Too many students overcommit when they get on campus. Even if you don't suffer academically, you will not learn as much as you would if you focused on a small number of activities. Spreading yourself too thin does not look good to future employers. As a human resources person from a major financial corporation said, "Our company wants to see someone with persistence and drive. We'd rather have you have one job and work your way up than many different jobs. That's an immediate red flag when I see applicants with a job list the size of their resume."

This applies to community service as well as internships and jobs. You should explore a variety of opportunities throughout your college career, but ultimately employers are wary of people who do too much and appear to have a shotgun approach.

Although student groups are a viable place to start either on- or off-campus activities, look for opportunities provided by the university faculty and administration. For on-campus activities, most colleges and universities want their best students to serve as student "hosts" to school visitors or as peer advisers. The competition for these positions is not as great as you would assume, and the payoffs can be enormous. A peer academic adviser works directly with a higher administration official and could end up as a student representative to the board of trustees. Some faculty members also use undergraduates as research assistants, teaching assistants, and tutors. If you find a faculty member who's looking for an assistant and are interested in the subject, take this path.

Your course work may help you get off-campus experiences even in your freshman year. A growing number of lower-division courses in colleges throughout the country have a field-service component. A political science course may give credit for your work on a political campaign. A freshman writing course may require community service to provide experiences about which you can write. Even if courses are not offered, most colleges have offices that place students in volunteer positions in all kinds of nonprofit and government agencies.

In addition to volunteering, or what is usually called "public or community service work," you can also seek paid positions, even in your freshman year. If you have college work-study, these positions cost the hiring department about fifty cents on the dollar, which places you in high demand. Even without work-study, college students are frequently hired on campus. A particularly valuable college job is to work for the alumni fund-raising office, in which you solicit alumni for contributions. People who can stand the rejection of cold-calling and can be successful at getting contributions are in short supply. It will give you a look at the field of sales and at the same time give you credentials as someone who can do a difficult job.

During your second year, build on those experiences you found most enjoyable and educational the first year. Perhaps you want to become a resident adviser, which provides both leadership experience and significant financial support. If you were active as a volunteer in residence hall associations the first year, your chances to win the RA position the second year are much greater. Or, if you liked the peer-advising program, perhaps you can be elected or appointed to the advisory board. Or, if you work with a professor, this might lead to more advanced work in which you learn how to use statistical software. Or, you might become a staff assistant to the campaign manager for the politician you worked for in your freshman year. Your paid positions can also lead to higher levels of work that develop many of your skills. You might manage other workers at sports events or supervise a small snack bar operated by the food service. Or, you might get hired at the local Boys and Girls Club to run a pregnancy prevention and self-esteem program for teenage girls because you were valuable as a volunteer to the person who ran the program the year before.

The trick is to make your initial position a learning experience for one or more of the ten Skill Sets. This does not necessarily mean finding an exciting and interesting experience like working in the chancellor's office to help set up receptions for the rich and the famous or becoming a statistician for the football team. It may mean dishing out food in the residence hall cafeteria or stocking books in the library. How can working for food service be a great learning opportunity? It will build and demonstrate your work ethic. If you do a good job and show leadership by suggesting to your supervisor a better way to do things, you will quickly move into a management position. Serving in a management position during your sophomore year will develop your people skills. It could lead to a high-paying summer job or a management position the next year. Employers salivate when they think they can hire someone who will relieve them of the people problems they face every day.

A former student obtained one of those dream summer internships with a consulting company during the summer between her junior and senior year. By the end of the summer, she had a firm offer with a sizable signing bonus because of her outstanding performance that summer. Her college career started off in social work but ended up in communications and arts and sciences. However, it was her extracurricular activities that made the difference.

That summer she worked for the consulting firm on a state government project in one of those high-paid dream internships discussed earlier. She was able to combine the knowledge from all her college experiences to serve the company well. At the end of summer, she received an offer for full-time employment when she graduated. She accepted the offer (with signing bonus) and was able to spend her senior year dedicated to things other than finding a job.

The steps that this undergraduate took to land the dream summer internship and also a very high-paying position for someone with just a bachelor's degree—equal to the starting salaries of many MBAs and MPAs—are interesting from a number of perspectives. First, in her freshman year she undertook some activities that were false starts, if not downright failures. Despite this, her eventual success was due to her ability to be decisive in changing programs and activities while having a firm idea that she wanted to develop her skills. Second, she undertook a variety of activities and stuck with them. Community service, research and teaching assistance to professors, and leadership in a sorority remained a constant throughout her career. Finally, luck played a role because it just so happened that a member of the consulting firm, who was also a former alumna of the program in which she was enrolled, made a classroom presentation and was looking for people to apply for the summer program. Good fortune is important, but those who work hard are more likely to get it.

Below is a list of activities from her first three years that helped her earn the internship:

FRESHMAN YEAR

- Joined the rowing team for a semester and then decided it was too time-consuming given the learning payoffs.
- Unsuccessfully ran for president of her hall council.
- Devoted a small number of hours to community service.
- Joined a sorority.
- Impressed two professors: one gave her an office job and the other some community service activities.
- Decided that her initial enrollment in the School of Social Work did not meet her long-term goals.

SUMMER BETWEEN FRESHMAN AND SOPHOMORE YEARS

- Obtained an internship as a marketing assistant for a cardiology firm in her hometown that provided priceless experience. She realized that marketing was not her aspiration, but that she enjoyed working with people.

SOPHOMORE YEAR

- Changed majors, choosing a dual major in policy studies in the School of Arts and Sciences and public relations in the School of Public Communications. Both programs supported applied learning.
- Elected to the position of recruitment chair for the Panhellenic Association, the governing body of the sorority system.
- Worked with a professor on class projects.

SUMMER BETWEEN SOPHOMORE AND JUNIOR YEARS

- Obtained an internship in Washington, D.C., with Independent Sector, a research and lobbying group that represents close to one thousand nonprofits.

- Became an undergraduate teaching assistant.

- Became a literacy tutor for the Center for Public and Community Service at an after-school program for Spanish-speaking children.

- Elected president of the Panhellenic Organization.

- Took a senior-level course in benchmarking that required a team project for a community agency. In February of that year, an alumna who worked for one of the top consulting firms made presentations to a senior-level class and recruited for its Summer Scholars Program.

- Interviewed and was selected for the position at the consulting company.

Paying your dues and doing well academically when you start college can open the doors for better volunteer and higher paying positions while in college. Most important, it will lead to a high Skills Score and many exciting job offers. With a solid base of experience early in your college career, you are ready to search for outstanding job and internship opportunities during your last two years of college. If you are reading this book as a sophomore, junior, or senior, you have not entirely missed the boat. You can do something right now to get on board.

Note: The appendix contains important times of the year that you should begin the search for internship experiences.

LAND GOOD SUMMER JOBS AND INTERNSHIPS

Landing a good internship or summer job is a result of two processes: (1) locating them and (2) convincing the organization that you are the one for the position.

THE SEARCH

The way you search for a community service project, an internship, or a part-time or summer job is no different from the way you will search for your first job after college, which means this is great practice. The first step is to figure out what kind of position you are looking for. You will need to be clear to yourself about your goals for the experience and then do a systematic search for a fit. Decide what kind of selection criteria you want to have—wage, stipend, credit, additional benefits, or company size. Don't be afraid to be selective in your search for the best position, even if you think you won't get your top choices. Eventually, you may have to ease up on your selection criteria, but aim high when you start out.

Your search for the "perfect" internship or job opportunity should employ both an inside and an outside strategy. The inside strategy depends on your contacts. Start with your family, friends, and neighbors. They can provide mutual contacts depending on their networks. If you have pursued my suggested course of action for your freshman and sophomore years, you'll have a solid network of people who might be able to lead you in the right direction. Use family and neighborhood ties to locate job and internship opportunities. Ask peers who are a year ahead of you for leads. They are in the same boat as you and should be willing to share information. Former interns will be able to call up their internship coordinator and give them a heads-up that your application is in the mail. Some professors, usually those who also have a "skills-oriented" approach to their courses, have a handful of direct alumni contacts who want to give back to their college and can offer good advice and possibly even work experiences.

The outside strategy is hard work. It involves consulting books, websites, and offices on campus to get advice and assistance. This strategy is time-consuming and, to an extent, hit-and-miss, but if you dedicate yourself to it, you are likely to gain a valuable internship. Matt and Susan are two of my students who found excellent summer internships early in their college careers using the outside strategy. The advice and recommendations below reflect their own experiences finding internships. They suggest you use books, the Web, and campus resources, especially career services.

BOOKS AND OTHER PUBLICATIONS

There are tons of internship reference guides available in annual editions that are described at the end of this chapter. These books list internships by field and location, and information such as selectivity, organization size, and application requirements. The books can be great springboards from which to launch the rest of your internship search.

These books are usually found in the reference section (along with college guides and SAT prep materials) in bookstores and libraries. Because libraries are apt to only carry outdated versions, Matt and Susan discovered that spending an afternoon or two at a large bookstore was the best way to go. Take along a notepad and pen and be prepared to find a lot of information.

One word of caution, though: don't take reference guide information as an ultimate, or a true, source. Matt and Susan found that the write-ups weren't always accurate and sometimes provided an overly flattering view of organizations. If you find an opportunity particularly appealing, investigate these agencies or companies by browsing their websites or contacting their internship coordinators.

There are also good books that give you more complete advice on the internship and job search as a whole—from finding one, to getting one, to making the most of your experience. In addition, you may find newspapers, magazines, and trade or other journals provide valuable leads.

WEBSITES

Several clearinghouse-type websites enable you to search for internship opportunities that match certain variables (for example, location, field, and time period) of your choice. Matt and Susan were primarily searching for nonprofit, government, or public service internships, but these websites also serve those interested in business, media, environment, science, and other fields. A few of the most helpful sites they found are listed at the end of this chapter.

Another excellent way to use the Web is to research agencies and companies you have identified as possibilities. Once you find an organization you might want to work for, bring up their web page and find out more information. Usually, internship information is located in the About Us, Contact Us, or Jobs and Opportunities section of websites.

If you find nothing on the website about internships or summer jobs, don't assume that the organization doesn't offer any: websites are often not kept up-to-date, especially at small organizations. In this case, email or the telephone is the best way to go. Ask the receptionist for an internship coordinator or the human resources department. Agencies may have never hired interns before and therefore will not publicize such opportunities. But, if you are highly motivated and very much interested in the work of a particular organization, contact that organization and inquire about the possibility of interning. If you demonstrate a specific knowledge or skill base, agencies may very well create a position just for you. Until you talk to an actual human being, don't assume anything.

One thing Matt and Susan found useful about websites is that they create a domino effect of leads upon leads upon leads. Look in the Sponsors, Partners, and Links sections of an agency's website to find links to other organizations that are similar in mission or field.

Finally, remember to work from the ground up. If you are interested in a particular subject or societal problem, do a general web search on organizations that attempt to address these issues.

CAMPUS RESOURCES

The most centralized source of information on your campus will be the career center or, if your college has it, the office for promoting and administering internships. These offices purchase a wide variety of publications. They have specialized sources for such fields as the media, music industry, animation, resorts, sports, and environmental positions.

Matt and Susan also jump-started their search with a visit to their campus internship office. Although they did not end up using the services of the office to get credit (discussed later in this chapter), they did take advantage of the resources that the office provided them. The office had decades' worth of internship search guides, file folders of newspaper clippings, recruitment flyers, and application materials. Don't underestimate the knowledge of the staff at these offices—they have helped students find excellent (and not-so-excellent) opportunities, and it's at least worth a conversation. In the best-case scenario, the staff may be a transition to the inside strategy: maybe they can hook you up with a former intern or an alumnus or alumna who can help you seal a position.

GETTING THE INTERNSHIP OR JOB

Using these strategies to find your internships is one thing; getting one is another thing entirely. Once you have decided what you are looking for, create a resume and a cover letter. Your cover letter and resume should highlight the experiences that best demonstrate your Skills Score. Talk about real-world experience in addition to your academic performance. Be sure to emphasize computer skills if you have them (and if you don't have them, develop them through computer classes or self-help books).

Those doing the hiring for your internship or part-time job are just like employers. They are interested in specific skills like writing, teamwork, and computer savvy. They will also want references, not just from faculty, but also from previous supervisors of community service, internships, or jobs.

One of the simplest ways you can impress a prospective internship agency is by sending your application, cover letter, and resume early. If you are applying for a summer internship, this means getting your application out by early January. Internship coordinators will not expect this timely behavior and will be impressed with the way you plan ahead. Susan, who interned with the Children's Defense Fund in the summer between her freshman and sophomore year, a feat in itself, can attest to the importance of being prompt:

> *"When I was doing my internship search, I had more than one agency place me high on their list of potential interns because they received my application in the first week of January. This is really rare for college students, who tend to put off the internship search and application process until a few days before the deadline, which for the summer is usually sometime in March. My internship coordinator at the Children's Defense Fund actually told me later that one of the biggest reasons she accepted me was because she was so impressed with my timeliness."*

Another easy way to show self-reliance and dependability, even in the application process, is to pick and choose what kind of assistance you get from your college or university. Getting academic credit for your internship experience is great if it will help you graduate on time or early. It also helps you get a better learning experience in most instances. However, if you don't need the credit, you're just paying the university extra tuition. Your internship coordinator may also be relieved at the absence of paperwork and evaluations to fill out as well as impressed that you are so willing to spend time doing something with no direct compensation (in the case of an unpaid internship).

The advice on credit needs to be tempered with caution. Some organizations demand that credit be associated with the internship so they do not have to treat you as a regular employee, and there is pressure on you to do well. This is particularly true in the media business. In addition, if you have a faculty member who will provide advice and help you reflect on your experience, the credit charge might be worth the cost even if you do not need credit. Ask other students about their experiences and then decide.

If this is your first time searching for an internship or part-time job, keep in mind that you may not get that "dream" position the first time around. If you are rejected from an organization that you really wanted to work for, call up their internship director and ask how your application could be improved the next time around. Your failure could be the ultimate learning experience and help you get the job in the future. In fact, sometimes the best opportunities may lie in the most unexpected (and sometimes unglamorous) positions.

For example, be willing to take pay-your-dues positions. Cold-call sales positions with reputable firms that give you ample training may be unspectacular and difficult, but you could have a great learning experience. These positions definitely will appeal to future employers in many fields. Working in a business like FedEx Office, where customer service along with the ability to learn how to operate different machines, can provide you with a base and ultimately lead to a management position.

Taking a position in something like data entry will help you improve and streamline your skills in highly useful computer programs. Though the job itself will likely be boring and monotonous, the skills you will learn are in such short supply that you will eventually make good money and be a target of recruitment for excellent internships and permanent employment. This tip is especially relevant if you are staying at your college for the summer or live in a college town. Many professors do research and will be looking for short-term employees to do data entry and preliminary analysis. Susan was able to use her computer software application skills as a selling point in her cover letter and resume: "I remember clearly two of the coordinators I interviewed with being absolutely floored that I, as a freshman, knew both Microsoft Excel and SPSS. When I actually started interning, I was amazed at how many times I was helping department heads with software programs. I even was able to show one staff member how to streamline a project using Excel. These skills can really get you far."

One final tip: go to temp firms. If you can demonstrate skills in demand, a temp firm will find you work, either part time or full time. The firm takes a cut, but the money you receive will be competitive with what you would get if you found the job yourself. Moreover, the firm will prepare you for the job and find you another one when the first is over. Temp positions get you inside the company so that you can build your own network and make it part of your inside strategy the next time you look for an internship or part-time or summer job. National temp firms like Robert Half and Manpower (listed in Useful Resources at the end of this chapter) provide a good starting point, but every city has local firms that can be equally useful.

MAKE THE MOST OF YOUR EXPERIENCES

Several books are discussed at the end of this chapter to help you get the most from your internship, but I want to emphasize that the key is your attitude. See your internship as an opportunity to raise your Skills Score and, at the same time, as an opportunity to be both proactive and professional. This attitude is crucial—not only with regard to internships but also to anything you do for your career future, whether it is an internship, a summer job, or your first job out of college. Look at all experiences as an investment in developing your basic skills.

There may be times after you have begun an internship that you do not see much potential for growth in your skills. If you have made a sincere effort to explore skills for all ten Skill Sets, you should move on unless there are financial, legal, or moral commitments that you made when you took the position. "Sincere effort" is the key phrase here. My first thought when students tell me that their internship supervisor was incompetent or did not keep them busy is that the student either did not try hard enough or was not capable of performing in that position. Whether in a volunteer, an internship, or a paid position, you must prove your worth to your supervisor. Search for additional work and for information that might help you identify additional work. If you are eager, your supervisor will want to hire you when you graduate and will be willing to provide you with a recommendation.

Or to put it in different terms, an internship or work experience is like a test you don't want to fail. It may be a lousy test or an unfair test, but treat it as a challenge that you will meet. A passive attitude of "they didn't have anything for me to do" is not acceptable, even if they really didn't have anything for you to do. Taking the initiative to find something to do is important if you have a weak supervisor. If you have a strong but busy supervisor, you need to make sure she or he recognizes your competence and talent the first day on the job. As soon as supervisors learn to trust your ability to do what needs to be done with as little supervision as possible, you will find yourself extremely busy. They don't want high-maintenance employees whose messes they have to clean up. Matt had firsthand experience dealing with these challenges as an intern for a political lobbying group in the summer of 2002:

> *"The first couple of days at my internship, no one was giving me anything to do. The majority of the other interns accepted this and sat around complaining of being bored. Every time I would start to get bored, however, I would remember a conversation I had with Professor Coplin during which he said that I was "self-motivated." This always inspired me to seek out more work, no matter how menial; I literally made thousands of copies during the first few weeks. Because of this work ethic, however, I was put in charge of a major campaign initiative and had a very rewarding experience."*

If you have a successful internship job experience, you should cultivate the relationships you developed with both your peers and your supervisors. Peers who interned with you may help you network in the future, just as you might help them. Supervisors can be instrumental in hiring you in the future, either directly or indirectly. They can provide a letter of recommendation, which you should try to obtain before you leave the job. Even more important, they could help you as a reference to be contacted by future employers through email or a phone call. When identifying a supervisor to serve as a reference, don't go after the big cheese like the CEO or the senator unless you had daily contact with him or her. Instead, go after your immediate supervisors because what they say will be more credible and specific. See chapter 20 for additional discussion of this kind of networking relationship.

If you have a poor experience in any of these apprenticeship-type activities, reflect on the reasons. Finding out that you are not cut out to be a journalist after a summer working on a local newspaper is not a bad thing. As Louis Blair, the former head of the Harry S. Truman Foundation, says, "The main difference between a successful person and an unsuccessful person is that the successful person has had a lot more failures!" Or to put it in the Zen perspective, "There are no wrong turns, only wrong thinking on the turns our life has taken."

Let me give you an example of wrong thinking in which a student placed his desire to get a great learning experience above the need to be professional. One of my students was an intern at a law firm and was supervised by a paralegal. When the paralegal asked him to make some copies to be provided to the court, the intern quit and was quite rude in the process. This student overlooked the fundamental reality that as an undergraduate intern in a law office, you are not going to write a legal brief. You pay your dues and make copies so you can attend professional meetings, do some very basic research, and get debriefed. In fact, many newly graduated lawyers do the same thing. In a field like law in which there is an oversupply of professionals, this little temper tantrum was not only unprofessional but it also helped reduce the supply by one.

Whether you get your apprentice experience from community service, a job, or an internship, enhance your skill development by recording daily (or at least weekly) what you did, what you learned from it, and how you could have done it better. These notes will help you refresh your memory a couple of years later when you are in a job interview. At the same time, they will help you learn more while you are going through the experience.

USEFUL RESOURCES

BOOKS

Internships for Dummies by Craig P. Donovan and Jim Garnett (John Wiley, 2001). This book tells you how to search for and land internships and, most important, how to gain an experience that will enhance your Skills Score.

Peterson's Internships (Peterson's Guides). This is one of the best internship directories available. It offers more than fifty thousand U.S. and overseas listings for summer, semester, and year-long internship opportunities at more than two thousand organizations. Get the most recent edition.

The Princeton Review Internship Bible by Mark Oldman and Samer Hamadeh (Random House). Thousands of internship entries listed by location and field of interest are found in this guide. It includes information on selectivity, compensation, academic requirements, and application procedures. Get the most recent edition.

WEBSITES

http://dcjobsource.com/internships.html This site is a reliable source of internships at the state level. Listings are given state by state.

www.craigslist.org Craigslist has regional job listings that are updated daily. Internships, apprenticeships, and part-time work are listed.

http://idealist.org Along with volunteer opportunities, this website has many listings for internships around the country.

www.internqueen.com The Intern Queen site provides advice on how to get experience in addition to internships.

www.internshipprograms.com You must register to use this site (it is free), but then you have access to searching thousands of opportunities in cities across the country. You can also post your resume on this site and allow prospective employers to recruit you.

www.internships-usa.com Internships-USA is one of the most comprehensive sources for internship information.

www.makingthedifference.org/federalinternships This U.S. government site lists sources for federal government internships around the country and advice on how to search for them.

www.vault.com/wps/portal/usa/internships The Vault site provides leads for internships and tools for self-assessment.

http://us.manpower.com/us and **www.roberthalf.com/JobSeekers** Manpower and Robert Half International are the two largest and best staff or temp firms, and are located in many cities.

"I LIVED A LIFE THAT'S FULL. I TRAVELED EACH AND EVERY HIGHWAY."

—PAUL ANKA, SINGER-SONGWRITER

CHAPTER 14

EXPLORING OFF-CAMPUS SEMESTERS

**BUILD YOUR SKILLS SCORE OFF CAMPUS •
WEIGH OVERSEAS EXPERIENCES AGAINST EXPERIENCES
IN THE UNITED STATES AND CANADA • EARN CREDIT
FOR COURSE WORK • EXPAND YOUR NETWORK •
CONSIDER THE NEGATIVES • FIND PROGRAMS**

Undergraduates are increasingly earning a semester's worth of credit in another location. Some students spend two or three semesters off campus and still graduate on time. A large array of opportunities for off-campus study exists both in the United States and around the world. From a skills and career exploration perspective, spending one or two semesters away from campus has potential benefits that usually outweigh the risks.

BUILD YOUR SKILLS SCORE OFF CAMPUS

Like everything you do in college, you can make the off-campus experience pay off for your Skills Score and career options. You can choose to use the experience to have a good time or explore a subject that interests you. In many cases, you can do both. Even if building your Skills Score or exploring a career is not your primary goal, it is pretty hard to be off campus for a semester and not raise your Skills Score and perhaps develop a better idea of what you want to do after college.

The following Skill Sets will be enhanced regardless of your primary goal for off-campus semesters:

- Taking Responsibility. An off-campus semester means that you will face a host of new logistical challenges, starting with the application process at your home institution. This will enhance your time-management skills as well as your ability to motivate yourself. Money management will be a major challenge. You not only need to have access to enough money, but you also need to use credit and possibly banking facilities in a new place.

- Developing Physical Skills. Staying healthy and well in a new environment will be an even bigger challenge than on your own campus. Spending a semester in a new location and environment will force you to adapt to the new obstacles that can prevent you from staying well or looking good.

- Communicating Verbally. You will need to communicate with a whole new set of people, including peers, administrators, and faculty. This may also be your first time in a place where the language is one that is not your own.

- Working Directly with People. You will have to work with a whole new set of people, including peers, administrators, and faculty.

- Using Quantitative Tools. You'll practice these skills particularly if your semester is overseas, where dealing with currency conversions requires more intense number crunching than most people are used to.

- Asking and Answering the Right Questions. Given the increased uncertainty surrounding your new environment, you will be more vulnerable to those who talk nonsense, and you will also have to pay attention to detail, especially when traveling.

- Solving Problems. You'll face new situations on a daily basis that require solutions.

These five Skill Sets will improve even if you are just taking college classes at a different location with a group of friends from your home institution. However, you will gain much more if you choose an off-campus semester in which the major learning component is field experience, through either an internship or assigned activities by the instructor. Students are increasingly choosing programs that have field experiences. They choose programs that have specific offerings like marine biology or archeological digs. They may also choose programs to develop their foreign language skills by living with a local family in a foreign country. In these types of programs, more than the basic skills listed previously are developed. Skills from the other Skill Sets are developed along with the type of skills listed in chapter 11. Some of these programs will also introduce you to professional skills not contained in the ten basic Skill Sets, such as learning to speak a different language, using exchange rates to determine prices in U.S. dollars, and reading maps.

Off-campus semester programs as a place to learn and enhance your Skills Score are uniformly recognized by graduate schools and employers. They know that students who like to deal with new situations and are able to take risks to improve themselves usually pursue off-campus programs. Graduate schools value foreign experiences because they help prepare students to work in professions that have a global reach. All employers like to hire people who can accept the risk of new challenges.

I strongly recommend that during your sophomore year, you start planning an off-campus semester for sometime during the following year. With two years of course work under your belt, you will be able to apply the skills you have been learning in the classroom in a different setting, which is key to being ready for a rewarding and exciting career.

If you are only going to take one semester off campus, you are faced with a decision to go overseas or to a program within the United States or Canada. What is the right decision?

The answer is like everything else in life: "It depends." The general rule is that going out of the United States and Canada is better than staying in the country because you will be challenged to experience another culture. However, there are many exceptions and considerations. First, there is the money question. Going overseas, if nothing else, requires significant travel expense. Second, if you have a specific interest such as politics or medicine, an internship-based semester working as a White House intern or for the National Institutes of Health would make more sense than an overseas placement that did not provide similar internships. Third, if you see going abroad for a semester as traveling for the sake of traveling or having a good time with your buddies, going to a more focused internship in the United States would be better for your career development.

More than 260,000 U.S. students participated in a study-abroad program in 2008–2009, according to the Institute for International Education.[1] That figure has tripled from fifteen years ago. While the majority of students go to Europe (55 percent), programs in Africa, Latin America, and Asia have increased in popularity over the past decade. The most popular options are one-semester programs, although some experts advocate a full year abroad.

An overseas experience means that twenty-four hours a day, seven days a week, you will be trying to make sense of the unfamiliar. The lack of familiarity with the physical environment, including toilets and transportation facilities, will be less important than your lack of familiarity with the language. Unless you go to an English-speaking country, your relationships will depend on makeshift attempts to communicate. If you are seeking to master that language and have taken some courses, the experience will sharply improve your language skills. The fact that you will have to learn conversational language to adjust to daily life will be a huge learning experience in itself.

The depth of the challenge will be directly related to the amount of time you spend away from peers from the United States. If you live with buddies from your college in a housing situation controlled by your university, you'll be much less challenged than if you live with a host family. Even so, you'll have plenty of opportunities to be confused by your inability to communicate when you leave the confines of the familiar.

Studying in an English-speaking country does have benefits. Because there won't be a language barrier, you will be able to immerse yourself in a different community and culture much more quickly. The depth of your experience may grow as you find it possible to communicate easily with the locals. If you try hard enough, you may find yourself experiencing small—but nonetheless important—parts of the social and community structure that you may have otherwise missed. This benefit also stands for domestic off-campus programs that send you to other areas of the country.

Almost any student who has had an overseas experience will rave about it, as this student did when she wrote me six months after graduation about her experience in Hong Kong:

> *"For eighteen years, I lived in a homogeneous bubble where Caucasian, middle-class Christians were the overwhelming majority. Diversity was a concept, not a reality. New York was enough of a culture shock! But I took a risk, hopped on a plane, and came back a different person—more educated and open-minded. Hong Kong was a learning experience—educationally, culturally, and professionally. I gained international experience that employers value in today's economy. I interned for the Fortune Global Forum in 2005 where every year,* Fortune *magazine hosts this forum for more than 250 of the world's top CEOs with prominent guest speakers. During my internship, I met and worked with leaders such as the CEO of AOL Time Warner, Bill Clinton, the prime minister of Japan, Thaksin Shinawatra (Thai prime minister), Jiang Zemin (president of the People's Republic of China), Jack Welch (former CEO of General Electric), and others. The forum was surrounded by political controversy and it became my responsibility to inform the Hong Kong and New York*

contacts of the international events around the world. Just last week I sat prepping a senior financial analyst for GE, who was traveling to Shanghai for a possible sales expansion opportunity, about the people, culture, and what to expect in Asia's economy today. You don't get that kind of exposure sitting around your sorority house discussing last week's episode of some reality TV show."

This student had unusually good overseas experiences, but you can see how being placed in a foreign environment can create rewarding learning experiences.

An off-campus experience within the United States or Canada will present you with fewer day-to-day challenges if only because differences in language will not permeate everything. However, you will be faced with new geography and the daily chores that were much easier at college.

If you choose off-campus semesters within the United States or Canada, you need to be more selective about the nature of the program, the quality of the course requirements, and the value of the internship or work environment in which you find yourself. In general, the stronger the local control by the university over the courses and hands-on experience, the better. Even if you get in an overseas program with poor courses and loose structure, you are still overseas.

Most domestic off-campus programs will require an internship experience of at least two, and as many as five, full days a week. The days will usually run the regular work hours of 9 to 5 and may involve overtime, plus you will have assignments and classes. Together, this experience will make you work much harder than you work on campus. The biggest challenge for many students with whom I have talked is learning to deal with "a real professional job."

One former student of mine thought he was a hard worker because he carried eighteen credits and was in all kinds of activities on campus, yet he almost had a meltdown during an internship at a high school in New York City. He had to get up at 5:30 in the morning and take the subway to arrive at the school by 7:30. He frequently did not get home until 9 p.m. because of classes held in another location and other activities. Not being able to run to the residence hall for a little nap or relaxation just about ruined him. It took eight weeks before he got adjusted to working in the real world because he had almost no free time. He reflects back on that experience as preparing him for working in his first job, and he found the experience valuable.

A domestic program off campus that requires a job-like internship can be more difficult than an overseas program in which there are no major internship opportunities. You may find a program with a four- or five-day-a-week internship overseas, but it's not as likely. This may be a crucial advantage to a domestic program.

EARN CREDIT FOR COURSE WORK

In any off-campus semester, your first goal should be to earn the academic credits you need to graduate on time. If you cannot earn a full semester's worth of credit, do not go into that program. Although most colleges accept most credits from many programs, check this out very carefully. You don't want to spend an extra semester at school because your college refuses to accept nine of the fifteen credits you took in Botswana. You want to see a written commitment either in a policy statement by your college or in a memo confirming what you have been told. Never accept the spoken word in a matter as important as this.

The best way to be sure you will get the credit is to enroll in a program run by your own college. This will keep your hassles to a minimum in getting credits accepted. If your school does not offer such programs, it probably has formal relationships with other colleges and organizations that do. If so, your next choice would be to enroll in one of those programs. Only after you have exhausted both of these alternatives should you enroll in a program run by a college, a university, or an institute that does not have a formal relationship with your home institution. If you do this, make sure your home college and program will accept the credit. You will probably be required to take a leave of absence from your home school and enroll in the college providing the experience. There may be some extra hidden fees if you do that. To ensure that you don't fall behind in credits from your off campus experience, you must begin the exploration two semesters before you go off-campus and have it buttoned down by the first month of the next semester. For example, start exploring options even as early as second semester of your freshman year and have the details worked out by the end of your sophomore year.

You can usually take twelve to eighteen credits during your off-campus experience. If you are ahead in the pursuit of your degree, drop to twelve credits because the more free time you have to explore your environment or just to have fun, the better. Most programs are designed to generate fifteen credits.

The benefits of course work off campus to your Skills Score and your preparation for your future career can best be explained by looking at their comparative advantage over courses you might take at your home college. The following statements are generalizations based on many conversations I have had with students over the years and therefore may not apply to your particular situation, but they provide a starting point.

Classes that are required for your degree but that you don't relish taking may be easier off campus. This assertion is true if only because the classes will be smaller. Many programs will not offer these kinds of required courses, but some will. You are more likely to find them if you take an off-campus program run by your own school or a program affiliated with your school. Taking such courses may not be optimal for your experience because the course may not make use of the new location, but occasionally it makes sense. Most programs will provide you with a syllabus in advance if you request one, and you can determine whether the required course will be tailored to the host culture in some way, such as with local speakers or field trips.

Classes are more likely to have fieldwork of some kind. Those programs that are well developed will try to offer courses that take advantage of the location. They will incorporate field trips, lectures by subject-matter experts and practitioners in the area, and actual fieldwork ranging from an internship at a nonprofit to studying vegetation in a nearby desert. Choose programs that have internship experiences for the same reasons I have emphasized throughout the book and particularly in the previous chapter. Fortunately, most overseas programs are increasing the fieldwork or internship elements of their course work.

Faculty members will be different from those in your home school. Even if the college ships someone over, the faculty member may be more relaxed and have a different attitude than they do when teaching the same course on campus. However, the use of local people is more common and likely to provide a very different educational experience. This applies to both domestic and foreign programs. In domestic programs, the faculty members are likely to be part-timers who have real-world applications to present to you. Foreign faculty will have a different take on most subjects than faculty at your college. In general, different is better.

EXPAND YOUR NETWORK

You may be going off campus for a semester with a group of your buddies or you may be meeting new students. Most programs have groups of students who are not necessarily from your home university. This will make for better class discussions and more peer learning than what occurs in your home school.

Even more important, the experiences you share with other students may develop into relationships that exist beyond the semester. You will face many challenges together and have a common set of experiences to help you bond. Some of your new acquaintances may have similar career interests and become part of your network, which, as chapter 20 describes, is a key to career success.

You may want to also use the experience to build your professional network in a different place, especially if you like to travel and you think you may end up working there. Given the forces pushing for globalization, contacts made in different parts of the world may work for you in your career.

The biggest single downside to off-campus programs is no matter what they tell you, it will cost you more (unless you get a paid position), and that is even more true for overseas programs. The tuition will be the same, but that does not include travel or daily expenditures in more expensive locales. You may not be able to get a job in another city or country to pay for these additional expenses. Occasionally, off-campus programs that require a substantial internship carry a stipend or the intern-hosting organization could provide a salary. You may also be able to find grants that support study in particular countries or through specific organizations—ask at your on-campus financial aid and study-abroad offices, and check the online financial aid and scholarship resources at the end of this chapter. In programs overseas where the standard of living is low, housing and food costs may be lower. In any case, carefully compare costs on campus and off.

The next biggest risk that you face in taking a semester off is breaking the continuity that might be needed by your academic program. You may take a course in the fall, leave in the spring, and get back in the fall but not be able to continue the course sequence until the next spring. This will depend on your academic program and the frequency with which courses are offered. You will also break the continuity of the extracurricular and academic commitments that you have developed during your first two years in college. This can be a major drawback, especially if going off campus means losing a good job or the progress you have made developing your own program or initiative. The only surefire way to mitigate this drawback is to adequately plan ahead. If you know in your freshman year that you are going to be studying off campus during the spring of your junior year, you can plan around that semester. This will give you time to schedule your classes so you don't miss a sequence, to negotiate with your employer, and to find a replacement to take over in leadership positions you may hold.

The chaos caused by going away one semester can use time and energy that would be better put to your course work or your career exploration. It could increase stress and cut down options for summer jobs and upcoming opportunities. If you want a summer internship in New York City but are in Austria for the spring semester, you could have trouble. If you want to apply for a scholarship or special award for your senior year, it may be difficult to get detailed information on application deadlines or to participate in selection processes. Email is wonderful but doesn't always work. Some places would like to conduct interviews in person (although Skype may be a suitable alternative). Moreover, you will not have as much support from the college's intern placement office and faculty members if you are away from campus.

The break from your home school can even be more serious if you are not sure what you want to do after you graduate. In my experience, most students put thoughts about the future on hold while they are away, especially overseas. The intensity of the experience seems to prevent long-range planning for many. If you are away during the fall semester of your senior year, you will miss most of the campus visits by the large corporations, and you will get back in the spring in a funk. Graduate school applications, and taking the tests for those schools, usually must be completed no later than February 1, which gives you little time if you arrive back in the United States in late December.

Finally, the question of safety and health needs to be considered. How serious those issues are depends on where you spend the semester off campus as well as your specific living arrangements. It also depends on the current status of your health and how careful you are about keeping yourself safe. The risks may be slightly, but not significantly, higher than remaining on campus. Other than staying away from countries where there is a civil war, or the potential for one, and taking the health precautions and safety recommended for tourists, most overseas locations are at least as safe from criminal acts and disease as your home college. Global terrorism and potential protests have made some areas more risky. Such events may not only put you at risk but could also disrupt your program in the middle of your semester. The State Department provides warnings on a regular basis through its website, http://travel.state.gov/travel, and university officials monitor conditions and provide advice and even support if a natural disaster or some political upheaval is likely to occur. Students studying in some programs Egypt during the spring of 2011, when public demonstrations led to the downfall of the existing government, were quickly removed to another country.

Much of the advice provided in the previous chapter on finding internships also applies to the search for off-campus semester programs. Decide on your goals and then do a search using books and websites. Your college career or internship office will also be a big help. The sites listed for finding internships can also be used for finding semester programs in the United States.

For overseas programs, most colleges and universities have a study-abroad/international office, or a study-abroad adviser who can review options and policies for off-campus study. Start with this office or person to save time and trouble. You'll receive a list of study-abroad programs offered by your college and also those approved for credit offered by programs outside your institution. You may be able to retain your scholarships and other institutional aid if you attend one of these programs. Study-abroad offices may also have a list of programs for which your home college will definitely not award credit. For instance, if you are a language major, you may be required to go to a foreign institution to study abroad rather than a U.S.-sponsored program that offers advanced language courses for Americans. The study-abroad adviser will be familiar with many of the programs you have heard or read about and can fill you in on a program's strengths and weaknesses.

Overseas semester programs vary. Most emphasize the geographical aspects of the experience and present a general program, but an increasing number of programs closely tie the geographical location to a topical focus of the experience. Broadly based university-supported programs like those offered by Boston University, the Institute for the International Education of Students (IES), the Semester at Sea, and Syracuse University are in the first category. Specialized topical programs like the Theatre Conservancy in England through Rutgers University and the Woods Hole SEA Semester, which focuses on marine biology and tropical conservation, are in the second category.

Given the large and growing options, I can only give you some leads. The section at the end of this chapter will suggest some general resources. The best source of information on the potential for all these programs for your Skills Score is from students who have experienced these programs, preferably from your own campus.

There are excellent study-abroad websites (see the list at the end of this chapter) that allow you to sort through the growing variety of options sponsored by universities, nonprofit organizations, and corporations. You can search by region, country, discipline, or language of study. Or you can search by duration of program: academic year, semester study, summer program, or intersession. Once you have narrowed your search to programs that seem to fit your needs and interests, consult the individual program websites for details about courses, living arrangements, and costs. Whether your search for programs begins with the Internet or with your school's study-abroad adviser, in the end it is your home school's study-abroad adviser or college dean who must approve a program so you receive credit.

The programs you find online will include everything from small "island" programs (with no connection to universities abroad) to "immersion" programs. Full-immersion programs will take you beyond the ten Skill Sets into specialized skills that could be useful if you plan to seek overseas employment. With full-immersion programs, you take classes alongside native students at the local university. The purpose of immersion programs is to allow students to more comprehensively learn about the local culture. These programs are challenging due to the cultural differences, but overcoming the challenges will be very beneficial for developing your Skills Score.

Nonimmersion study-abroad programs will also help you improve your skills but will not include the challenges of immersion programs. These programs are still in foreign countries, but you will take courses alongside both native students and your home university classmates. Programs like these are usually in English-speaking countries and do not have prerequisite language requirements. You may also have the option to do a full-semester internship while abroad. Not only will that look good on a resume when you apply to jobs, but it will also help you develop your skills.

Over the past decade, colleges have increased the number of short summer programs (two to six weeks) as well as quickie one-week programs during the winter or spring break. Although the college's motivation for these programs is to increase revenue, many of them have exceptional value. They usually have a very enthusiastic professor in charge, and they are focused on specific topics like health care or the media. They are usually expensive, and the credits you get may not help you complete your degree earlier and therefore the program doesn't save you money. They also rarely have an internship associated with them, and the relatively short period of time limits the amount of experience you will get in living in a foreign country. Whether or not you should take advantage of them depends on your interests and your pocketbook. They may not be as valuable as a summer internship or job to your Skills Score or career exploration.

If none of the hundreds of formal program offerings that now exist suits you, you can create your own fifteen-credit-hour-semester-away-from-campus experience. If you are a very strong student and can find the right on-campus program or at least a faculty member, you can find yourself a placement at a nonprofit and ask for some portion of the credit. Usually nine credits is an upper limit for experience credit (graded pass/fail), but you can sometimes get up to fifteen through independent study courses. To get to fifteen credits, you could propose two independent study courses for a grade that you can complete while you are away. Alternatively, you could take any number of distance-learning courses offered by your school or some other school that will be accepted by your home school. Making your own semester-away program requires a strong and trusting relationship with at least one faculty member. If you think you might want to try a self-designed program, get started on building that relationship right away.

USEFUL RESOURCES

BOOK

Peterson's Study Abroad (Peterson's Guides). This is one of the most widely used directories for study abroad. It is updated frequently, so be sure to get the most recent edition.

WEBSITES

www.ciee.org This valuable and friendly site of the Council on International Educational Exchange (CIEE) provides comprehensive coverage of educational exchange programs. CIEE offers some good services, but the study-abroad programs listed on this site are strictly their own. It administers work- and travel-abroad programs for students and recent graduates, such as international volunteer opportunities and teaching English in Asia.

www.iesabroad.org This website guides you to the programs offered by the Institute for the International Education of Students, which has strong relationships with universities in more than a dozen countries and will help you transfer credit to your home college.

www.iie.org The Institute of International Education's site lists some substantial financial aid and scholarship programs for undergrads and grad students studying abroad, particularly in Asia and other non-Western sites.

www.studyabroad.com This user-friendly site of Study Abroad Information Source provides comprehensive coverage and claims it is the number one online search site. Unlike others, the site takes browsers directly to sponsors' web pages. Also, it lists internship opportunities.

www.transitionsabroad.com/listings/work/internships This site assists students looking for internships in their abroad experience.

www.washingtoninternship.com The Washington Internship Program site provides information on opportunities for a variety of semester-long internships and course programs in government agencies and nonprofit organizations in Washington, D.C. For other websites for programs outside of Washington, see the Useful Resources section in chapter 13.

"WE DON'T LIVE TO EAT. **WE EAT TO LIVE.** IN THE SAME WAY, OUR LIVELIHOOD EXISTS **TO SUPPORT OUR LIFE,** NOT THE OTHER WAY AROUND."

—BERNARD GLASSMAN AND RICK FIELDS, IN *INSTRUCTIONS TO THE COOK: A ZEN MASTER'S LESSONS ON LIVING A LIFE THAT MATTERS*

CHAPTER 15

DOING WELL BY DOING GOOD DURING YOUR COLLEGE YEARS

**BUILD YOUR SKILLS SCORE BY VOLUNTEERING •
VALUE VOLUNTEER OPPORTUNITIES—EMPLOYERS DO •
EXPLORE AND NETWORK FOR CAREERS •
CULTIVATE INTEGRITY**

You were probably introduced to the idea of community service in your high school or through your family or religious institution. You may think that working in a food pantry, tutoring economically disadvantaged youth, or reading to someone in a nursing home is only for the unselfish and pure. In my book *How You Can Help: An Easy Guide to Doing Good Deeds in Your Everyday Life*, I called this misconception one of the "curses" of Mother Teresa. The other "curse" is the misconception that one must dedicate every single waking hour to doing good. They are "curses" because people use this unreachable model as an excuse for not doing anything.

If Mother Teresa were to be viewed as a role model, it would be best to examine how she got things done and follow her lead. Except for computer skills, which became important in the last years of her life, Mother Teresa had a very high Skills Score. She was a master of communications, a person who knew how to find answers to the tough questions, a stellar problem solver, a first-rate nonsense detector, and she was great with people. The standards she set for leadership are hard to match, but if you are going to do anything to honor her life, be as effective as she was in promoting a better world.

Just as Mother Teresa honed her skills by serving others, you can do the same in preparing for a successful work life. Working for the public good during your college years and after can provide you with valuable experiences in the job force.

But that is not really the point of the quotation by the Zen master at the beginning of this chapter, is it? His point is that money is not everything. It is a tool for your happiness, not the definition of your happiness. That point is very hard to deliver to beginning college students who are spending and/or borrowing huge amounts of money in order to have a rewarding career. That is why I'm not going to tell you to do good because it will make you happy and spiritually satisfied, even though it is true. This chapter tells you why doing good in college will lead to a great life of work.

Doing good for the purposes of this chapter means any kind of work you do as a volunteer or for credit either on or off campus. It applies to volunteering at the rescue mission or a local community tutoring program as well as what you might do for student organizations and for faculty and staff committees. These volunteer activities, especially if they involve leadership positions, can be a critical source of Skills Score development.

BUILD YOUR SKILLS SCORE BY VOLUNTEERING

It might seem harsh to say, but the truth is that nonprofit organizations usually have no choice but to give you experiences before you are really ready for them. For example, a local community center might like to have a monthly newsletter to distribute but does not have the funds to hire a professional. If you have some basic skills in Microsoft Publisher or have taken an introductory public relations course but have no real experience in producing a newsletter, the center might be willing to give you a shot. From someone with no experience, you now have an opportunity to be a newsletter designer, an editor, a writer, and a publisher. If you do a reasonably good job, you could have a product to put in a portfolio when you seek a paying job with a private organization.

One of my students did a study for a local nonprofit on how members of the organization liked the organization's newsletter. He conducted a phone survey and wrote up the results for this organization.

The study was helpful to the organization but even more helpful to the student. He brought a copy of his study to a job interview with a national association in the construction business. One of the major jobs they wanted him to do was conduct yearly surveys on their publications. My student said, "Well, I just happen to have a study I did for an organization in Syracuse on its newsletter, and here it is." He was hired on the spot and never looked back.

Summer and semester internships are easier to get at nonprofits than businesses for the same reasons that they provide viable sites during the semester—namely, lack of skilled staff. Businesses are likely to have paid internships, except in areas of high student interest like TV stations and law firms. Many nonprofits may not be able to offer a salary or a lump sum stipend, but some do.

Volunteering will teach you the entire Skill Set of chapter 1, Taking Responsibility. You will meet the typical joiners who overcommit to too many volunteer activities and forget to go to meetings. You will see the devastating effect of poorly managed meetings that start late and end later. Many of these volunteer organizations struggle to keep track of money in an accurately and timely way. You will also see how good intentions lead to perks enjoyed by the leaders of the group at the expense of the rank-and-file members or clients. All of these negative lessons can be learned just about anywhere, but they are most abundant in organizations dependent upon volunteers.

But not all nonprofits are so poorly managed, especially those that have a national affiliation. Teach for America, for example, is one of the best-run nonprofits. It has created a recruitment machine that competes with the biggest companies in the country.[1] TFA trains college graduates so they perform as well if not better in the classroom as students with master's degrees in education. The leaders of many nonprofits use modern business practices and at the same time maintain a deep commitment to the public good. These organizations are likely to have well-developed programs to manage volunteers. You can learn a lot no matter what type of organization you work for—nonprofit, government, or business.

VALUE VOLUNTEER ACTIVITIES—EMPLOYERS DO

Volunteering and working in nonprofit internships can give you critical experience that will enable you to build your Skills Score. For that reason alone, it is valuable to prospective employers. You can grow from someone who has little experience with Excel or Access to one with substantial experience. It is one thing to say to an employer, "I took a course where I learned Excel" and quite another to say "I worked for the Salvation Army creating Excel spreadsheets to generate graphs for a grant proposal."

Doing good without a credit or monetary payoff is viewed by many employers as valuable for another reason. Such work can mean that you are the type of person who can work for something bigger than yourself. The step from good citizen in the volunteer sector to being a team player within the business world is small.

Most companies want to hire someone who is both competitive and a team player. If you can do both, you are more likely to get the job and more likely to excel on the job. They want to see students who helped their college host applicants, served on the residence hall council, participated in student government, or tutored kids in a community center. They know that fitting such activities into your busy schedule shows good time-management skills and a good heart.

A word of warning is in order, however. Employers become concerned if they see a lot of scattered activities, especially if it comes with a weak GPA. You need to focus on a few do-good activities and still maintain a respectable GPA. Don't become a community service junkie!

EXPLORE AND NETWORK FOR CAREERS

Working as a volunteer for a nonprofit or government agency will expand your contacts for future job exploration. Nonprofits have boards of directors from all over the community. You can meet them at social functions or meetings, and talk to them about your future. Adults love to play Daddy or Mommy to college students, and they frequently have very good advice. If you are sitting next to the right person at a dinner, you can conduct an informational interview before dessert. Contacts make through volunteer activities can build your professional network, which is described in chapter 20.

If you undertake volunteer activities and internships with government and nonprofit organizations during your college years, you may find a career that you want to pursue. You may discover you want to teach, do police work, work as a district attorney, or run a community center. You may learn that you do not want to sit in front of a computer all day or that you do not like the chaos of a small, underfunded organization. Even if you don't go into nonprofit work, you may find the skills you exercise as a volunteer are the type of thing you like to do. If you enjoy performing statistical analysis for a nonprofit in the summer, you may want to think about a position in market research when you graduate. If you enjoy meeting people and explaining the mission of your nonprofit, you might want to explore a sales position after you graduate.

On the other hand, from your experience with a nonprofit, you may decide that you want to work for one when you graduate. More than 20 percent of the American workforce is employed by nonprofit organizations or federal, state, and local governments.[2] Every job you can do in the business world, you can do in the nonprofit and government world. By volunteering during your college years and then taking internships, you can explore the advantages and disadvantages of employment outside of business.

The yearly salary of people working in these positions ranges from the low teens to the high six figures. People who help others or work in public service are not necessarily going to be poor. It depends on their talents and on what they want to do with their lives.

But the truth of the matter is that a person performing the same duties as someone in a for-profit business will receive less money working either for the government or for the nonprofit sector. Accountants working for the government make less than those who work for private firms. But there are other advantages. Government positions sometimes carry lucrative pensions. For example, some teachers in New York State who retire after twenty-five years of service receive close to 100 percent of what they were paid when working. Even where the pensions are not as generous, government workers can retire at fifty, get a pension, and take on a new career. These pensions are likely to become smaller in the future as a result of the pressures to lower government costs, but they will continue to be part of government employment. Nonprofits do not usually have strong pension programs, but they are much more generous about vacations and family-friendly policies.

The bottom line is that the money is not as good as it is in the business sector, but the perks may offset it. Moreover, if you work in a field in which you help others, you can be happy that you are making a difference. A feeling of doing something good for others can be another bonus to a rewarding job.

You should also see volunteer activities as an opportunity to build your career network, as we will discuss in chapter 20. You probably have a better chance of bonding with someone with whom you volunteer than some random social acquaintance or someone in one of your classes. In addition, you will share similar challenges that you can talk about after the experience, which is a powerful source of bonding. Also, some of the professionals who supervise you could also become part of your network, especially if you perform at your best.

CULTIVATE INTEGRITY

The final reason for doing good during your years at college is that it will help build and reinforce a sense of integrity in everything you do. *Integrity* is the practice of being open and truthful toward others. Employers want to see evidence of integrity in their employees because that is the basis of trust.

One way to develop and show integrity during your college years is to present a record of consistent volunteer work with one or two nonprofit organizations. If you devote four years to Habitat for Humanity on campus and take part in at least one of their spring-break trips, you demonstrate integrity. If you work your way up through the Greek system from being an officer in your fraternity or sorority to a position on a university-wide body, you show that you have persistence and commitment to serve others.

Moreover, taking on volunteer positions enhances your capacity for integrity, if only because you associate with a group of people who can see beyond their own narrow self-interest. As Miguel de Cervantes has Don Quixote say, "Tell me what company you keep, and I'll tell you what you are." If you move up through a student organization, you will face additional responsibilities, including dealing with people who have competing interests and who lack integrity. Working with people who ask you to break the rules will give you a taste of what you will face in whatever profession you pursue. It will prepare you for a world where integrity is in short supply.

USEFUL RESOURCES

BOOK

How You Can Help: An Easy Guide to Doing Good Deeds in Your Everyday Life by William D. Coplin (Routledge, 2000). A no-guilt approach to doing good, this book will provide you with the range of activities that can be undertaken as a meaningful but limited part of your life.

WEBSITES

www.idealist.org For those interested in a public service internship, fellowship, summer job, or volunteer opportunity, this is the website to search for thousands of opportunities by country, state, area of focus, and time period. The site also includes a "career center" with lots of resources and helpful hints for those interested in the nonprofit world.

www.serve.gov Supported by the Corporation for National and Community Service, this site provides information and help in creating your own volunteer opportunities, as well as a nation-wide search for opportunities already established near you.

www.volunteer.gov Volunteer.gov is federally run and allows you to search for opportunities with state parks and federal environmental agencies, such as the Fish and Wildlife Service, the Army Corps of Engineers, and others.

www.volunteermatch.org Volunteer Match is an easy-to-navigate website where you can search for local volunteer opportunities based on interest and time frame.

"IT'S DÉJÀ VU ALL OVER AGAIN."

—YOGI BERRA, FORMER CATCHER, OUTFIELDER, AND MANAGER FOR THE NEW YORK YANKEES

CHAPTER 16

THINKING ABOUT EDUCATION
BEYOND COLLEGE

**CONSIDER NOT GRADUATING OR GRADUATING EARLY •
VIEW GRADUATE SCHOOL AS A RISKY INVESTMENT
ALTERNATIVE • GET PAID TO LEARN**

This book is about what you need to learn in college, so why would I have a chapter on thinking beyond your college days? The answer is that if you know what is ahead, you can take action starting in your freshman year to be prepared after college.

Whatever you do after you leave college will be "going to school." In fact, everything you do throughout your work life should be viewed as enhancing your Skills Score and exploring careers. "Lifelong learning" is no empty phrase. It is the key to a successful career.

If you approach your job as this book suggests you approach your college education, you will acquire more skills and you will be constantly on the lookout for professional paths worth taking. Your twenties is the perfect time to learn skills and explore career options. That is why some of the strongest companies set up training programs, sometimes two years in length, and create a long-term plan for "professional development." An employee who stops learning is an employee who is not likely to move up—and who is quite likely to be moved out.

If your job requires that you continually learn, the strategies suggested in this book for college will also serve you well at work. Your decisions about career paths and projects as well as your volunteer activities within and outside your organization will determine how much you learn.

The long-term benefits of a commitment to learning in your career are substantial. You will be excited to go to work every day because you learn new things. Your employer will see that excitement and be ready to assign you new tasks. You will have opportunities that will open many paths to you. As you grow, your skills grow, too—and vice versa.

You will develop more skills and acquire more career-related knowledge in the first few years following college than during your college years. This is true whether you go to graduate school, get a temporary job or internship, or start on a full-time job in your career area. Think of your first five to ten years after graduating college as mostly educational. It will be a time when you do even more career exploration or skill development than you did in college.

If you accept my viewpoint and treat your college experience as a way to develop skills and explore careers, you will see the wisdom of the quotation at the beginning of the chapter by the famous New York Yankee catcher, Yogi Berra: "It's déjà vu all over again." To continue with the baseball analogy, going to college is like playing baseball in the minor leagues. You start to develop your skills, and then after college, you join the major leagues—but in the major leagues you're still practicing and improving on the same skills you developed in the minors. Very few baseball players are successful in the majors if they skip the minor leagues, just as a similar percentage of people skip college and have very successful careers. For the vast majority of successful baseball players, the minor leagues are necessary, just as for the vast majority of people with successful careers, some college is required. However, the skill level of baseball players is much higher when in the majors, just as your skill level will be much higher as you proceed through your career.

This viewpoint leads to some pretty startling ideas. The first is to get out of college as fast as you can, preferably with a degree, but not necessarily. The second is that graduate school right after college in most cases is not a good choice. The third is that getting paid for your postcollege education is better than paying for it.

CONSIDER NOT GRADUATING OR GRADUATING EARLY

When most people think about students dropping out of college for better, more lucrative opportunities, they think of athletes. It is common in Division I schools for exceptional athletes to leave college for the opportunity to go pro right away. These athletes are often criticized for not getting their degrees. However, accepting a great opportunity that can be useful for your career without graduating college is not a terrible idea. If a college degree and a dollar will get you four quarters and the most important thing you do in your four years of college is to develop your skills and explore careers, it stands to reason that leaving school before you graduate is an acceptable choice. If you have the skills and have a clear career path, it may not make sense to graduate, at least not right away.

I say this for several reasons other than that you have the skills and career focus. First, college is very expensive and you may not want to add to your debt. Remember that every $10,000 in debt is at least $100 a month for ten years. If you are in debt beyond $30,000, you need to think hard and long about that.

Second, while you are in college you may get a job—with a clear career direction and potential—that pays very well. It may make sense to take it, if only because it may not be there a year later. If you only have one or two semesters' worth of credit left, you can be earning a good wage and finish up the degree part time. I know several students who went to a college with a strong co-op program—that is, a full-semester paid program as part of their degree requirement— and never came back to college. They chose not to spend their senior year paying tuition and enjoying student life, but instead chose to start working at a very good salary with high career potential. The ones I know may have never finished their degree, but they gained two years more of full-time experience than those who chose to wait until they graduated to get a job.

Third, you may figure out that you want to get a certificate that doesn't take four years to acquire and leads directly to a job. For example, you can get a pharmacy technician certificate in a nine-month program and earn up to $60,000 a year.[1] That may be a better decision than completing your degree in another year or two and then going to a certificate program in some skilled field. I know several students who have completed their degree and then entered a certificate program or a two-year technical program. That choice needlessly added to their overall debt and diminished time not in a full-time job.

This advice is only a suggestion because it carries risks. Many employers want to see a college degree. They see the degree as a measure of persistence, and persistence is in short supply in the workforce.

It really depends on how far along you are on the ten Skill Sets, if you have a career focus, and how much debt you have.

Some professions require an undergraduate degree. If you are interested in law or education, you have no choice. Graduate schools require undergraduate degrees, except if a student has substantial professional experience. Choosing to graduate also depends on how adamant your parents are about your getting a degree and how much you want to live in the now by having fun in college.

If dropping out before graduation doesn't suit you, but you also don't want a lot of debt, seriously think about graduating early. If you bring college credits earned in high school or take 18 credits a semester instead of the normal 15 and your degree requires 120 credits, you may be able to graduate a semester or even a year early. Not only will you save money on college costs, but you also will be able to start earning money and getting work experience earlier. Another bonus, besides saving time and cash, is that employers will see this as a sign that you are a go-getter.

VIEW GRADUATE SCHOOL AS A RISKY INVESTMENT ALTERNATIVE

Graduate school is becoming increasingly popular—maybe too popular according to Randall Collins. In an editorial titled "The Dirty Little Secrets of Credential Inflation!" in the *Chronicle of Higher Education*, he writes, "Many people believe that our high-tech era requires massive educational expansion" and if it keeps up, "janitors will need PhDs and baby sitters advanced degrees in child care."[2] In an article, two Stanford Business School researchers, Jeffrey Pfeffer and Christina Fong, maintain that with the exception of some of the elite schools, an MBA is not correlated with higher salaries over the long run.[3]

Keeping these comments in mind, ask yourself, "Is graduate school a good investment for me?" If you are going to be a doctor, lawyer, or professor, you have no choice. You have to get what is called the "union card."

However, even when graduate school is required, you may be better off getting some work experience before you go to graduate school. Many of my former students who are lawyers suggest getting a job with a law firm as a case assistant through which, in effect, you would be trained as a paralegal. You will get a decent salary, benefits, and opportunities to build your professional network, and, most of all, see whether you really want to become a lawyer. Moreover, you will get into a better law school and be a lot better prepared than those who come right out of college. You can get internships or one- or two-year job programs in companies, government, or nonprofit organizations, as I will discuss later in this chapter, which will allow you to develop more skills and explore careers fields related to these internships or jobs.

If you are thinking about getting your master's in business administration (MBA) or a master's in public administration (MPA), consider entering the workforce before going to graduate school. These graduate programs are highly competitive and are more likely to accept and provide financial aid to students who have a few years of work experience. Additionally, the company you work for may even pay for your graduate education. In most cases, they will require you work for them for a certain number of years after completing your graduate studies, but this far outweighs the debt you would accumulate if you paid for graduate school yourself.

For most other fields, neither a PhD nor even a master's is required, and in some cases an advanced degree may make you look overeducated for the job you want. The most important question to ask yourself is what a graduate degree can do for your skills and your career exploration. If you already developed your basic Skills Score in college, the answer is that graduate school will introduce you to new skills, especially in quantitative analysis and research. It should also reinforce existing people, analytical, and problem-solving skills. Graduate programs will also help improve your grasp of professional concepts and terminology specific to the career field you are pursuing. Programs that have a deep commitment to fieldwork-based learning will be the most powerful in improving your skills.

If for some reason you left college without developing the basic Skill Sets, graduate school can accomplish what your college education did not. First of all, most of your peers, if you go to a halfway decent program, will have those skills. Just associating and competing with them will raise your level. In addition, they will have other more advanced skills than you might have, which they will help you learn. Second, graduate programs tend to be more skill oriented. They will have some courses that provide the opportunity to develop basic and advanced skills. Third, most good graduate programs will have significant internship or fieldwork requirements.

If you go to a graduate program, follow the advice throughout this book on how courses and non-course activities can be used to develop the skills you need. Choose the programs and courses that emphasize skill development. For example, if you are in law school, take as many clinic credits as possible. Choose a graduate program that requires a semester or even a yearlong internship.

It makes more sense to go to graduate school for a master's program if your undergraduate program left you poorly prepared. But if you already have a high Skills Score, the advantages to graduate school do not lie primarily in acquiring critical skills. Instead, they are related to career exploration and development. First, graduate programs will help you explore careers by getting you closer to practitioners than you were in your undergraduate program. Faculty members in graduate programs are usually accomplished in their profession or have had at least some experience. Moreover, some of the students in your classes will have already been in the field, and you can learn a great deal from them. Second, any good graduate program will have a lot of resources devoted to getting you a job or at least an internship leading to a job. Third, the friends you make in graduate school will be in fields related to the one you choose. Consequently, you will have a built-in network that will help you find and keep jobs.

Another value to graduate school is what might be called "the growing-up factor." Many people in the work world are not ready to take anyone under twenty-five seriously. The four years of college fills the time until you are twenty-one, if you started college right out of high school. If you look young or feel you are not quite ready to deal with professionals over the age of thirty, taking a couple of years to mature may not be a bad idea.

Graduate school, however, is a costly way to tread water. If warehousing yourself to grow up is the only reason you plan to go to graduate school, work for at least two years in an entry-level job instead. Many companies hire people right out of college with the assumption that they are really "interns" and will leave after two years. Consulting companies, which are best viewed as high-class temp firms, will send you off here and there for six-month gigs. A job with a consulting company may be viewed as a short-term commitment to figure out what you want to do when you grow up. At the same time, consulting firms put you in different job positions at different companies, which improves your networks and could even lead directly to a job.

A special word about law school is needed because too many people are going to law school with no commitment to becoming a lawyer or without a clue about how the law degree will help them. Many of my students went to law school in the early 2000s, and they are not happy campers because of these negatives:

- Law school costs $150,000, and financial aid is minimal compared with undergraduate programs.

- Law school, according to most students I have talked to, is HELL. Many law professors are brutal to their students.

- Law schools tend to attract highly competitive and insecure people who help to make it even more HELL than intended by the professors.

- People with law degrees have serious trouble getting jobs.

- Many jobs, especially at the entry level, in the legal profession tend to be boring—some recent law school grads might even say "soul crushing."

According to a 2011 article, "a generation of JDs face the grimmest job market in decades. Since 2008, 15,000 attorney and legal staff jobs at large firms have vanished." Moreover, the author, David Segal, indicates that he does not believe the statistics law schools provide on job placement. He quotes a law professor who says, "Every time I look at this data, I feel dirty."[4]

Approaching law school with a healthy dose of skepticism is a good idea. You may want to pursue law school despite its cost and risks if any of these statements is true:

- You have relatives in the law business who will hire you.

- You have wanted to be a lawyer for as long as you can remember.

- You like to argue and your parents said, "You should be a lawyer"—unless they are secretly thinking, "You should suffer the hell of going to law school."

- You want to pursue careers high up in government circles, which frequently require having the law credential and being able to read legislation. Like it or not, a large number of elected officials started out in law.

- You have this burning desire to lock up bad guys, to protect others from the arbitrary and capricious application of the law, or to fight some injustice (like child abuse or consumer fraud).

The growing trend for students to obtain a combination degree consisting of a law degree and a master's of public administration (MPA) or a master's of business administration (MBA) does not make much sense, especially given the cost. An MPA or MBA is good enough for most jobs. As mentioned above, appearing to be overeducated can be a negative. Employers may feel the salary they can offer is not high enough to compensate for the extra degree, or they may see your accumulation of degrees as a sign of insecurity and lack of direction. A combination degree may help in some cases, but the key to employment beyond the entrance level is experience (unless degrees are a requirement for the job).

The message about graduate school is mixed. Except for professions requiring the credential, it should not be viewed as a requirement for a successful career. Even for such professions, two or three years of work will clarify your decision to go to graduate school. As far as your Skills Score is concerned, graduate school can raise your general levels and introduce you to the more specialized skills and the perspectives of the profession you choose. The primary value, however, of most graduate school programs is to help you explore careers and get you into a career network.

I have not mentioned PhDs in this discussion for two reasons. First, very few readers should be considering the PhD given its limited utility. The PhD is designed for college teaching and advanced research jobs for which the degree itself is a credential for getting into the job. The investment costs are very high and the chances of landing a job are low.[5]

I am not saying that a graduate degree may not be right for you, but do weigh the benefits, costs, and risks, and work for a while after college to help you make the right choice. The best graduate programs frequently will not accept students who don't have a few years of work experience, because they see the experience as a way for students to gain focus, skills, and knowledge they can use in their graduate program.

GET PAID TO LEARN

Going into the workforce in either a permanent or a temporary job after college is a win-win. You get paid, and at the same time you develop skills. You also learn more about yourself and the field in which your job is located—more than you learned in your four years of college. You might even think of your first job as an internship. Most employers think it of that way, and some even call it a paid internship. This is true for the business, nonprofit, and government sectors.

Going after a job in business is the course most frequently chosen by new college graduates. This is because more than 70 percent of jobs in the United States are in the business rather than the government or nonprofit sectors.[6] Although the job market is competitive, persistence pays off. Many companies have a training period, which itself is valuable.

If you are hired by a big corporation, you will participate in extensive training programs that provide as good or better education than graduate programs and you get a reasonably good salary at the same time. The programs can last from one month to two years. The General Electric website (www.ge.com/careers/students/fmp/index.html) says this about its Financial Management Training Program (FMP), which is widely considered to be the premier program of its kind. It is the first step in many successful GE management careers. "FMP develops leadership and analytical skills through classroom training and key assignments." This statement may be self-serving for GE, but from my experience with several alumni, it is true. Don't think the "key assignments" phrase means only classes. For the FMP participants, it means rotating every six months into different business sectors run by GE. The GE rotational programs for college graduates are highly respected in the corporate world. If you are able to work in one of these programs after graduating, you will be a highly competitive candidate for positions elsewhere. Other companies like Johnson and

Johnson, Lockheed Martin, Microsoft, and the Lincoln Financial Group have similar programs.

If you cannot land a satisfactory entry-level position, all is not lost. In fact, an excellent option, which could have as good, if not better, long-term payoff than a traditional entry-level corporate job, is to go to a temp agency. Some of my students were hired through a temp agency, and they are now on a path to success. To give you a clear idea of how the temp scene works, one of my former students provides a description of her experience. She writes:

> *"After graduation, my dad suggested I sign up with a temp agency immediately and . . . look for a 'real job.' A temp agency interviews you and tests your competency in some basic skill areas like word processing, alphabetizing, and arithmetic. Then you call every morning (this is really important) until they give you an assignment. I had no corporate experience, but basic office skills got me a position in an operational department of a stock broker-age firm. The temp salary was about $25K. My first two days were entirely spent filing account paperwork—the test of whether I was a complainer or willing to work hard. I spent the next weeks and months preparing daily man-agement reports for the staff to work from, supervising other temps, analyzing client accounts for compliance with industry regulation, and executing cashiering trans-actions in client and house accounts. After two months, I was offered a permanent position, at about $28K. [This is in 2000 money.]*
>
> *"I was promoted quickly through the operational levels, found a good mentor, and with his help landed a career opportunity in project management about a year after I was hired. So after five years, I'm making $58,000 using my knowledge and skills—gained on the job and from some of my college experience—to solve problems in technical and operational processes that have regula-tory or financial impact on the company."*

With a reasonable salary and a future in the company, this alumna has many options. She could have a profitable career in the company. She could go on the job market and search for a better job, or she could go to graduate school to hone her skills and move up faster in the field she is in. Her five years of experience and outstanding performance would enable her to get into a much stronger graduate program than if she had applied right out of college. And indeed, after completing graduate school at the Maxwell School of Syracuse University, she now has the career she wanted working in Washington, D.C., for the federal government. All this from a temporary position!

Any business job you get, regardless of whether there is a corporate training program or not, will provide you with the opportunity to develop skills and explore careers. Joining a small company provides a lot of opportunity for creativity and flexibility in what you learn because you will be cross-trained to do different jobs. You might not receive the formal training that GE provides, but you will be rewarded if you have the skills outlined in this book.

Another solid alternative is to join a program offered by nonprofit organization like Teach for America or a government organization like the Peace Corps or AmeriCorps. These organizations provide two years of experience that will help you figure out what you want to be, money to pay off loans or additional schooling together with a salary, and a network for career building. Alumni of Teach for America and the Peace Corps have gone to the best graduate programs and landed jobs in the most well-established corporations. Many smaller and less known non-profits have one- or two-year programs where you get a small salary, perhaps without benefits. To learn more about these options as well as others, check out the websites listed at the end of this chapter.

Another option is to join the military. If you are in good physical shape and not risk averse, the military offers college graduates enormous opportunities. If you were in an ROTC program as an undergraduate, you are already set for this option. If you did not take one of these programs in college or did not go to a service academy, it is not too late to join the military once you graduate. You can apply to an officer candidacy training program, which requires a four-year commitment. This is a competitive option, but I have had students take it and benefit greatly. If you decide to stay in the military for twenty years, you can retire with a solid pension and start a new career.

While you are in college, you can take steps that will prepare you to obtain a position right out of college where you can continue your learning and get paid. If you are interested in landing a job in GE's FMP program, you can develop leadership qualities, take courses in finance (not necessarily a major), and apply for a summer internship. If you are interested in Teach for America, you can work as a volunteer tutor or mentor in a disadvantaged school. If you are thinking about law school or some other graduate school, you can intern in organizations that hire graduates from those schools to broaden your network as well as take some courses similar to those offered in graduate school. The skills and experiences you have in college can lead to a very productive life right after college.

USEFUL RESOURCES

BOOK

Graduate Programs in Business, Education, Health, Information Studies, Law & Social Work (Peterson's, 2011). This book details more than 14,000 graduate programs in 158 disciplines, and will point you in the right direction for whichever graduate program interests you.

WEBSITES

www.americorps.gov A network of national service programs, AmeriCorps engages more than fifty thousand Americans each year in intensive service to meet critical needs in education, public safety, health, and the environment.

www.lucasgroup.com/military This is one of the many websites of an organization that helps place military officers. The site lists the range of jobs that ex-military people get as well as salaries for those positions.

www.peacecorps.gov The Peace Corps was formally authorized by Congress in 1961, and its mission is to "promote world peace and friendship." There are seven thousand Peace Corps volunteers currently serving in seventy countries around the world. All assignments are for two years plus three months of training in your country of service. Peace Corp alumni have a strong network and use their experience to pursue graduate study and rewarding careers.

www.petersons.com/graduate-schools.aspx This site provides advice on making a decision about going to graduate school. It also helps you locate a graduate school that fits your needs.

www.teachforamerica.org Teach for America is the national corps of outstanding college graduates of all academic majors and backgrounds who commit two years to teach in urban and rural public schools. Since its inception in 1990, more than ten thousand exceptional individuals have joined Teach for America.

PART THREE

LAUNCHING YOUR CAREER

"I ALWAYS WANTED TO BE SOMEBODY, BUT I SHOULD HAVE BEEN MORE SPECIFIC."

—LILY TOMLIN, COMEDIENNE

CHAPTER 17

EXPLORING CAREER FIELDS

BEGIN THE SELF-REFLECTION PROCESS • SCAN CAREER FIELDS • GET MORE SPECIFIC INFORMATION ABOUT CAREERS

Believe it or not, you have been exploring career fields your whole life. Remember when you wanted to be a police officer or teacher, or when you thought you'd be a basketball superstar, TV news anchor, hot-shot lawyer, or U.S. senator? Those were ways of "trying out" different careers. Now it's time to move beyond fantasy and deal with reality.

"Dealing with reality" doesn't mean you can't shoot for the stars. You should always aspire to achieve your dreams. Throughout junior and senior high school, many students aspire to high-profile jobs that are portrayed in the media or are viewed as high paying. Many continue to pursue their dream job in college without ever looking at what else is possible. They don't realize that there are hundreds of thousands of different jobs that might be interesting and pay a decent salary. During your college years, you have the time and opportunity to explore other options even as you seek to be a brain surgeon, a famous lawyer, a successful politician, or a TV sportscaster.

A major goal of your four years in college is to explore what kinds of careers would be best for you. This is a difficult and complicated process. It takes time and, like the process of developing skills employers want, a serious commitment. I see the process as three interrelated steps: (1) self-reflection, (2) scanning professional options, and (3) testing the waters through action. Unlike traditional stairs in a two-story house, these three steps are not sequenced. Self-reflection will lead to scanning and perhaps more self-reflection, which of course will be informed by your apprenticeships and other educational activities in college. The three steps are more a circle.

Using tools provided by your career services office can help with self-reflection. You can find a variety of tests and computer programs that can help you see what kind of career would be satisfying to you. Although these tools will not provide definitive answers, they will help you think more systematically about yourself.

The earlier you start your career exploration, the sooner you will be able to narrow down your choices, and therefore develop the skills, knowledge, and experience you will need to succeed in those fields. To get started, complete the Career Preference Questionnaire. It will help you think about what you prefer in a career and possibly even your first job.

CAREER PREFERENCE QUESTIONNAIRE

1. **Work with People:**
   Mostly __ About half the time __ Much less than half the time __

2. **Work with Information:**
   Mostly __ About half the time __ Much less than half the time __

3. **Work with Things:**
   Mostly __ About half the time __ Much less than half the time __

4. **Salary after 10 Years:**
   Over $200,000 __ Between $75,000 and $200,000 __ Under $75,000 __

5. **Hours:**
   Part-time __ Less than 40 __ No more than 40 __ 40–60 __ Over 60 __

6. **Field Type:**
   Solely doing good __ Mostly doing good __ Doing good and making money __
   Mostly making money __ Solely making money __

7. **Proximity:**
   Very close to where I live __ Within 3 hours of where I live __
   Across the country __ Out of the country __

8. **Travel for Job:**
   No travel __ Travel 1–12 times a year __ Travel once a month __
   Travel once a week __ Travel more than once a week __

9. **Economic Risk:**
   Very risky ___ Somewhat risky ___ Neither risky nor secure ___
   Somewhat secure ___ Very secure ___

10. **Working Environment:**
    Very orderly ___ Orderly ___ Neither orderly nor chaotic ___
    Chaotic ___ Very chaotic ___

11. **Region:**
    Northeast ___ Mid-Atlantic ___ South ___ Southwest ___ Midwest ___ West ___

12. **Education:**
    Some high school ___ High school diploma ___ Some college ___
    4-year college diploma ___ Graduate education ___

13. **Neighborhood:**
    Urban ___ Suburban ___ Rural ___

Now that you have completed the questionnaire, you may want to reflect on several questions. Were there career categories that you had not considered before? Were some questions more difficult than others? Did completing the questionnaire give you a more complete perspective on the trade-offs you will have to make in choosing your career?

The first three items in the questionnaire asked you to estimate how much time you would like to spend working with people, working with information, or working with things. "Work with People" would lead to careers like teaching, counseling, and nursing where most of your time is spent helping others. "Work with Information" would lead to careers in which you gather and analyze information (for example, accounting, engineering, finance, and law). "Work with Things" can best be described as working with your hands (for example, dentistry, plumbing, surgery, and outdoor jobs).

The distinction among "people," "information," and "things" only serves as a starter question, because all jobs require working with people to some extent as well as dealing with information or things. Your responses to the questions suggest a direction. Also, as your career progresses, the emphasis on each area may change. For example, lawyers may start out working with information more than people, but if they become partners in the law firm, they will spend more time managing staff and getting new clients. If you want to become the president of a big construction firm, you might start out as a plumber or carpenter but demonstrate to your superiors your interest in intensive work with people.

Because you may have a job that will mix working with people, information, and possibly even things, and because managerial work may be in your distant future, try to figure out what you like to do best: work with people, information, or things. This will help you think about which career fields are more interesting to you than others.

The other questions in the Career Preference Questionnaire may seem somewhat trivial, but they are key factors in career and job decisions for most people. Use the questionnaire as a way of thinking about those factors rather than as a system to make a decision. The goal is for you to be self-reflecting in your pursuit of a career path.

Completing this questionnaire helps point you in some career direction, but it cannot tell you exactly which career to follow. This is because the thirteen factors interact with each other so, for example, a high-paying job may or may not require education beyond college depending on what it is and where you live. The questionnaire is designed to help you think about what is important to you as you think about careers.

SCAN CAREER FIELDS

Career fields can be grouped into two categories: those that require either a specific undergraduate or postgraduate degree and/or a specific certification (like an accountant, a nurse, a physician, or a lawyer) and those that have no degree or formal certification requirement. In some cases, you need both a degree and to pass a certification examination (to be a lawyer or an accountant, for example). Although many companies, government, and nonprofit organization say "a college degree" is required, a significant number say that solid experience can substitute for a degree.

If neither of the two lists below provides you with an appealing option, use other resources, including counselors, family, books, and websites. The purpose of this scanning process is to help you start to think about your future. Spend a limited amount of time in making your initial selection, because the purpose of the scan is to help you figure out what skills you want to develop in college rather than require you to settle on a specific career.

SELECTED ENTRY-LEVEL PROFESSIONAL POSITIONS REQUIRING ADVANCED STUDY AND/OR CERTIFICATE

PROFESSION	DEGREE AND/OR CREDENTIAL REQUIREMENT	WEBSITE
Accountant	Degree in accounting or a closely related field; some work experience may be required.	American Institute of Certified Public Accountants www.aicpa.org
Architect	Professional degree in architecture (usually acquired from a five-year program at a four-year school), a period of practical training or internship, and a license, which includes the two former requirements as well as passage of all sections of the Architect Registration Examination.	American Institute of Architects www.aia.org
Archivist	Master's degree in history and/or library science and substantial practical or work experience.	Society of American Archivists www.archivists.org
Audiologist/ Speech Pathologist	Most states and the District of Columbia require the following for licensing: a master's degree, 300–375 hours of supervised clinical experience, a passing score on a national examination, and nine months of postgraduate professional clinical experience.	American Speech-Language-Hearing Association www.asha.org
Clergy	Many denominations require that clergy complete a bachelor's degree and a graduate-level program of theological study.	The Academy of Parish Clergy www.apclergy.org
Clinical Psychologist	Master's degree, and frequently a doctoral degree, is required for employment as a psychologist in most fields. Psychologists in independent practice must meet licensing or certification requirements in all states and the District of Columbia.	American Psychological Association www.apa.org
College and University Administrator	Most positions require at least a master's degree, and some require a doctoral degree.	Student Affairs Administrators in Higher Education www.naspa.org
Food Scientist	Master's degree or doctoral degree is required for basic research.	Institute of Food Technologists www.ift.org

PROFESSION	DEGREE AND/OR CREDENTIAL REQUIREMENT	WEBSITE
Instructional Coordinator	Master's degree is required to work in this profession.	National Education Association www.nea.org
Lawyer	Four years of undergraduate study followed by three years in law school. To practice law, you will also need to pass the bar examination in the state you wish to work. Advanced law degrees may be desirable for those planning to specialize, do research, or teach.	American Bar Association www.americanbar.org
Librarian	Master's degree in library science is required for positions in most public, academic, and special libraries, and in many school systems.	American Library Association www.ala.org
Medical and Psychiatric Social Worker	Master's degree in social work is generally required for positions in the mental health field and public agencies, and is usually necessary for supervisory, administrative, or research positions. A doctorate usually is required for teaching and some research and administrative jobs.	National Association of Social Workers www.naswdc.org
Medicine and Health Services Manager	Master's degree in such areas as health services administration, long-term care administration, and health sciences is the standard credential for most generalist positions in this field.	American College of Healthcare Executives www.ache.org
Operations Researcher/ Analyst	Master's degree and high level of computer skills are required.	Institute for Operations Research and the Management Sciences www.informs.org
Optometrist	Four-year professional degree program at an accredited optometric school preceded by at least two or three years of preoptometric study at an accredited college or university. All states require optometrists to be licensed.	American Optometric Association www.aoanet.org
Pharmacist	Pharmacists must be licensed. To obtain a license, one must graduate from an accredited college of pharmacy, pass a state examination, and serve an internship under a licensed pharmacist. Most colleges of pharmacy require one or two years of college-level prepharmacy education.	American Association of Colleges of Pharmacy www.aacp.org

PROFESSION	DEGREE AND/OR CREDENTIAL REQUIREMENT	WEBSITE
Physical Therapist	All states and the District of Columbia require physical therapists to pass a licensure exam after graduating from an accredited physical therapy program.	American Physical Therapy Association www.apta.org
Physician	Four years of undergraduate school, four years of medical school, three to eight years of internship and residency, and a diplomate depending on medical specialty. Some fields have additional requirements.	American Medical Association www.ama-assn.org
Researcher and/or Professor	Master's degree for more professional opportunities; doctorate, which takes four to ten years of graduate school, for most positions in postsecondary institutions.	Search under the specific profession you are pursuing—example: "Economist"
School/ Vocational/ Career Counselor	All states and the District of Columbia require school counselors to have state school counseling certification. Depending on the state, a master's degree in counseling and two to five years of teaching experience may be required for a counseling certificate.	American Counseling Association www.counseling.org
Teacher	All states and the District of Columbia require public school teachers to be certified and require at least a bachelor's degree (in education or another field) and completion of an approved teacher training program with a prescribed number of subject and education credits and supervised practice teaching.	American Federation of Teachers www.aft.org
Veterinarian	Prospective veterinarians must graduate from a four-year program at an accredited college of veterinary medicine with a doctor of veterinary medicine (DVM or VMD) degree and obtain a license to practice. All states and the District of Columbia require that veterinarians be licensed.	American Veterinary Medical Association www.avma.org
Vocational Rehabilitation Counselor	Most vocational and related rehabilitation agencies usually require a master's degree in rehabilitation counseling, counseling and guidance, or counseling psychology.	National Rehabilitation Association www.nationalrehab.org

SELECTED ENTRY-LEVEL PROFESSIONAL POSITIONS NOT REQUIRING ADVANCED STUDY AND/OR A CERTIFICATE

Administrative Services Manager

Artist

Athletic Trainer

Audio-Visual Specialist

Budget Analyst

Computer and Information Systems Manager

Computer Programmer

Computer Security Specialist

Computer Support Specialist

Computer Systems Analyst

Construction Manager

Consultant

Cost Estimator

Credit Analyst

Data Communications Analyst

Database Administrator

Dietitian/Nutritionist

Editor

Employee Training Specialist

Employment and Placement Specialist

Employment Interviewer

Farm Products Purchasing Agent

Financial Counselor

Forester

Government Service Executive

Graphic Designer

Health and Safety Engineer

Human Resources Manager

Industrial Production Manager

Insurance Claim Examiner

Interior Designer

Interpreter/Translator

Job and Occupational Analyst

Loan Officer/Counselor

Market Research Analyst

Medical/Clinical Laboratory Technologist

Meetings and Convention Planner

Newscaster

Parole and Probation Officer

Postal Worker

Property Manager

Public Health Educator

Public Relations Specialist

Purchasing Agent

Real Estate Appraiser

Recreation Facilities Manager

Recreation Worker

Reporter

Residential Counselor

Sales

Set Designer

Social Services Manager

Social Worker

Tax Examiner/Revenue Agent

Technical Writer

Transportation Manager

Utilities Manager

Wholesale and Retail Buyer

Writer

Once you have identified some professions that interest you, you are ready to acquire information on those fields. Gathering specific information on a field should be done one field at a time. Your college career center will have access to electronic career exploration databases that allow you to gather information on specific career fields, and also help you match your interests and competencies to specific career fields. SIGI (System of Integrated Guidance Information) is a software program that uses personality analysis to help with career exploration. If your college or university does not currently have access to programs like SIGI, you can often ask the career center to purchase them.[1] A program that you can access from your own computer free of charge is O*NET, which is referenced in the Useful Resources section at the end of this chapter. O*NET is an excellent way to explore specific job fields, and will provide details about the job you're interested in (for example: typical tasks of the job; specialties and similar occupations; skills and attitudes; education, training, and work experience needed; transferable work-content skills; suggested school courses; physical demands; work hours and travel; national earnings; and more).

As part of your study of a field, conduct at least one informational interview. *Informational interviewing* is a technique in which you find someone who has the job or career you think you might want, and you ask him or her all about it. These interviews will help you decide whether you really want to pursue that career. You might ask questions like "How did you get to your current position?" or "What do you like best and least about your current position?" Internships, part-time jobs, and job shadowing (following an employee around for a day or two) can help you get a more complete picture by giving you an experience in the field and access to people whom you can interview. By the time you enter your senior year, you should have in-depth information for at least three professional fields.

Once you have identified some career fields that interest you using the Career Preference Questionnaire on page 210, you are ready to acquire more specific information on those fields. Select three fields to explore using the five steps described below. You can start this process early in your freshman year or even before, but preferably not later than the beginning of your sophomore year.

STEP 1:
EXAMINE THE WEBSITES OF THE PROFESSIONAL ASSOCIATIONS THAT SUPPORT YOUR FIELD.

These organizations frequently have national, regional, state, or even city branches. Once you have looked at their websites, attend one of their meetings. They usually give a discount to students. Offer to volunteer at their sign-in desk. Not only will this activity give you more information about the career field, but it could also help you build your professional network as we will discuss in chapter 20. Everybody knows that lawyers join the American Bar Association, but most people don't realize that there are professional organizations for every career field. For example, one of the largest professional organizations is Strategic Human Resource Management (SHRM). Every company has a human resources department that is responsible for recruiting and retaining employees. Many of these professionals join SHRM to share knowledge about the human resources profession. Students looking for jobs in the field of public relations could attend the national or regional meetings of the Public Relations Society of America (PSRA) and even join as a student member at a reduced rate. For most of these organizational meetings, especially local ones, you may be able to talk them into letting you in for free.

You can find the websites for other professional organizations in the table on pages 213–215.

STEP 2:
EXAMINE THE WEBSITES OF SPECIFIC COMPANIES OR ORGANIZATIONS (GOVERNMENTAL AND NONPROFIT) THAT HIRE PEOPLE IN THE CAREER FIELD YOU'RE EXAMINING.

Having a better understanding of the companies and organizations in the field in which you're interested can help you learn more about the specific career field as well as the company you are studying. Knowledge of relevant companies will help you ask better questions once you get to informational interviews in step 3. Employers will often ask you in an interview what you know about the company or organization. Be prepared with knowledge of the company and its competitors. By having general knowledge and understanding of the company, you should be able to ask the interviewer questions about the organization, which makes you look like you are genuinely interested in the position. If you can talk to those who make campus recruiting visits, that would be ideal. You can also look on the organizational websites for internships.

STEP 3:
CONDUCT INFORMATIONAL INTERVIEWS WITH PROFESSIONALS IN THE FIELD.

Reviewing professional association and company websites leads you to the next step: informational interviews, which I mentioned above. Do not expect these interviews to lead directly to a job or an internship and don't bring it up because the person will feel used. However, if they offer, take them up on it.

To get informational interviews, work with your career services program staff. The staff may have alumni contacts in the field, and they will help you make an initial contact. Attend speeches and panels of people in your field who visit campus. They can provide insight on how their organizations work and may even know about opportunities for students within their organizations.

STEP 4:
FOLLOW THE ADVICE IN CHAPTER 13 ON INTERNSHIPS AND APPRENTICESHIPS.

If you have followed the research steps just outlined, you will most likely uncover internships. This may be with a specific company, but it could also be with the relevant professional organization. Think about the implications of being an intern at the American Bar Association (ABA). You might work at an ABA conference by helping out at the sign-in table. You will meet lawyers and support staff and be in a position to help them out. You might establish enough of a relationship to add them to your network, especially when you help someone get a new badge, which they lost in the bar. Internships will help you explore the career, prepare for interviews, and build a network, and may even result in a permanent job, as it does for about 64 percent of people who have corporate internships.[2] While working at internships in your desired career field, make a list of the relevant skills you will need to be successful in that field. This will be important in the next step of your career research.

STEP 5:
BUILD RELEVANT SKILLS AND KNOWLEDGE.

Once you have done some investigation on career fields, you can start to work on the skills and knowledge that are most important to your fields of interest. Although all the Skill Sets described in the first ten chapters are important, some may be more important for your chosen career path.

In addition to the ten Skill Sets, specific knowledge about the career field will be required. The knowledge component will vary for each career field. Your most crucial task is to learn the history of the field and the terms most frequently used in the field. It's also important to be familiar with the organizations—business, nonprofit, or government—that might employ you or have a major impact on careers in the field. Your web research, informational interviewing, and internships will help you build a knowledge base that enables you to ask more questions about the history and terminology in the field.

You should also develop technical skills beyond the skills mentioned in chapters 1 through 10.

Every career field requires skills beyond the basic ten Skill Sets—skills that employers would expect their employees to have or develop. For many fields, the specialized skills are higher levels of the skills listed under our basic ten. This is true for the field of journalism, for example, in which higher levels of writing and asking questions are required. In other fields, such as graphic design, there may be skills not listed in our basic ten. Most businesses would like to see some familiarity with accounting and finance even if you don't intend to go into those areas.

For those interested in law, training in legal research most associated with paralegal training is a very good idea. Many colleges will not offer formal courses that count toward degree requirements in the liberal arts for such training, and some will not accept transfer credit from a community college. However, if you want to do well in law school and be a lawyer, it makes sense to pick up such training sometime during your four years of college.

Finally, it is never a mistake to develop skills in as many computer applications as you can while in college. Become a whiz at Microsoft Excel and Access. Do as much web design as you can. Also, don't ignore all the tricks using Microsoft Word. If you are into a career that requires visuals, familiarity with Macs and graphic design programs would be useful. Although you may not want to have a techie job, having some basic techie skills beyond the average could get you a job and lead to faster promotions.

USEFUL RESOURCES

BOOKS

Do What You Are: Discover the Perfect Career for You Through the Secrets of Personality Type by Paul D. Tieger (Little, Brown and Company, 2007). This is one of many books that connects psychological research to advice on careers and job success.

Occupational Outlook Handbook 2011–2012 by the U.S. Department of Labor is issued annually. This is the most thorough source of information on the more than three hundred top jobs, which accounts for

90 percent of jobs in the United States. The book provides information on the type of work, qualifications, training, earnings, and job outlook.

What Color Is Your Parachute? A Practical Manual for Job-Hunters & Career-Changers, 40th edition, by Richard N. Bolles (Ten Speed Press, 2012). This book has sold more than ten million copies since it was first published in 1970. The book is revised frequently. Written primarily for people changing jobs and careers, *Parachute* provides a more elaborate discussion than the questions raised by this chapter. If you want to explore further, complete the activities presented in Bolles's "Flower Exercise: A Picture of the Job of Your Dreams." You may also find his website helpful (see below).

You Majored in What?: Mapping Your Path from Chaos to Career by Katharine Brooks (Viking Adult, 2009). Mentioned in chapter 12 as a compass for finding careers through academic programs, this book can also help you deal with the chaos you face in thinking about careers.

WEBSITES

www.CareerBuilder.com and **www.Monster.com** These are job-search engines that also provide advice and career tests for those seeking to better define their career goals. They include resources for both beginning job-seekers and professionals contemplating a change in fields.

www.JobHuntersBible.com This is the website of Richard N. Bolles, author of *What Color Is Your Parachute?* (see above).

www.leadershipdirectories.com The Leadership Library website is a commercial database to which your college library probably subscribes. The site provides job titles and individuals in those jobs for corporate, nonprofit, and government organizations. It can help you see what kinds of jobs are out there and also find people you hope to add to your network.

www.onenetcenter.org The Occupational Information Network (O*NET) can help you narrow down career fields and discover what is necessary to succeed in them. According to the O*NET website, "The O*NET program is the nation's primary source of occupational information. Central to the project is the O*NET database, containing information on hundreds of standardized and occupation-specific descriptors. The database, which is available to the public at no cost, is continually updated by surveying a broad range of workers from each occupation." Information from this database forms the heart of O*NET OnLine, an interactive application for exploring and searching occupations. The database also provides the basis for a Career Field Scanning Questionnaire, an instrument for workers and students looking to find or change careers. O*NET is being developed under the sponsorship of the U.S. Department of Labor/Employment and Training Administration (USDOL/ETA) through a grant to the North Carolina Employment Security Commission.

www.naceweb.org This website of NACE, the National Association of Colleges and Employers, is partially open to nonmembers and helps you understand how the career services program at your school can help you.

"ONE HOUR SPENT PLANNING IS WORTH FOUR HOURS OF EXECUTION."

—CRAWFORD GREENWALT, PRESIDENT OF THE DUPONT COMPANY

CHAPTER 18

PLANNING YOUR SKILLS AGENDA

ASSESS YOUR SKILLS • MONITOR AND PLAN YOUR SKILL IMPROVEMENT

Think about how you would go about achieving any personal goal whether it is losing weight, running faster, or improving your grades. They all require practice. The same holds true for improving the skills you need for a successful career. College is a good place to practice your skills both inside and outside the classroom. In fact, the term "gymnasium" was first used in ancient Greece to mean a place for physical *and* intellectual education. Undergraduates should see college as a sort of "skills gym"—a complex and multifaceted place to develop skills through continuous practice.

This chapter will help you create your own plan to improve your skills during your undergraduate years. The purpose of any plan is to achieve your goals, whether it is a football game plan, a business plan, or, in this case, a plan to develop the skills you need to succeed in the workplace. A plan is never set in stone; you need to make adjustments to it if your opposition throws up an unexpected defense. In the career game, your "opposition" can be other job applicants you compete against, the changing labor environment, or new technologies.

The appendix provides three tools to help you plan your college years so you can increase your Skills Score:

1. Assessing where you are now on each skill (Initial Skills Self-Assessment Form, page 274)

2. Monitoring your progress through your Skills Score (Semi-Annual Skills Self-Assessment Form, page 277)

3. Developing a plan for what you need to do to achieve your goal (Four-Year Calendar, page 266)

The first and most crucial step in improving your skills is to assess your current level of performance. If you don't know where you are, you can't possibly figure out where you are headed, let alone when you get there. Ask yourself how you are doing on each of the ten Skill Sets. Self-assessment can be informed by the views of others or, in a few cases, by an objective test.

Unfortunately, most skills can only be assessed in the context of a specific activity and by the outcomes of what you do. Your skill at selling might be assessed by how many items you sell if you are in retail sales or how much money you raise working for your college's alumni fund-raising operation. The grades you get on a paper or a test give you some evidence of your skill in writing, for example, but teacher assessments rarely are real-world tests of your skills. For most skills, the best way is to assess yourself and provide what evidence you can find to support your assessment.

For that reason, with the help of many college students I have developed an Initial Skills Self-Assessment Form that you should use in determining your own performance on the ten Skill Sets. The form generates an Initial Skills Score that ranges between 1 and 4 (just like a GPA) and can be used as a guide to your own self-improvement. Blank forms are available in the appendix and on billcoplin.org.

When completed, you will have an assessment similar to the one that appears below.

To illustrate how this form might be filled out, I've included a form that Marybeth, a student of mine, filled out the summer before she entered her freshman year of college.

SAMPLE SKILLS SELF-ASSESSMENT FORM

SKILL SET	SKILL	RATING	EVIDENCE
Taking Responsibility	Motivate Yourself	4	At the beginning of the school year, I committed myself to making the varsity lacrosse team. I practiced for at least half an hour every day, and I attended all of the captain's practices and scrimmages. During this time I held at least a B+ average in all of my classes. I did have to sacrifice my job and my commitments to other clubs and friends.
	Be Ethical	3	I've never cheated on an exam or a test, but I have let friends study my homework. I have also seen cheating occur and I didn't alert my instructors.
	Manage Your Time	2	I always hand in my assignments on time, but I am often up late working on papers, or working on them the morning that they are due.
	Manage Your Money	1	I don't have a checkbook, and I rarely look at bank statements or my savings account. Most of the money I earn at my part-time job becomes spending money for food and gas.
Developing Physical Skills	Stay Well	2	I missed three classes due to illness, but besides that I have never overslept, been late to school, or missed class. I take gym class and play sports to stay physically fit.
	Look Good	3	I dress appropriately for interviews with college representatives. My coach also makes me dress up on game days. I do wear sweatpants and T-shirts to class, which makes me look as if I don't think class is important.
	Type Well	2	I can type efficiently enough to write papers well, but I cannot type 35 words per minute without making errors. I often look at my hands while I type and later have to correct typing errors.
	Write Legibly	3	I come prepared with a pen and paper to every class. However, sometimes my notes are disorganized or hard to read.

SKILL SET	SKILL	RATING	EVIDENCE
Communicating Verbally	Converse One-on-One	2	I ask questions in class when I don't understand something, and I listen to my teacher's responses. I have miscommunications with my friends, parents, and teachers when trying to explain myself. I tend to be quiet with people who are not my closest friends.
	Present to Groups	2	I make presentations that receive good grades, but my teacher has told me I need to work on my tone of voice and that I should avoid sticking to a scripted, memorized speech. I also practice giving speeches while speaking in front of a small committee at Model United Nations meetings.
	Use Visual Displays	3	I helped develop and present two PowerPoint presentations in my global history class. I also created a PowerPoint presentation for my statistics class where I used graphs and charts to present data.
Communicating in Writing	Write Well	2	I received A's on my persuasive and argumentative essays, but these writing assignments were narrow and not the type of writing I would do in some professional settings.
	Edit and Proof	3	I write one or two rough drafts for most of my papers, and I review them for grammatical errors, but my teachers still find grammatical errors in some of my final papers.
	Use Word-Processing Tools	3	I draft essays and resumes using Word, but I don't use all of the functions offered by the program often enough to be considered proficient.
	Master Online Communications	3	I use my school's email account to send information and attachments to my teachers and peers. I don't store my information online, but parts of my class documents are stored online.
Working Directly with People	Build Good Relationships	3	I maintain good relations with most people I talk to, but I could make more of an effort to build stronger relationships with my teachers.
	Work in Teams	3	While participating in Model United Nations, I worked with a group of students from my school to create a position paper representing our country. I pulled my own weight while writing this paper, and I held the other members of my group accountable. I also work in my church youth group to organize events.
	Teach Others	3	I've worked as a coach, teaching soccer and lacrosse skills to young girls. I also tutor my neighbor in math once a week.

SKILL SET	SKILL	RATING	EVIDENCE
Influencing People	Manage Effectively	3	As captain of my soccer team, I help manage my twenty-four teammates, but I've never had to manage anyone in a work setting.
	Sell Successfully	3	Each year I go door to door asking neighbors to donate money for my high school's fund-raiser for Camp Good Days and Special Times, but I need to pursue more opportunities to practice this skill.
	Politick Wisely	3	I am a member of my student government, and we have to make decisions regarding budgets and event planning. I can always seek more opportunities to do this.
	Lead Effectively	3	I am a captain of my soccer team, and I take on leadership positions in group projects, but I have never pursued a leadership position at work.
Gathering Information	Search the Web	2	I know how to use multiple search engines. I have located the contact information of government officials and found government data when I participated in Model UN. I cannot locate internships or jobs on the Internet effectively.
	Use Library Holdings	4	I use my school library's online card catalog as well as the online databases to do research for some of my papers.
	Use Commercial Databases	3	I've used many of the databases my school library offers, including ProQuest, FirstSearch, LexisNexis, and online subscriptions, but I am not proficient in all of these.
	Conduct Interviews	1	I have spoken to college representatives and my school counselor about which colleges would be best for me, but I need to practice this skill more often. I should work on conducting more informative and effective interviews.
	Use Surveys	1	I've produced some basic surveys in math and psychology classes. I've also taken similar surveys, but I need to practice being more critical of survey results and survey design.
	Keep and Use Records	2	I have kept a log of my hours while working a babysitting job. I also practice using a time-management sheet in my home economics course, but I don't keep records of my daily activities.

SKILL SET	SKILL	RATING	EVIDENCE
Using Quantitative Tools	Use Numbers	2	I know general calculus functions and calculate percentages in my head, but I haven't had many opportunities to look at budgets and crunch numbers.
	Use Graphs and Tables	2	I create and analyze graphs and charts in math and science classes. I should work on using graphs, tables, and charts to identify problems.
	Use Spreadsheet Programs	2	I have entered data into Excel and made graphs from data in science class. I am not proficient in this program.
Asking and Answering the Right Questions	Detect Nonsense	3	I can detect when my peers are giving me nonsense excuses, especially when they try to get out of an activity they committed to, like a meeting for a group project. I read critically whenever I have reading to do in class, but I could always work on this skill and acquire more knowledge in order to get better at it.
	Pay Attention to Detail	3	I often read and reread texts, in and outside of class, in order to understand the true meanings, the hidden meanings, and the motives of each text. I can always work to improve this skill.
	Apply Knowledge	3	I take science classes and I understand the scientific method. I apply hypothesis testing to psychological experiments. I also read the newspaper every morning to stay up-to-date on topics covered in my global history and American history classes. I should work harder to apply the things I learn in school to things I do outside of the classroom.
	Evaluate Actions and Policies	2	As a member of a high school sports team, I set personal goals at the beginning of the season. At each practice, we constantly evaluate our progress toward these goals. We also make changes to the way we play and practice in order to fix problems. I didn't, however, apply this practice to school, work, or my other activities.

SKILL SET	SKILL	RATING	EVIDENCE
Solving Problems	Identify Problems	3	In my church youth group, I help organize events. Here I identify potential problems in order to avoid them. I need to pursue more opportunities to identify problems, and I need to work on identifying problems sooner.
	Develop Solutions	2	In Model UN, we work to come up with solutions to the problem of emissions of greenhouse gases and pollution. These solutions included making recommendations to the Kyoto Protocol and convincing more nations to sign the treaty. Besides this example, I haven't had much experience with this.
	Launch Solutions	2	As class secretary, I help launch solutions, including the solutions we came up with to create a successful prom on a slim budget. Again, I need more opportunities to develop solutions and then put them into action.

To determine your Skills Score, total your ratings and divide by 38
Marybeth's overall score: 99/38 = **2.6**

Filling out the assessment as described above is a lot of work, if you take it seriously. However, doing so tests your self-motivation, and the potential payoffs are enormous. By thinking about what you do well and what you need to improve, you can both plan how to improve all your skills and also monitor your improvement over time. Thousands of students have used this simple procedure to make decisions about courses, internships, jobs, and careers.

You may think a 2.6 is not very good, but for a high school senior it is outstanding. I have met very few freshmen who I would rate as highly as Marybeth rated herself. I think she did a realistic job, because she is serious about using college to develop the skills she needs for a successful career. She is now a junior and has been working hard to develop the skills employers want. When she graduates, she will probably have a score above 3.5. It is important to realize that no one can be perfect on all skills in the ten Skill Sets, and on any given day, you may perform worse that you usually do. However, you should practice the skills and reflect on your performance all of the time.

The following table will help you think about how you would rate yourself on all of the skills in the ten Skill Sets. The table lists activities that may indicate a high score.

TIPS FOR COMPLETING THE SKILLS
SELF-ASSESSMENT FORM

SKILL SET	SKILL	BEST PRACTICES FOR DEVELOPING HIGH SKILL LEVELS
Taking Responsibility	Motivate Yourself	• Maintain a high GPA • Document goals or priorities • Record a goal I set and then met • Keep commitments (for example, I hand papers in on time)
	Be Ethical	• Keep promises made to friends • Avoid cheating and lying
	Manage Your Time	• Use a planner to plan and set priorities • Plan and follow a schedule that allows for the completion of tasks and assignments • Be able to meet multiple and coinciding deadlines
	Manage Your Money	• Keep expenses in line with income (for example, list how much money I make and spend each month) • Keep checkbook balanced • Pay bills on time • Consider costs and benefits before making a purchase
Developing Physical Skills	Stay Well	• Maintain a good diet • Exercise routinely • Sleep adequate number of hours each night • Limit number of absences due to illness
	Look Good	• Dress appropriately for an interview, a presentation, or a formal occasion • Maintain appearance in an effort to make a good impression for different occasions
	Type Well	• Achieve 35 wpm or more on a typing test
	Write Legibly	• Maintain legible notes for studying • Write legibly so other students can use my notes to study or copy when they've been absent • Bring a pen and paper to classes and meetings
Communicating Verbally	Converse One-on-One	• Answer questions clearly • Explain something to another person clearly • Ask a question and receive a clear answer
	Present to Groups	• Present successfully to class for grade (indicate grade or teacher's assessment) • Volunteer to give a speech in class • Speak publicly
	Use Visual Displays	• Use PowerPoint during presentations • Create a map or an outline • Create a flyer or handout to make a point

SKILL SET	SKILL	BEST PRACTICES FOR DEVELOPING HIGH SKILL LEVELS
Communicating in Writing	Write Well	• Write memos, resumes, proposals, agendas, persuasive essays, argumentative essays, or other materials
	Edit and Proof	• Look over papers for grammatical and spelling errors before handing them in • Write and revise multiple drafts for papers • Edit other students' papers • Do not lose points on a written assignment for poor organization/grammar/spelling/word choice
	Use Word-Processing Tools	• Create a professional-looking resume or memo • Use specific functions like Spell-Check and Grammar-Check, Cut, Copy and Paste, Tracking, and others
	Master Online Communica-tions	• Use email, Facebook, or Twitter to communicate • Use web storage for papers and resumes
Working Directly with People	Build Good Relation-ships	• Talk to someone to resolve a conflict • Build a relationship with a teacher, boss, coworker, teammate, or peer despite differences
	Work in Teams	• Work on group project(s) • Play on a sports team • Work with a group in an extracurricular activity • Work with others in a job setting
	Teach Others	• Explain something to someone else • Work as a mentor and/or coach • Act as a role model or example for others
Influencing People	Manage Effectively	• Assign jobs and/or deadlines to others (for example, for a group project or at a job or on a team) • Act as a third party to resolve a conflict
	Sell Successfully	• Raise funds successfully for a cause • Convince someone to agree with my way of thinking
	Politick Wisely	• Propose action to a group or someone in power • Win an elected position in some student group • Speak to several players on both sides of an issue
	Lead Effectively	• Motivate others to accomplish a goal • Hold minor or major leadership positions at work, on a sports team, or in an organization or team project
Gathering Information	Search the Web	• Use the Web to locate newspaper articles • Understand that opinionated blogs and many other websites are not credible or reliable sources • Use various search engines • Locate a job or an internship online

continued

SKILL SET	SKILL	BEST PRACTICES FOR DEVELOPING HIGH SKILL LEVELS
Gathering Information, continued	Use Library Holdings	• Use an online database to find research material in the library
	Use Commercial Databases	• Use commercial databases to gather research, including LexisNexis or ProQuest Direct
	Conduct Interviews	• Interview an adult • Ask another person about himself or herself • Speak with a professional about the path he or she took to get into a career and beyond
	Use Surveys	• Create a survey • Analyze survey results • Take a class that uses survey data • Read about surveys and question their design
	Keep and Use Records	• Keep a list of accomplishments, courses, and credits taken • Keep a list of people who you might want in your network • Keep track of expenditures and income through filing system or computer database • Document hours for a job or community service
Using Quantitative Tools	Use Numbers	• Use percentages • Calculate a tip without a calculator
	Use Graphs and Tables	• Create or analyze a graph or table • Explain a graph or table to others
	Use Spreadsheet Programs	• Use Microsoft Excel for personal information • Use a table for science class • Use a data table for a job
Asking and Answering the Right Questions	Detect Nonsense	• Ask questions to uncover the truth • Question the facts of a document or the source of information
	Pay Attention to Detail	• Create proper citations in papers • Write accurate research papers with references • Follow directions closely and specifically
	Apply Knowledge	• Recognize errors in someone's thinking because I have knowledge of the subject • Apply knowledge from the classroom in the real world • Apply experience in the real world to the classroom
	Evaluate Actions and Policies	• Set clear goals • Determine whether goals are met or not • Reach a goal • Determine a certain policy was effective or ineffective

SKILL SET	SKILL	BEST PRACTICES FOR DEVELOPING HIGH SKILL LEVELS
Solving Problems	Identify Problems	• Verify that specific problems exist using reputable evidence from reliable resources • Measure a problem
	Develop Solutions	• Provide logical and creative ways to solve problems • Conduct research to ensure the solution being developed is the best solution • Use benefits and costs to evaluate a solution's quality
	Launch Solutions	• Implement a plan created by a club or during a class project • Look at possible solutions to a problem and decide which solution should be implemented • Take action to get your ideas accepted

MONITOR AND PLAN YOUR SKILL IMPROVEMENT

The main advantage of completing the Initial Skills Self-Assessment Form is that you can look at it every month or so to see where you practiced and improved your skills. Skills are not something you learn once and have, but something you improve through practice and self-assessment. In addition, the appendix has a Semiannual Skills Self-Assessment Form that you update every six months, so by regularly monitoring your skill level you can track your improvement over the four years of college.

In addition to monitoring your skills monthly, plan to undertake activities that will give you practice in the skills you need to improve or that are crucial to a career path you are considering. Write weekly or biweekly plans on selected skills that guide you. For example, if you are not good at editing and proofing and you have a paper due in two weeks, finish it early so that you can spend more time than you usually do in editing and proofing a hard copy.

In addition to short-term planning, undertake long-term planning that includes each semester and the summers you are in college. The following table, Model Skills Curriculum, will help you build your skills strategy. The model is provided for a two-semester system, but you should be able to apply it to colleges that use a quarter or tri-mester system. Please note that a course requiring twenty pages of papers refers to turned-in assignments and does not mean in-class exams that add up to twenty pages. It can be one big paper, two ten-page papers, or four five-page papers. And remember, the model is for the general skills and does not include specialized skills that you might need for a specific field.

MODEL SKILLS CURRICLUM

YEAR	SEMESTER	COURSES	NON-COURSE ACTIVITIES
FRESHMAN	Fall	One course requiring at least 20 pages of papers.	Residence hall governance; campus job or sport activity.
	Spring	One course requiring at least 20 pages of papers; one course requiring applied statistics.	Volunteer position as campus tour guide; 20 hours offcampus community service.
	Summer	Take a skills-based course, like web design or intro-duction to legal research, at your local community college that you can't get at your school, or com-plete some core require-ment course for your degree.	Office or retail job, unless you can find something more directly related to careers you wish to explore.
SOPHOMORE	Fall	One course requiring at least 20 pages of papers.	Resident adviser or leader-ship position in a student organization and 20 hours of community service; job in a university office.
	Spring	One course requiring at least 20 pages of papers; one course requiring a team project; one course requiring oral presentation.	Resident adviser or leader-ship position in a student organization and 20 hours of community service; job in a university office.
	Summer		Job or internship to develop sales, computer, statistical, or writing skills.

YEAR	SEMESTER	COURSES	NON-COURSE ACTIVITIES
JUNIOR	Fall	One course requiring at least 20 pages of papers; one course requiring a team project; one course requiring applied statistics.	Leadership position in a student organization; management job position on or off campus.
	Spring	Off-campus semester.	Travel; immersion in another culture; community service.
	Summer		Competitive internship at a business, government, or nonprofit agency.
SENIOR	Fall	One course requiring at least 20 pages of papers; one course requiring a team project; one course requiring at least 20 percent fieldwork.	40 hours on job search or 20 hours on job search and 20 hours on graduate school search and test preparation.
	Spring	One course requiring at least 20 pages of papers; one course requiring an oral presentation.	Relaxation, nail down the job, avoid senioritis.

This Model Skills Curriculum will help you move your Skills Score close to 4.0. Note that the number of credit hours listed is half of the average 120 needed to graduate. The other 60 credit hours can be used to develop your other interests, to pick up more career-specific knowledge and skills, or to complete requirements that do not do much for a high Skills Score. It is always a good idea to pick up areas of knowledge and skills outside of the ten Skill Sets, just as chapter 11 suggests. It will certainly make you less boring, and it may even help you in your career.

This book's appendix has key dates that serve as deadlines for when you should undertake actions throughout your entire four years as an undergraduate. The Model Skills Curriculum (above) can help you think about ways to meet the goals and complete the activities suggested in the planner.

USEFUL RESOURCES

BOOK

The Career Adventure: Your Guide to Personal Assessment, Career Exploration, and Decision Making by Susan Johnston (Prentice Hall, 2005). This book provides concrete tools to assess your skills, including exercises and case studies.

"CAREERS TODAY REQUIRE BRAND MANAGEMENT. WHAT DO PEOPLE THINK OF ME?"

—A SLIDE PRESENTED TO EMPLOYEES AT ONE OF THE WORLD'S LARGEST CORPORATIONS

CHAPTER 19

BRANDING YOURSELF THROUGH RESUMES, COVER LETTERS, AND INTERVIEWS

SELECT THE SKILLS YOU WANT TO EMPHASIZE • DECIDE WHERE TO SHOW OFF YOUR SKILLS

Employers want to know what you can do for their organization. They need to be convinced that you will deliver the services they want. To that end, you need to market yourself as a responsible, trustworthy, and skillful employee—and the best way to do that is to create an image or "brand" of yourself that appeals to potential employers.

A "brand," at least for our purposes, refers to the qualities, skills, and attitudes that we attribute to a product or a person. For any given position, an employer may review hundreds of resumes, and spend less than a minute on each. This time pressure makes "branding" the key to a successful, stand-out resume. "Brands" can communicate a lot in just a second. The way you build your brand is by communicating consistent and relevant information in your resume, cover letter, and interview. There are other ways to build and communicate your brand, most notably by using social media (which will be discussed in the next chapter); however, these modern tools are not as important as the "big three"—resume, cover letter, and interview. Several websites and services that will get you thinking about your own personal "branding" are listed in the Useful Resources section of this chapter.

This chapter discusses the resume first and the cover letter second, even though both may arrive at the employer simultaneously. This is because resumes are usually the first screening device for employers—especially for entry-level or internship positions. With the use of electronic delivery and online social networks like LinkedIn, the resume may arrive first with no cover letter.

When developing your "brand," focus on creating a message that is not only easy to remember but also rings true. For years, Toyota branded itself as the most reliable car. After a series of highly publicized incidents leading to recalls, the reliability picture became less valid. Predictably, Toyota car sales declined. So branding yourself is not just about presenting a clear and consistent image; it is also about being true to your brand. Don't prepare a cover letter that tells the employer you are a detailed-oriented person and forget to put a date on it.

This chapter discusses how you can develop your resumes, cover letters, and interviews to highlight your strongest skills in the ten Skill Sets. It does *not* discuss how to communicate other specialized skills like graphic design, previous experience within the field, detailed knowledge of the field, or outside interests. Although skills and attributes beyond the ten Skill Sets are important, they are too diverse to discuss in this chapter. This chapter is not a comprehensive primer on writing resumes and cover letters and performing well in interviews. Several outstanding books and websites are available that will help you do that. In addition, your college career services office will review and suggest revisions for your resume and cover letter, and provide practice interviewing.

Although you may be tempted to put off thinking about your resumes, cover letters, and interviews until you approach the end of your college career, build your brand starting today. If you construct a picture of how you want future employers to see you when you graduate college, you will have a much better idea of what you are trying to do with your college education. Visualizing where you want to be on your skill development will help you get there more effectively. Hypothesizing about your own personal brand is a great way to figure out how to get there. Sure, the end product will change between now and when you finish college—it should!—but your end product will be much better if you begin to work on it long before your senior year.

Don't delay considering how to brand yourself another day. Create a resume as soon as possible. If you take my advice on getting internships as soon as possible (see chapter 13, Creating Your Own Apprenticeships), you will realize that you need a resume ready to go as soon as you hear of an opportunity. Don't miss out on a job or an internship opportunity because you don't have a solid resume ready to send out as soon as you see a job opportunity.

SELECT THE SKILLS YOU WANT TO EMPHASIZE

Let's return to cars in thinking about branding. Car makers may want to brand their cars as reliable, a good value for the money, and comfortable—but they also know that buyers are looking for a minimum level of competence in acceleration, interior design, and safety. They choose to emphasize what they "brand," but they also make sure they have satisfied through their advertising and design all of the other minimum expectations customers have.

Think of the ten Skill Sets as the "minimum level of competence" employers expect you to have. Your resume and interview should somehow provide evidence that you can perform all or nearly all of the skills in the ten Skill Sets.

When you choose to brand yourself, focus on skills that you are more than just "competent" in. You never want to brand yourself as an "average" writer. If you cannot brand yourself as an *excellent* writer, then writing skills should not have a prominent place in your resume, cover letter, or interview. Emphasize some other skill that you are stronger in.

Select no more than five of the ten Skill Sets (or specific skills) to emphasize in your resume, cover letter, and interview. Without a doubt, the entire first skill set, "taking responsibility," should be part of your brand. If it's not, you need to rethink who you are. No employer wants to hire someone who can't motivate his- or herself, be ethical, manage time, or manage money. Many employers are concerned with the work ethic of today's college graduates, and they will always be on the lookout for slackers. Brand yourself as someone employers can depend on.

Beyond the Skill Set of "taking responsibility," you can choose from any of the remaining Skill Sets. Your choices must be based first on what you are good at, and second on what you like to do. Just because you don't *like* sitting at a computer and creating spreadsheets, don't be too quick to dismiss the skill if you are really good at it. Remember, your first job is a stepping-stone to a career.

In choosing how you want to brand yourself, ask the question "Can I provide concrete evidence that I have a high level of competence in the skill?" Talking about how wonderful you are without giving concrete examples weakens your credibility.

When I interview students for the position of undergraduate teaching assistant for my freshman course, I ask the interviewee, "Would you be a good teaching assistant (TA)?" The response is usually, "Yes, because I know the material," or "Yes, because I am good at teaching," or "Yes, because I am a leader." I then say, "Don't give me your opinion of yourself. What evidence can you give me?" This frequently throws the candidate off balance. But what I am looking for is concrete evidence, such as "I have a 95 average in the class, which demonstrates my mastery of the material," or "I taught Sunday school and was considered good enough to be invited back every year until I went to college," or "I was president of my class in high school, which demonstrates the leadership needed for the TA position." So, when branding yourself, find convincing evidence to demonstrate skills in which you excel. You should choose skills that allow you to discuss your accomplishments, especially during interviews.

In chapter 18, I suggested that you do what Marybeth did: Evaluate your skills using the tools in the appendix, and monitor your improvement over time. If you have completed this self-assessment, you will be aware of where your strengths are. "Emphasize your strengths" may seem to be a simple piece of advice, but unfortunately it is not the only principle to follow in preparing a resume, cover letter, or interview. An equally important principle is, "Emphasize the skills that best fit the needs of employers." Employers whose highest priority is "manage effectively" will want you to be an adequate writer but not a great writer. In fact, branding yourself as a great writer could cost you the job.

What if your best skills do not fit the needs of the employer? You may be tempted to fake it in your resume, cover letter, and interview. Faking it (or overselling your skills) carries the risk of being discovered and not receiving the job. Worse yet, you could get the job and then be penalized for misrepresenting your skills. If you know the employer wants strong number-crunching skills and yours are mediocre, don't brand yourself as "good with numbers." You may not lose your job immediately, but you will lose credibility with your employer that could damage your chances of long-term success.

When weighing the needs of the employer and your own strengths, you may decide that you are relatively good—not great—at the required skills. The best policy is to be honest: suggest to the employer that you are strong in those skills, but might need some help developing them further.

DECIDE WHERE TO SHOW OFF YOUR SKILLS

Taken together, your resumes, cover letters, and interviews should accomplish two tasks: they should (1) demonstrate that you are competent in most of the ten Skill Sets, and (2) show that you are spectacular in the three to five skills or Skill Sets most relevant to the job or internship position you are seeking. This section will provide guidance on which of the three tools are most suited for each of the skills.

You can't fit all the information about all your skills into a cover letter and a resume. Save much of the information for your interview, and even then, you will not be able to get it all in. The resume and cover letter are like the headline and opening paragraph of a newspaper article. Just as a newspaper headline's job is to get you to read the rest of the story, your goal is to get to the interview stage, where you can provide information on the Skill Sets not easily mentioned in the resume and cover letter. Your interview will also give you a chance to provide added depth to those skills that you mention in your resume and cover letter.

The following table provides general guidelines for Skill Sets that should be placed in your resume and cover letter and those that you will have to cover in your interview. Some are mentioned in more than one place.

SKILLS TO SHOW OFF IN A RESUME AND COVER LETTER

CHAPTER 1   Motivate Yourself, Manage Your Time (both indicated by high GPA and quantity of activities), Manage Your Money (indicate on your resume whether you pay for your college education)

CHAPTER 2   Type Well (indicated by zero typos and grammar mistakes)

CHAPTER 3   Use Visual Displays (create a visually appealing resume)

CHAPTER 4   Write Well (list internship or job in which you wrote a lot), Edit and Proof (make sure there are no mistakes in your resume), Use Word-Processing Tools (list on resume)

CHAPTER 5   Build Good Relationships, Work in Teams, Teach Others (list positions as teaching assistant or substitute teacher in a high school)

CHAPTER 6   Manage Effectively (list job or internship where you were responsible for people, such as a resident advisor position), Sell Successfully (list sales job), Lead Effectively (give an example of leadership skills in action)

CHAPTER 7   Use Commercial Databases (list specific ones in which you are proficient), Conduct Interviews, Use Surveys, Keep and Use Records (list projects that used one or more of these skills)

CHAPTER 8   Use Numbers (provide specific numbers for experiences on resume), Use Spreadsheet Programs (list Excel, SPSS, and other programs you have worked with in a project)

CHAPTER 9   Pay Attention to Detail (make sure there are no mistakes on your resume)

CHAPTER 10   Identify Problems, Develop Solutions, Launch Solutions (list specific examples from your extracurricular activites)

SKILLS TO SHOW OFF IN A RESUME

To better illustrate how to demonstrate your proficiency in the ten Skill Sets on a resume, I have listed some sample content that Marybeth could use in her resume. You can compare it to her Skills Self-Assessment Form in chapter 17 (see page 227).

EXCERPTS FROM MARYBETH'S RESUME

WORK AND LEADERSHIP EXPERIENCE

Intern, Home HeadQuarters, Inc.

- Coded and compiled data from customer satisfaction surveys *(Chapter 7, Gathering Information)*
- Analyzed survey results. Analysis used to write grant proposals *(Chapter 8, Using Quantitative Tools; Chapter 9, Asking and Answering the Right Questions)*
- Drafted reports on client satisfaction *(Chapter 4, Communicating in Writing)*
- Facilitated instruction of financial literacy classes for English as a Second Language Students *(Chapter 6, Influencing People)*

Manager/Managing Editor, 3CSkills Collaborative, Syracuse University

- Designed high school curriculum materials *(Chapter 10, Solving Problems)*
- Managed twelve students *(Chapter 6, Influencing People)*
- Oversaw the drafting, revising, and editing of materials *(Chapter 4, Communicating in Writing)*

Undergraduate Teaching Assistant, An Introduction to the Analysis of Public Policy, Syracuse University

- Advised eight students learning to analyze public policies *(Chapter 3, Communicating Verbally; Chapter 6, Influencing People)*
- Graded thirty papers on education policies *(Chapter 4, Communicating in Writing; Chapter 9, Asking and Answering the Right Questions)*
- Trained seventeen teaching assistants to grade worksheets *(Chapter 1, Taking Responsibility; Chapter 6, Influencing People)*

SKILLS

- Proficient in the Microsoft Office Suite and PASW Statistical Analysis *(Chapter 4, Communicating in Writing; Chapter 8, Using Quantitative Tools)*
- Experience with ArcGIS Mapping System *(Chapter 8, Using Quantitative Tools)*

EDUCATION

Syracuse University, Syracuse, NY

- Maxwell School of Public Affairs, College of Arts and Sciences
- Policy Studies Major; GPA: 3.77 *(Chapter 1, Taking Responsibility)*
- Three-time Dean's List Honoree

SERVICE

Youth Service Opportunities Project, Washington, DC

- Worked directly with homeless population for one week in March 2010 *(Chapter 10, Solving Problems)*
- Raised money for homeless population selling newspapers written by homeless people *(Chapter 6, Influencing People)*
- Prepared and hosted dinner for homeless population at a shelter *(Chapter 10, Solving Problems)*

Say Yes to Education, Syracuse, NY

- Tutored fourth graders in writing during an after-school program *(Chapter 6, Influencing People)*
- Supervised first graders in an after-school program *(Chapter 6, Influencing People)*

ACTIVITIES

Syracuse University Club Soccer

- Organized practices and tryouts for fifty teamates *(Chapter 6, Influencing People)*
- Three-year starter *(Chapter 1, Taking Responsibility)*

Marybeth's resume is impressive but not something that is "out of this world." Most college graduates who are serious about developing the skills employers want could have this content in their resume. She didn't build a clinic in Africa or raise $100,000 for a charity or win a prestigious graduate scholarship. Her GPA is high, but what will impress employers most are her experiences and the concrete evidence of her success. The resume brands her as outstanding in "taking responsibility," "influencing people," "communicating in writing," and "gathering information." Employers can't help but see a cluster of skills that would make her a great hire for a variety of jobs.

SKILLS TO SHOW OFF IN A COVER LETTER

A cover letter allows you to elaborate in complete sentences on the skills you want to highlight. The two major rules are that your cover letter has to be short and that it must give concrete examples, not superlatives. The cover letter below was written by Marybeth in an application for a job with a consulting company that provides services to government and nonprofit agencies. I've noted the relevant skills or Skill Sets in parentheses within the body of the letter.

Dear Ms. Robinson,

I would like to be considered for the research assistant position posted by your company. I admire your company's mission in providing consulting services to government and nonprofit agencies and see myself pursuing a career in applied research to help improve government programs and policies. [Skill: Build Good Relationships (chapter 5)]

Five months ago I began working at a local nonprofit organization, Home HeadQuarters, Inc., which provides programs to improve neighborhoods in the city of Syracuse. I helped collect data, entered it into a spreadsheet, and prepared an initial draft of several reports. [Skill Set: Using Quantitative Tools (chapter 8)] I started as an unpaid intern and was put on the payroll after the first month. [Skill Sets: Taking Responsibility (chapter 1), Using Quantitative Tools (chapter 8), Asking and Answering the Right Questions (chapter 9), and Solving Problems (chapter 10)]

As a rising senior in the Public Policy Program at the Maxwell School, my course work includes creating surveys and analyzing results. In my Methods of Policy Analysis and Presentation course, I analyzed a customer satisfaction survey for Home HeadQuarters, Inc., using Microsoft Excel. I wrote a fifty-page research report for the same organization presenting my analysis. In my Statistics for the Social Sciences course, I analyzed data from the General Social Survey using Microsoft Excel and PASW Statistics. In this course and my Introduction to Statistics course, I created presentations in PowerPoint. These presentations required me to display significant relationships between two or more variables. [Skill: Use Suveys (chapter 7)]

As a teaching assistant for an upper-division policy studies course, I had to clearly communicate information and instructions to ten students. [Skill: Converse One-on-One (chapter 3), Skill Set: Working Directly with People (chapter 5)] I was a managing editor for the same course. I edited the work of ten students for both content and grammar before the final products were submitted. This gave me experience with Microsoft Word and written communication. [Skills: Write Well and Edit and Proof (chapter 4)]

I have experience working in community-based organizations. I volunteered with the Say Yes to Education program, where I led after-school programs for first and fourth graders in the city of Syracuse. I also spent a week with the Youth Service Opportunities Project in Washington, D.C., where I worked directly with the homeless community. [Skills: Motivate Yourself, Be Ethical, and Manage Your Time (chapter 1)] I am a responsible student who has taken on leadership roles as a teaching assistant and a managing editor. [Skills: Manage Effectively and Lead Effectively (chapter 6)]

Attached is a copy of my current Syracuse University transcript. I look forward to the opportunity to discuss this position with you. For any additional information, please email me. Thank you for your time and consideration.

Along with her resume, this cover letter reinforces Marybeth's brand as a hard worker, a good writer, solid at using quantitative skills, and a people person. It is rare to find such a combination in the workforce. No wonder supervisors at the nonprofit she started working with decided to put her on the payroll one month later.

SKILLS TO SHOW OFF IN AN INTERVIEW

You have much more "space" in interviews to elaborate on your strengths. Make sure the skills you emphasize in the interview build logically upon what you wrote in your resume and cover letter. Be sure to back up your skills with concrete examples. Before going into your interview, review your cover letter and resume. The interviewer will likely use those documents to generate questions for you, so you need to remember what you wrote.

EXAMPLES OF HOW TO PRESENT THE TEN SKILL SETS IN AN INTERVIEW

TAKING RESPONSIBILITY	Arrive on time
	Be responsive to the interviewer's questions
	Say things that are consistent with your resume and cover letter
DEVELOPING PHYSICAL SKILLS	Dress appropriately
	Send a handwritten follow-up note
COMMUNICATING VERBALLY	Listen to your interviewer and answer appropriately
	Provide a convincing example of how you present to groups
GATHERING INFORMATION	Discuss a project where you collected data or conducted interviews

In deciding which experiences to cover in your resumes, cover letters, and interviews, use the ten Skill Sets as a guideline. Cite experiences both in and outside the classroom that provide concrete evidence that you have used and excelled at specific skills.

Your non-course activities are more important than your course work for landing a good job. You will notice that mentioning majors and course work is not emphasized. Presenting your experiences outside of the classroom is. This is not because the course work is unimportant. Rather, it is because employers want to see that you applied what you learned in class to what you can do. Technical majors like accounting or journalism in professional schools, or the physical sciences in liberal arts, can be critical, but for the majority of fields and jobs the degree and the courses are not as important as demonstrating the ten Skill Sets.

Usually, jobs requiring technical majors clearly indicate that in the advertisements. For the majority of jobs, employers require you to have mastered the skills that are part of the Skill Sets. If you use a lot of space in your resume, cover letter, or interview to describe your major, you will reduce your chances of success, unless you talk about outside experiences required by the major. In your interview, however, you may be able to talk about how some great courses and your major specifically prepared you for this job.

Having warned you about overemphasizing your academic program, I do not mean to suggest you cannot introduce some information. However, be strategic about it. For example, you could talk about taking a speech course because you know how important it is to speak to groups effectively, or you could discuss a conflict resolution course in which you picked up specific techniques on how to defuse a tense situation. You could talk about a course in writing in which you wrote grants for a nonprofit agency. You can indicate that your history classes were great because you wrote long papers that your professor tore apart. This point is to show that the courses you took demonstrated your commitment to improving a specific skill.

Although this chapter is about how to brand yourself in your resumes, cover letters, and interviews, it also serves to emphasize the main point of the book. See college as an opportunity to develop the skills employers want. If you don't, then you cannot produce the kinds of resumes, cover letters, and interviews that will get you on a viable career path. Always think of the interconnections between what you do in your college years and what you will be saying in your resumes, cover letters, and interviews when you enter the job market. Pursue the strategies for boosting your skills discussed in chapters 12 through 16, and use the information about professions and the planning tools presented in chapters 17 and 18.

USEFUL RESOURCES

BOOKS

Guerrilla Marketing for Job Hunters 3.0: How to Stand Out from the Crowd and Tap into the Hidden Job Market Using Social Media and 999 Other Tactics Today, revised edition, by Jay Conrad Levinson and David E. Perry (John Wiley & Sons, 2011). Levinson and Perry provide practical advice for a job-seeking climate that is increasingly dependent on social media.

What Color Is Your Parachute? Guide to Job-Hunting Online, 6th edition, by Mark Emery Bolles and Richard N. Bolles (Ten Speed Press, 2011). The authors discuss uses of the Internet to search for and obtain jobs.

Job Interview Skills 101: The Course You Forgot to Take by Ellyn Enisman (Hudson House, 2010). This book offers instructive ideas on how to interview well for jobs, regardless of whether you are looking for an internship, first job, or new job.

The *Knock 'em Dead* series by best-selling author Martin Yate (Adams Media, 2010) periodically releases new editions of cover letter, resume, and job-searching manuals that include samples and advice on leveraging power with social media.

"IT'S NOT WHAT YOU KNOW BUT WHO YOU KNOW."

—*THE ELECTRICAL WORKER*, A JOURNAL OF THE INTERNATIONAL BROTHERHOOD OF ELECTRICAL WORKERS, 1914

CHAPTER 20

DEVELOPING YOUR CAREER NETWORK

USE SOCIAL NETWORKING · BUILD PROFESSIONAL NETWORKS · DEVELOP ONLINE NETWORKING

Some people take the quotation at the beginning of the chapter to be an absolute truth, but networking alone will not make you successful. Only your skills, character, and careful consideration of the risks and benefits of various careers will guarantee success. However, the size of your career network and the number of contacts you make through face-to-face communications or social media can be the difference between getting a job two months after you graduate or two years later. When looking for a job, "who you know" and "who you ask" are critical to securing advice and identifying opportunities.

One very important caveat here! Members of your career network should appreciate your skills; if they don't, they may not be an asset. Many students want to include me in their formal networks. I am selective about whom I allow to do this. Some students who make the request would not be pleased if someone contacted me for a reference. I always tell the truth, cautioning that it is just my opinion. This is why it is important to build your networks carefully and to build them through professional activities where you have excelled.

Career networking is not something you do as a senior. You should begin as soon as you arrive on campus and even before. You can establish contacts with college staff, particularly the career services program, and peers who help guide to you a successful career path. Starting early makes sense because networking is like depositing money in a bank account where your interest compounds. Your contacts grow continuously, with one contact leading to other contacts that lead to more contacts.

This chapter discusses three types of networking activities—social, professional, and online. Each of the three can impact the others, and all must be a part of your networking strategy.

USE SOCIAL NETWORKING

I use the term "social networking" to identify relationships you develop from your day-to-day contact with people. The primary purpose of the ties you establish in your social network is not to get a job or explore careers, but—sooner or later—they can lead to career help directly or indirectly.

FAMILY

Family can sometimes provide meaningful contacts. These trusted individuals may not be able to give you job leads directly, but they may put you in touch with others who can.

Older relatives interact with lots of professionals outside of your inner circle, or they themselves may be in a career field that interests you. So ask family members about their careers and whom they know in chosen industries, product/service categories, or organizations. For instance, if you dream of an internship at a leading marketing firm, ask about external agencies retained by a relative's employer. Push for a few names. Then mention that relative up front when you call, because name-dropping is a common way to "break the ice."

FRIENDS

College friends may be part of your social network, but they also can assist in the pursuit of your career. If you've made friends through your courses, Greek life, student activity groups, or special events like fund-raisers, these friends become part of your social network. However, some of these contacts can also become part of your career network after the initial social bond is established.

The student groups you choose to join will shape these social networks. Working with peers on a volunteer initiative, such as Habitat for Humanity over spring break, frequently results in long-term relationships for career help down the road. You and people with whom you work as a team in a particularly challenging course may have a special bond after completing a class project. These people, too, may come in handy as you move through your career.

When it comes to social connections, the primary goal is not to enhance your employment opportunities, but rather to have fun. Social relationships could eventually help in your career pursuits. For example, you and a fraternity brother may be very close when reminiscing about your escapades in college, and you may eventually end up in the same field or even company. In this case, your social relationship melds with a professional relationship. If this happens, it is more a function of happenstance than an action to build your career network.

A word of caution is in order here. Moving from a social relationship with a friend to a career contact is not automatic and carries some risks. If you ask for your fun-loving fraternity brother to help you land a job at his company five years out of college, he may feel uncomfortable. He may see you as an airhead but a lot of fun as a drinking partner. Such a shift should be approached in a way that recognizes that you are asking a favor and not assuming that because you are friends, he is obliged to help you. Throwing out some hints at the beginning of the conversation, such as "Your job sounds like it has a lot of potential" may avoid an awkward situation. If he responds with details and thinks of you as a good hire, he might ask whether you have interest in his field. If not, you should be hesitant to ask more before you provide information on how you are no longer just a great party animal. Think of it as a preinterview.

You can also establish relationships with individuals who share similar career interests or who might be mentors, references, and generators of job leads. These include professors as well as college staff and professionals you contact via your internships and jobs during your college years.

PROFESSORS

Some undergraduates believe that faculty members are their best sources of career mentoring, references, and even jobs. This view is true if students are planning to follow in a professor's footsteps, which in the liberal arts means becoming a professor or at least a professional researcher. It may also be true for students in professional schools like management, communications, and education, especially if those professors have had a significant amount of job experience and continue to be in touch with trends in the field.

Although your professors may not be the best source for career mentoring and job opportunities, they usually are important for your list of references on your resume and sometimes as writers of letters of recommendation for graduate school and nonprofit organizations like Teach for America and AmeriCorps. If you plan on going to graduate school or applying for a scholarship or a government program like the Peace Corps, you will need a letter of reference from a faculty member.

You will need at least one faculty member to list as a reference on job applications and your resume. Corporations may want to call the professor to ask whether you were a hard worker and a responsible person or have a specific skill. From my own experience, corporations rarely call professors for job references. For students who list me on the resumes, I might get one call, and it is usually after the company has already decided to make an offer. The call is usually just to check to make sure the candidates are not lying or whether there are some massive skeletons in their closets. Even so, employers like to see at least one professor's name on the resume.

Many students arrive at their senior year with no professor they feel comfortable asking for a reference. Don't be one of those students. Target a few professors in your sophomore year who you think may be able to write you a good letter or answer questions a job interviewer may ask. The best target would be a professor in a small class where you did well and with whom you visited a few times to discuss your work or just ask general questions. This is one reason that you might volunteer to do research with a professor on a project, if you have an interest in that area.

In addition, be nice to your adviser for your major if he or she is a faculty member. Always answer emails and show up for advising meetings when you are supposed to. This little attention to detail and time management will differentiate you in a positive way from most of your adviser's advisees. Take a course from that professor and do well in course. Also, if you are in a student organization in which a faculty member has a deep interest, offer to assist that person in his work with the organization, and demonstrate your commitment by taking on a leadership role in the organization.

When you pick a faculty member as a reference or a source of career advice, your decision should be based on more than the grade you earned in his or her class. Don't seek a recommendation from a top-ranked faculty member unless you are looking to attend graduate schools and want to become a professor. Adjunct faculty, who are part-time instructors with jobs in a field that you are considering, may deliver better feedback because of their "boots on the ground" immersion with an organization or industry.

Sometimes a low-performing student will approach me for a letter. I tell the student that I will write a letter, but they might be better off looking for someone who would write a stronger letter than I would. If they persist, I will write a letter that usually says "the student has potential that he did not live up to in working with me." My experience is that a lukewarm recommendation such as this does not necessarily mean the students will not be admitted to the graduate program. High scores on the GRE or LSAT will usually counteract lukewarm letters.

When you do approach a professor to serve as a reference or recommender, be organized. Clearly identify yourself and what course or courses you took with the professor. If your grade was an A, you could mention the grade. Ask the professor whether he or she feels comfortable serving as a reference. Clearly explain whether the request is just to be listed as a reference or to write a letter. If it is for a letter, provide details about yourself and where you are applying so that the professor can use those details in the letter. Include the length of time the professor has known you and what relationship you have with the professor other than taking a course. If you have served on a committee together or the professor is an adviser, be specific. Be sure to give clear instructions on where the letter is to be sent or picked up and whether some forms, which might be provided electronically, are required. Don't assume the professor can read your mind.

I get in a very bad mood when a student asks for a letter to be written but doesn't include the address. That means I have to write back and wait until the student gets back to me. If it takes the student a week, I am even angrier. A face-to-face meeting may not be required. A brief, concise email that provides the professor with "talking points" about you on what you studied or related activities can be just as effective as a face-to-face meeting. In your email, offer to meet in case the professor would prefer to handle the conversation face-to-face.

These suggestions are based on the assumption that most faculty members would be more likely to provide a good letter if you make it easy to write the letter. If they have to look up information or email you to find out where to send the letter, they may put off writing the letter and when they write it, not be inclined to give you a high rating on organization and responsibility.

OTHER PROFESSIONALS

During your four years of college, talk with a range of professionals in career fields you have under consideration. By your junior year, you should have the beginnings of a network outside of college, based on people you met in your internships, jobs, and interviews, as well as those you met who were campus visitors.

The best way to get a good start on building a professional network is to schedule an appointment with staff members at the on-campus career services office in your freshman year. These counselors are knowledgeable about a variety of careers (plus, they are paid to support you). Most undergraduates don't use these services fully or early enough. Instead, they show up in their senior year for the first time and act is if the career services office is an employment agency. You can get the jump on other students by showing up early and often.

A particularly powerful tip is to pursue a part-time job with career services because you will get a first look at internship and job opportunities. Even if you can't get a job with career services, make sure you participate in its programs. Career services sponsors workshops and employment/internship fairs that are held many times throughout the year. Attend as many as you can. Also, sign up for the online services offered by career services. Make sure your career services people like and remember you. You could exercise your legible handwriting by sending a short thank-you note, which will be remembered for a long time.

Career services can help you build your professional network by putting you in touch with alumni in fields in which you may have interest. Many alumni want to give back to their alma mater, are eager to provide advice, and sometimes have internship and job leads. Some career services programs have alumni mentoring systems. All have contacts with employers and frequently bring company representatives to campus.

One of the best ways to meet alumni and other professionals is to attend events on campus where talks are given by alumni and professionals. You might not meet the featured speaker or guest, but you will meet those who hosted him or her. You can also offer to help the administrators in setting up the events, which can get you access to some of the professionals who are invited.

If you are given the name of an alumni mentor, don't do what one of my students did. He sent an email to a top executive in an association and asked for advice. The alum gave the student three different times to meet, and the student didn't respond right away. When he did, he said he was busy all of those times and offered no alternatives. The alum just deleted his email and never responded to him again. The alum emailed me asking what was wrong with the student.

Career services staff members will carefully screen you and remind you to act professionally when contacting alumni. They live in fear of a phone call to the fund-raising office or to the college president from an alumnus complaining about rude, naïve, and spoiled-brat students. To earn trust, inform staff that you will research the executive's background before you meet. This habit ensures that you are prepared.

You need to earn the staff's respect to have them help you connect not only with alums but also with employers looking for new hires.

Career services programs on most college campuses work closely with employers to provide opportunities for contact. Employers offer both internships and jobs, and often participate in career fairs. Occasionally, these employers may offer what they call leadership programs or information programs that describe not only their company but also information on their fields. Career services staff will publicize these programs. Like their support of your contact with alumni, career services staff are also concerned about your behavior toward employers. They don't want employers to get a bad impression of their students and to cross their college off the list of places they will visit.

Your work on a professional network should move by your junior year to contacts outside of the college. In chapter 17, I discussed how your career exploration should include identifying relevant associations, job shadowing, doing informational interviews, and obtaining internships. These activities can help you build a career network. The most important of these is the internship where your immediate supervisors can not only provide career advice but also, if they like you, provide job leads and recommendations. Many of my successful students leave their internships with a couple of people interested enough in their future that the students can contact them for advice and job leads.

From experiences with my students over the past forty years and from surveys of corporations, the relationships you build at your jobs or internships during the college year can lead directly to jobs. In fact, every year three or more of my students who had summer internships are given jobs in the early fall by the organization where they interned.

In all of your contacts with people on and off campus, be aware that they look for many of the skills in our ten Skill Sets. In particular, they look for proactive people who have good communication skills. For example, presidents of fraternities and sororities have interaction with officials at the national level, which opens up an entirely new set of potential members of your network. Job supervisors who want you to take management positions with them are likely to want to make you part of their professional network.

College students are most familiar with Facebook, but this social media tool is not as useful for careers as LinkedIn or even Twitter, which is discussed below. One of your "friends" on Facebook may provide you with some information about job openings or internships, but Facebook should be used to maintain only social relationships. In fact, Facebook may have done as much harm as good for today's college students due to inappropriate sharing of lifestyle details.

Make sure your personal profile on Facebook is kept private. If your profile is open for every Facebook user to see, this means that you have no idea who could be looking at your profile and your pictures from last weekend's raging party. Users can limit their profile so that when their name is searched, only certain information appears, such as their name and profile picture. Make sure your profile picture is something appropriate, because you can bet that when recruiters review your resume, they also check your Facebook profile. Bottom line: it's better to be safe than sorry. The more private your Facebook profile, the less information can come back to haunt your job hunt.

Also, make sure your email uses a professional address. You may have thought it was cute to have an email like loverboy@yahoo.com when you were in high school. It is a career and internship killer in college. The same goes for your phone message on your cell phone or answering machine.

LINKEDIN

By the company's own definition, LinkedIn is a means to reconnect with past colleagues and friends, power your career by networking with professionals, and get answers to questions about industries that interest you. It is a business-oriented social networking website that allows users to create profiles that display all of their career and work-related experiences. This profile can then be shared with potential employers and networking contacts. A strong LinkedIn profile will allow recruiters to get a broad idea of your expertise and work capabilities. LinkedIn is all about connecting with the right people. This means that you do not send a "connect request" to every friend you know, but you try to keep your profile open to those who can comment on your career work. An example of this would be peers with whom you worked on an important group project. You should connect with as many coworkers as you can, too. This will spread your name throughout the workplace and allow your contacts to keep you in mind when a job opening comes around.[1]

Many companies will post current job openings on their LinkedIn accounts. This provides you with inside information that may not have hit their company website yet. Connecting on LinkedIn demonstrates that you are truly interested in the company and the industry.

A senior who works in my office and majored in my Policy Studies program had three internships before graduating. Over her winter break, she was contacted by each of her past internships. She had been in touch through email with those with whom she had directly worked during her time at the agency, and she had been connected with them on LinkedIn since her second week at her internships. A senior vice president at her most recent internship connected with her via LinkedIn after hearing her name several times as a potential hire. This professional wanted to view her profile to see all of her experience, and then once he was able to gain more information on her background, he followed it up with a phone call about full-time opportunities at the agency.

To build your LinkedIn network, first create an account and build your profile. You can choose to post as much information as you feel necessary. Post all relevant work experience that you would include on a resume. Once your profile is complete, you can begin to add people to your network. Start with the peers and adults whom you have met and with whom you have worked in a meaningful way, on and off campus. If you have worked closely with certain people, either on campus or at a past internship, you can send a request for them to write a recommendation on your work, which will then appear on your profile. You can also follow companies on LinkedIn, enabling you to see any jobs they may post.

It's important to begin building your network of contacts right away. You can import contacts from your address book and look through the list for people marked with the blue "in" logo to the right of their name. (This means they're already on LinkedIn.) But be selective about whom you invite. Invite current classmates, colleagues, current and former supervisors, and close family friends to join your network.[2]

TWITTER

Twitter is a popular social networking service that allows the user to send and read brief messages of 140 characters or less, called "tweets." Many companies have their own Twitter accounts, and their social media experts will update it each day with company information or industry trends. Nowadays it is actually quite difficult to find even a mid-sized company that does not have a Twitter account.

To get the most out of your Twitter experience for career purposes, you should follow the companies or organizations with which you are most interested in working. If you are trying to get noticed by a company, try tweeting about industry trends or retweeting their posts that you find valuable by providing your own commentary. This allows employers to see that you are a mature, proactive thinker. When the time comes to hire for an internship or a job, they will see that you have been following their organization for some time instead of just checking out their website quickly before writing a cover letter. This activity will build your knowledge of the industry and the company, which is a must in the interview process.

WARNINGS ON THE USE OF ONLINE TOOLS

While online tools are useful, they are not a substitute for face time at professional meetings, career and internship fairs, interviews, and informal conversations. Online tools like LinkedIn require some kind of shared experience. The Internet has never made an internship or job offer—only people hire people. You must periodically step away from the computer to meet and greet humans. By doing so, you can make a lasting impression.

Don't misuse electronic communications by being a pest. For example, sending excessive emails or calling repeatedly is unacceptable. Don't say things like "hi" or, believe it not, "hey." Be sure to use a salutation. Follow the skills you developed in mastering online communications described in chapter 4.

It is fitting to end the book on the topic of networking. Students with impressive personal and online networks get valuable internships and jobs quicker than those who come to ask me to give them my network. Students with strong networks based on professional relationships with others have high Skills Scores. This is an unbroken circle. Students who have strong career networks have better Skill Sets, and students who have better Skill Sets have better internships and jobs, and are about to embark on impressive career paths.

USEFUL RESOURCES

BOOKS

A Foot in the Door by Katherine Hansen (Ten Speed Press, 2000). The main purpose of this book is to help you establish contacts for job hunting. It also contains a useful section on informational interviewing.

Guerrilla Marketing for Job Hunters 3.0: How to Stand Out from the Crowd and Tap into the Hidden Job Market Using Social Media and 999 Other Tactics Today, revised edition, by Jay Conrad Levinson and David E. Perry (John Wiley & Sons, 2011). This widely used book will help you in your job hunt, especially with LinkedIn and social media.

What Color Is Your Parachute? Guide to Job-Hunting Online, 6th edition, by Mark Emery Bolles and Richard N. Bolles (Ten Speed Press, 2011). This book discusses how to use the Internet to build your professional network.

The Power Formula for LinkedIn Success: Kick-start Your Business, Brand, and Job Search by Wayne Breitbarth (Greenleaf Book Group Press, 2011). This book can be used as a primer for LinkedIn.

WEBSITES

www.govloop.com Similar to LinkedIn, this website is used as a social networking tool for professionals, specifically government employees.

www.linkedin.com LinkedIn will let you upload your resume and connect with professionals across networks that range from your workplace, to your hometown, to your alma mater. Recruiters and headhunters frequently use this site to search for and review candidates for employment.

This planner has two purposes. The first is to encourage you to choose activities that teach you skills and help you explore careers throughout your four years in college. The second, and less obvious, purpose is to help you develop the ten Skill Sets presented throughout the book. Take this planner seriously and use it consistently; if you do, your career path will be on solid footing when you graduate.

Go to www.billcoplin.org to download the blank forms that appear throughout this planner.

PLANNER CONTENTS

NETWORKING PROSPECTS

Throughout your four years of college, whenever you meet people who might be able to offer job advice or leads, record their name, email, phone, mailing address, a short note reminding you of who they are, how you met them, and whether you have added them to your social media network (e.g., LinkedIn). The list should be fluid; you might decide to eliminate some and add others. It can also be as long as you want it to be, which means it would be best to set up a computer file.

Ultimately, it should consist of people like professors, guest speakers, graduate students, supervisors at work or at community-service locations, and organization advisers with whom you would eventually like to connect through LinkedIn (if not today, some day in the near future when your career goals are better established).

NAME	EMAIL	PHONE	ADDRESS	COMMENTS

FOUR-YEAR CALENDAR

This Four-Year Calendar provides tentative due dates between the July prior to your first year and the June of your last year of college that will help you develop the ten Skill Sets. These are not firm deadlines, but rather they are the ideal dates by which you should have begun work on each activity. The planner does not have all the deadlines required by your college, such as when to enroll in classes or decide on a major. Each college has different expectations and standards, and they will send you many reminders when their deadlines are looming. This planner is filled with the deadlines that colleges *don't* spell out for you—and if you fulfill each activity by the designated time, you will be a step closer to being career-ready when you graduate college.

Following the calendar is an explanation of the items listed in the calendar. Most of the items are self-explanatory but the notes immediately following the calendar provide more detailed information. Forms to be used for the items mentioned in the calendar follow this section.

YEAR 1

JULY	AUGUST	SEPTEMBER
1st Initial Skills Self-Assessment Form **5**th Degree Check **10**th Preliminary Course Schedule for Next Semester **15**th Semiannual Budget Form	**1**st Annual Goal Setting **15**th Academic Year Jobs, Activities, and Leadership Experiences	**1**st Academic Year Jobs, Activities, and Leadership Experiences **15**th Career Service Visits
OCTOBER	**NOVEMBER**	**DECEMBER**
1st Faculty Member Contact **15**th Summer Jobs and Internships Search	**1**st Preliminary Course Schedule for Next Semester **15**th Summer Jobs and Internships Search	**15**th Summer Jobs and Internships Search **27**th Semiannual Budget Form
JANUARY	**FEBRUARY**	**MARCH**
1st Semiannual Skills Self-Assessment Form **15**th Summer Jobs and Internships Search	**15**th Summer Jobs and Internships Search	**15**th Summer Jobs and Internships Search
APRIL	**MAY**	**JUNE**
1st Degree Check **10**th Preliminary Course Schedule for Next Semester **15**th Summer Jobs and Internships Search	**15**th Summer Jobs and Internships Search	**15**th Off-Campus Semester Exploration **20**th Semiannual Budget Form

YEAR 2

JULY	AUGUST	SEPTEMBER
5th Semiannual Skills Self-Assessment Form **10th** Preliminary Course Schedule for Next Semester **15th** Semiannual Budget Form	**1st** Annual Goal Setting **15th** Academic Year Jobs, Activities, and Leadership Experiences	**1st** Academic Year Jobs, Activities, and Leadership Experiences **15th** Career Services Visit
OCTOBER	**NOVEMBER**	**DECEMBER**
1st Faculty Member Contact **15th** Summer Jobs and Internships Search	**1st** Preliminary Course Schedule for Next Semester **15th** Summer Jobs and Internships Search	**15th** Summer Jobs and Internships Search **27th** Semiannual Budget Form
JANUARY	**FEBRUARY**	**MARCH**
1st Semiannual Skills Self-Assessment Form **15th** Summer Jobs and Internships Search	**15th** Summer Jobs and Internships Search	**15th** Summer Jobs and Internships Search
APRIL	**MAY**	**JUNE**
1st Degree Check **10th** Preliminary Course Schedule for Next Semester **15th** Summer Jobs and Internships Search	**15th** Summer Jobs and Internships Search	**15th** Off-Campus Semester Exploration **20th** Semiannual Budget Form

YEAR 3

JULY	AUGUST	SEPTEMBER
5th Semiannual Skills Self-Assessment Form **10**th Preliminary Course Schedule for Next Semester **15**th Semiannual Budget Form	**1**st Annual Goal Setting **15**th Academic Year Jobs, Activities, and Leadership Experiences	**1**st Academic Year Jobs, Activities, and Leadership Experiences **15**th Career Services Visit

OCTOBER	NOVEMBER	DECEMBER
1st Faculty Member Contact **15**th Academic Year Jobs, Activities, and Leadership Experiences	**1**st Degree Check **10**th Preliminary Course Schedule for Next Semester **15**th Academic Year Jobs, Activities, and Leadership Experiences	**15**th Academic Year Jobs, Activities, and Leadership Experiences **27**th Semiannual Budget Form

JANUARY	FEBRUARY	MARCH
1st Semiannual Skills Self-Assessment Form **15**th Summer Jobs and Internships Search	**15**th Summer Jobs and Internships Search	**15**th Summer Jobs and Internships Search

APRIL	MAY	JUNE
1st Degree Check **10**th Preliminary Course Schedule for Next Semester **15**th Summer Jobs and Internships Search	**15**th Summer Jobs and Internships Search	**15**th Off-Campus Semester Exploration **20**th Semiannual Budget Form

YEAR 4

JULY	AUGUST	SEPTEMBER
5th Semiannual Skills Self-Assessment Form **10**th Preliminary Course Schedule for Next Semester **15**th Semiannual Budget Form	**1**st Annual Goal Setting **15**th Explore Career Path Options	**15**th Explore Career Path Options

OCTOBER	NOVEMBER	DECEMBER
15th Explore Career Path Options	**1**st Degree Check **10**th Preliminary Course Schedule for Next Semester **15**th Explore Career Path Options	**15**th Explore Career Path Options **27**th Semiannual Budget Form

JANUARY	FEBRUARY	MARCH
1st Semiannual Skills Self-Assessment **15**th Explore Career Path Options	**1**st Degree Check **15**th Explore Career Path Options	**15**th Explore Career Path Options

APRIL	MAY	JUNE
15th Explore Career Path Options	**15**th Explore Career Path Options	**1**st Semiannual Skills Self-Assessment Form (Final) **10**th Personal Budget for 1st Year after College

NOTES ON KEYWORDS USED IN THE CALENDAR

1. **SEMIANNUAL SKILLS SELF-ASSESSMENT FORM:** This form consists of two parts. The first is the Initial Skills Self-Assessment Form introduced in chapter 18 on pages 227–235 with an example completed by a high school senior and tips on how to assess yourself. Complete the first form and record your ratings on the second part, the Semiannual Skills Self-Assessment Form, where you will record the rating you give yourself every six months. Following the guidelines and instructions that appear in chapter 18, estimate your Skills Score each July and January, starting two months prior to your first year in college. Be honest in your self-assessment. By doing this, you will be able to chart your progress in developing the ten Skill Sets throughout your college years.

2. **DEGREE CHECK:** Before you start to think about course selection for the next semester, perform a degree check to see what requirements you have left. Check total credits needed, core requirements, major requirements, and minor requirements. Be sure to do this before the first semester of your first year, especially if you are bringing in credits from the outside. You don't want to waste time fulfilling a requirement you already completed in high school.

3. **PRELIMINARY COURSE SCHEDULE FOR NEXT SEMESTER:** By the date indicated, you should have a good idea of what courses you will take the coming semester with a few alternatives in case you can't get your first choices. Selection will change up to and perhaps even including the first week of classes, but hopefully not after that. When choosing courses, follow the guidelines provided in the "Courses" sections found in chapters 1 through 10.

4. **SEMIANNUAL BUDGET FORM:** This form appears on page 279. Complete the form starting in July prior to your first year, then update it every December and June for the next three and a half years.

5. **ACADEMIC YEAR JOBS, ACTIVITIES, AND LEADERSHIP EXPERIENCES:** Use your college website and the people with whom you talk as well as fairs and presentations to explore all kinds of out-of-class activities you might want to undertake during the next two semesters. If you plan to work, go to the student employment office. On-campus jobs should be your first choice, especially if you have a work-study grant. If you plan to explore off-campus jobs, look for ones that are close to your college, unless you have prior connections with a company or the possibility of significantly higher pay. Other kinds of activities—such as participating in student government, writing for the school newspaper, or volunteering with one of the many community-service groups—also need to be explored.

6. **CAREER SERVICES VISIT:** Frequent visits to career services starting in your first semester will allow you to register for online services, attend training sessions, and explore internship and job opportunities throughout your four years. Frequent visits will also put you in good standing with the career services specialists and may even lead to better access to new job listings.

7. **FACULTY MEMBER CONTACT:** Visit at least one faculty member with whom you think you can connect each semester. You may select the professor from class or advising, or you may identify this professor through campus news coverage. Sign up to receive daily Internet news releases from the college that will help you identify possible faculty and staff contacts who may help you with career exploration and skill development.

8. **SUMMER JOBS AND INTERNSHIPS SEARCH:** Search and apply for summer jobs and internships until you land something, which could take up to seven months. This item appears on the calendar every month and can obviously be ignored once you have obtained one. "Jobs" and "internships" are lumped together because they could be combined and because, in many cases, there is no difference between the two.

9. **OFF-CAMPUS SEMESTER EXPLORATION:** You need to plan your course work if you will be off campus for one or two semesters. This requires that you make decisions long before the semester you plan to go. Once you have made the decision, no more

reminders are provided because the organization running the program you are planning to take will have different dates and requirements.

10. **ANNUAL GOAL SETTING:** Review your grades, progress on degree completion, student and leadership activities, internship and job search activities, Semiannual Skills Self-Assessment Form, and Semiannual Budget Form to identify up to ten goals you hope to accomplish by June of your next year.

11. **EXPLORE CAREER PATH OPTIONS:** Although you will explore career opportunities that include jobs, nonprofit programs like City Year, government programs like the Peace Corps, and graduate school before August prior to your senior year, you will need to get more specific and narrow your options. Decide whether you will go directly to graduate school, which, as discussed in chapter 16, is not a good idea in the majority of cases. Make this decision no later than the fall of your senior year because you will have to complete applications, get recommendations, take tests like the GRE or LSAT, and do detailed research by the end of the first semester. You should narrow down your graduate school choices by then. Whether or not you are thinking about graduate school, make plans during August and September of your senior year to search for interesting job opportunities in order to apply for positions as early as October. Continue the process for the next nine months. Make the necessary applications as needed. Check the Internet information from career services weekly and participate in training provided by career services. Attend career fairs and relevant presentations.

12. **PERSONAL FIRST-YEAR BUDGET AFTER COLLEGE:** Prepare a spreadsheet similar to the form on page 279 that allows you to examine your income and costs during your first year after college. This exercise will help you make important decisions so that you begin on a sound financial future.

This initial assessment should only be completed once, in July before your freshman year. The second is the Semiannual Skills Self-Assessment Form, where every six months you record the ratings you give yourself for the ten Skill Sets. (Both are available for download online at www.billcoplin.org.) The ratings you give yourself on the initial assessment should be recorded in the first column of the second form. For each of the skills, rate what you believe to be your current proficiency from 1 (poor) to 4 (excellent) using the guidelines below, and in no more than two sentences explain why you gave yourself that rating in the "evidence" column.

Example on how to complete the form:

1 (POOR)	2 (FAIR)	3 (GOOD)	4 (EXCELLENT)
I have no skill; I'm not even sure I understand the skill.	I have some experience and competence in exercising the skill.	I have exercised the skill competently on several occasions.	I can exercise the skill at the level of a professional with many years of experience.

Please use the examples below as a point of reference for providing your evidence. Remember that your evidence for each skill must support the rating you give yourself.

SKILL	RATING	EVIDENCE
Motivate Yourself	1	I usually don't do well in math, but I was really worried about an upcoming test so I sucked it up and studied two extra hours. My grade ended up being a lot higher than normal. However, despite this one solid effort, I do not study enough to get my grades where they should be.
Master Online Communications	2	I send emails and text messages all the time, so I am good at knowing how to do all that, but I often use Internet slang and don't exactly reread my messages before sending them. One time I even sent my boss an email full of spelling errors and slang, and he didn't understand what I was trying to say.
Keep and Use Records	3	Every month when I get my paycheck, I store my pay stubs in a chronological file folder in a safe drawer; I also do the same with my cell phone bills and my receipts from when I spend money. This helps me keep track of the money I get and my biggest expenses.

INITIAL SKILLS SELF-ASSESSMENT FORM

SKILL SET	SKILL	RATING	EVIDENCE
Taking Responsibility	Motivate Yourself		
	Be Ethical		
	Manage Your Time		
	Manage Your Money		
Developing Physical Skills	Stay Well		
	Look Good		
	Type Well		
	Write Legibly		
Communicating Verbally	Converse One-on-One		
	Present to Groups		
	Use Visual Displays		
Communicating in Writing	Write Well		
	Edit and Proof		
	Use Word-Processing Tools		
	Master Online Communications		
Working Directly with People	Build Good Relationships		
	Work in Teams		
	Teach Others		
Influencing People	Manage Effectively		
	Sell Successfully		
	Politick Wisely		
	Lead Effectively		

continued

SKILL SET	SKILL	RATING	EVIDENCE
Gathering Information	Search the Web		
	Use Library Holdings		
	Use Commercial Databases		
	Conduct Interviews		
	Use Surveys		
	Keep and Use Records		
Using Quantitative Tools	Use Numbers		
	Use Graphs and Tables		
	Use Spreadsheet Programs		
Asking and Answering the Right Questions	Detect Nonsense		
	Pay Attention to Detail		
	Apply Knowledge		
	Evaluate Actions and Policies		
Solving Problems	Identify Problems		
	Develop Solutions		
	Launch Solutions		

After completing the Initial Skills Self-Assessment Form, record the ratings on the form below. Every six months, record your ratings by looking at your previous ratings and thinking about the criteria presented in chapter 18. You can look at the trend for each of the thirty-eight skills as you progress through your four years to view improvements.

SKILL SET	SKILL	1ST YEAR JUL	1ST YEAR JAN	2ND YEAR JUL	2ND YEAR JAN	3RD YEAR JUL	3RD YEAR JAN	4TH YEAR JUL	4TH YEAR JAN	POST-GRAD JUL
Taking Responsibility	Motivate Yourself									
	Be Ethical									
	Manage Your Time									
	Manage Your Money									
Developing Physical Skills	Stay Well									
	Look Good									
	Type Well									
	Write Legibly									
Communicating Verbally	Converse One-on-One									
	Present to Groups									
	Use Visual Displays									
Communicating in Writing	Write Well									
	Edit and Proof									
	Use Word-Processing Tools									
	Master Online Communications									

SKILL SET	SKILL	1ST YEAR JUL	1ST YEAR JAN	2ND YEAR JUL	2ND YEAR JAN	3RD YEAR JUL	3RD YEAR JAN	4TH YEAR JUL	4TH YEAR JAN	POST-GRAD JUL
Working Directly with People	Build Good Relationships									
	Work in Teams									
	Teach Others									
Influencing People	Manage Effectively									
	Sell Successfully									
	Politick Wisely									
	Lead Effectively									
Gathering Information	Search the Web									
	Use Library Holdings									
	Use Commercial Databases									
	Conduct Interviews									
	Use Surveys									
	Keep and Use Records									
Using Quantitative Tools	Use Numbers									
	Use Graphs and Tables									
	Use Spreadsheet Programs									
Asking and Answering the Right Questions	Detect Nonsense									
	Pay Attention to Detail									
	Apply Knowledge									
	Evaluate Actions and Policies									
Solving Problems	Identify Problems									
	Develop Solutions									
	Launch Solutions									

Skills Score: Add the ratings you have given yourself and divide by 38: __ /38 = __.

SEMIANNUAL BUDGET FORM

Estimate all sources of funds and costs in July of your first year. Then every six months thereafter enter in your actual funds and costs and adjust your estimates for the future. An electronic version of this spreadsheet is available for download at www.billcoplin.org; I advise you to save it to your computer and update it every January and July for the next three and a half years.

SEMIANNUAL BUDGET FORM

DATE COMPLETED								
SOURCE OF FUNDS								
My Own Savings								
My Job During School Year								
Parents								
Scholarships								
Grants								
Loans								
Other								
TOTAL								
COSTS								
Tuition								
Room and Board								
Other Charges								
Books								
Travel Costs								
Spending Money								
10% Contingency Fund								
TOTAL								
BALANCE (total funds minus total costs)								

INTRODUCTION

1. Estimated full-time year-round work for 1997 to 1999 according to the U.S. Census Bureau, "Current Population Surveys," March 1998, March 1999, and March 2000. www.census.gov/prod/2002pubs/p23-210.pdf.

2. Philip Oreopoulos and Salvanes G. Kjell, "Priceless: The Nonpecuniary Benefits of Schooling," *Journal of Economic Perspectives* 25 (2011): 159–84.

3. Institute for College Access and Success, "Student Debt and the Class of 2011," November 2011. http://projectonstudentdebt.org/files/pub/classof2010.pdf.

4. The Project on Student Debt, "Student Debt and the Class of 2010," 2011. http://projectonstudentdebt.org/files/pub/classof2010.pdf.

5. Erica Ho, "Survey: 85% of New College Grads Move Back in with Mom and Dad," *Time News Feed,* May 10, 2011.

6. Harvard Graduate School of Education, "Pathways to Prosperity: Meeting Today's Challenge of Preparing Young Americans for the 21st Century," February 2011. www.gse.harvard.edu/news_events/features/2011/Pathways_to_Prosperity_Feb2011.pdf.

7. Doug Lederman, "Graduated but Not Literate," *Inside Higher Education News*, December 16, 2005, reporting on the U.S. Education Department's National Center for Education Statistics Report titled "The National Assessment of Adult Literacy."

8. U.S. Department of Education, National Center for Education Statistics, *Digest of Education Statistics, 2010*, published in 2011. http://nces.ed.gov/fastfacts/display.asp?id=76.

9. U.S. Department of Education, National Center for Education Statistics, "National Postsecondary Student Aid Study," 2009. http://nces.ed.gov/surveys/npsas.

10. Reprinted from *Job Outlook 2010*, by permission of the National Association of Colleges and Employers.

11. Kate Zernike, "Tests Are Not Just for Kids," *New York Times*, August 4, 2002.

CHAPTER 1: TAKING RESPONSIBILITY

1. David Glenn, "Procrastination in College Students Is a Marker for Unhealthy Behaviors," *The Chronicle of Higher Education*, August 26, 2002. http://chronicle.com/daily/2002/08/2002082602n.htm.

CHAPTER 2: DEVELOPING PHYSICAL SKILLS

1. Benjamin Franklin, "Silence Dogood, No. 4 on Higher Learning," in *Benjamin Franklin on Education*, ed. John Hardin Best (New York: Columbia University Teachers College, 1961), 34.

CHAPTER 4: COMMUNICATING IN WRITING

1. William Strunk Jr. and E. B. White, *The Elements of Style* (Boston: Allyn & Bacon, 1999), 23.

CHAPTER 5: WORKING DIRECTLY WITH PEOPLE

1. Dale Carnegie, *How to Win Friends and Influence People* (New York: Pocket Books, 1982), xiv.

CHAPTER 7: GATHERING INFORMATION

1. Wikipedia, s.v. "Verifiability," http://en.wikipedia.org/wiki/Wikipedia:Verifiability.
2. Frank Bettger, *How I Raised Myself from Failure to Success in Selling* (New York: Fireside, 1992), 12.

CHAPTER 12: MAKING SMART ACADEMIC CHOICES FOR SKILL DEVELOPMENT

1. Dave Moniz, "In Quest for Workers, Firms Search Ranks of U.S. Military," *Christian Science Monitor*, August 26, 1999. www.csmonitor.com/durable/1999/08/26/fp2s2-csm.shtml.

CHAPTER 13: CREATING YOUR OWN APPRENTICESHIPS

1. National Association of Colleges and Employers, "2010 Internship and Co-op Survey," 2010. www.naceweb.org/products/2010internship_co-op_survey.

2. "In Pictures: Top 10 Internships of 2010," www.forbes.com/2010/01/13/best-internships-jobs-leadership-careers-employment_slide_11.html; "Internships: The Best Places to Start," January 13, 2010 www.forbes.com/2010/01/13/best-internships-jobs-leadership-careers-employment.html; U.S. Drug Enforcement Administration, www.justice.gov/dea/resources/careers/opportunity/student-employment.htm.

CHAPTER 14: EXPLORING OFF-CAMPUS SEMESTERS

1. Institute for International Education, "Expanding Study Abroad Capacity at U.S. Colleges and Universities," Issue 6, May 2, 2009; Megan Rooney, "Keeping the Study in Study Abroad," *Chronicle of Higher Education*, November 22, 2002, A63–64.

CHAPTER 15: DOING WELL BY DOING GOOD DURING YOUR COLLEGE YEARS

1. Patricia Sellers, "Schooling Corporate Giants on Recruiting," *Fortune Magazine*, November 27, 2006.

2. William D. Coplin, *How You Can Help: An Easy Guide to Doing Good Deeds in Your Everyday Life* (New York: Routledge, 2000), 83.

CHAPTER 16: THINKING ABOUT EDUCATION BEYOND COLLEGE

1. Joanne Jacobs, "In a Tough Economy, New Focus on Job-Oriented Certificates," *Hechinger Report*, January 16, 2011. http://hechinger report.org/content/in-a-tough-economy-new-focus-on-job-oriented-certificates_4968.

2. Randall Collins, "The Dirty Little Secrets of Credential Inflation!" *The Chronicle of Higher Education*, September 27, 2002, sec. 2, B20.

3. Jeffrey Pfeffer and Christina Fong, "The End of Business Schools? Less Success Than Meets the Eye," *Academy of Management*; vol. 1, no. 1, (September 2002).

4. David Segal, "Is Law School a Losing Game?" *New York Times*, January 8, 2011. www.nytimes.com/2011/01/09/business/09law.html?_r=1&emc=eta1.

5. "The Disposable Academic: Why Doing a PhD Is Often a Waste of Time," *The Economist*, December 18, 2010, 156–58.

6. Employment Projections Program, *Occupational Outlook Handbook*, (Washington, DC: U.S. Department of Labor, US Bureau of Labor Statistics, 2009).

CHAPTER 17: EXPLORING CAREER FIELDS

1. www.sigi3.org.

2. "The Importance of Working an Internship in College," June 20, 2011. www.onlinecollegecourses.com/2011/06/20/the-importance-of-working-an-internship-in-college

CHAPTER 20: DEVELOPING YOUR CAREER NETWORK

1. This discussion of LinkedIn is adapted from material published by the Maxwell Career and Alumni Office of Syracuse University. See www.maxwell.syr.edu/career.aspx?id=208.

2. "What is LinkedIn?" Accessed December 2, 2011. http://learn.linkedin.com/what-is-linkedin.